Teaching and Learning in Further Education

Diversity and change
Fourth edition

Prue Huddleston and
Lorna Unwin

Routledge
Taylor & Francis Group

LONDON AND NEW YORK

Fourth edition published 2013
by Routledge
2 Park Square, Milton Park, Abingdon, Oxon OX14 4RN

Simultaneously published in the USA and Canada
by Routledge
711 Third Avenue, New York, NY 10017

Routledge is an imprint of the Taylor & Francis Group, an informa business

First edition published by Routledge 1997
Third edition published by Routledge 2007

British Library Cataloguing in Publication Data
A catalogue record for this book is available from the British Library

Library of Congress Cataloging in Publication Data
Huddleston, Prue.
  Teaching and learning in further education: diversity and change/
  Prue Huddleston, Lorna Unwin. – 4th ed.
  p. cm.
  1. Continuing education – Great Britain. 2. Adult learning –
Great Britain. 3. Teaching – Great Britain. I. Unwin, Lorna.
  II. Title.
  LC5256.G7H76 2012
  374.941 – dc23
  2012026089

ISBN: 978-0-415-62316-2 (hbk)
ISBN: 978-0-415-62317-9 (pbk)
ISBN: 978-0-203-10539-9 (ebk)

Typeset in Bembo and Gill Sans
by Florence Production Ltd, Stoodleigh, Devon, UK

Printed and bound in Great Britain by
TJ International Ltd, Padstow, Cornwall

Contents

Figures

Preface

This book differs from many other texts on teaching and learning in further education (FE) colleges as it argues that teachers need to understand the wider socio-economic, political, historical and cultural contexts that help to shape their professional activities. Its ideas are rooted in social theories of learning and in a substantial body of research literature on FE, and on teaching and learning more generally. Teaching in an FE college in the UK is a very demanding job. At first glance, it would seem that the FE teacher shares few of the advantages enjoyed by colleagues in schools and universities. Unlike schools, colleges are open to their students from early in the morning to late at night, often at weekends, and throughout the traditional summer holiday period from mid-July to early September. Unlike universities, colleges are open to people of all abilities, from adults who may be learning to read and write to those who are technically highly skilled and, again increasingly, to those who are following undergraduate and postgraduate courses. Some school pupils aged 14–16 spend up to three days a week in colleges, a development that has significant implications for curriculum design, student support and teaching styles.

There is, therefore, a heterogeneity about the student body, structures and curricular offerings in FE colleges that would send some school and university teachers running for cover. That very diversity, however, helps to make FE colleges stimulating and exciting environments in which to work as a teacher.

Change is the name of the game in education and training in the UK, particularly in England. Since the third edition of this book was published in 2007, colleges have had to cope with further changes to qualifications, assessment procedures and funding regimes. As authors of a book that seeks to present a comprehensive analysis of the FE sector, we face the challenge of trying to be as up to date as possible. We acknowledge, however, that given the way in which successive governments, particularly in England, seem intent on reorganising some aspect of the architecture of education and training every few months, some of the initiatives covered in this book may have been further amended or even withdrawn in the time it takes for the manuscript to be published. All colleges have to strive to incorporate externally imposed change in such a way as to cause as little disruption as possible to their students and staff, but change is endemic and, therefore, many staff will find themselves under unwelcome pressure at various times.

Working in any sector of education means we must be prepared for change and periods of upheaval, much of which may be imposed from outside our sector or organisation. However, the majority of FE teachers still spend much of their working day focused on helping their students to learn, to progress and to achieve. Throughout this book, we have tried to portray the realities of college life in order to emphasise that FE teachers must be capable of adapting to many different situations and circumstances. In any one day, an FE teacher will employ a range of strategies, moving from a traditional didactic style in one lesson to being a facilitator of group work in another, from the company of mature adult students to a group of disaffected 14 year olds, and from teaching and assessing in the college classroom to the variable conditions of the industrial or commercial workplace.

This book has been written primarily for people who are embarking on a teaching career in colleges of further education and for those already teaching who may wish to review their approaches to and understanding of the process of teaching and learning. It may also be of use to managers in FE and to people working in organisations that have a relationship with FE colleges. Researchers engaged in studying FE colleges and post-compulsory education and training more broadly may also find this book a useful resource for information and potential research topics.

The book is divided into three parts: Part I: Further education in context; Part II: Teaching and learning; and Part III: Professional development. Part I has been fully revised to take account of changes to the way in which FE is structured, the student body and curricula and qualifications. Chapter 1 pulls together the different facets of the FE world to show how colleges are funded and the external constraints that govern the ways in which they can go about their business. Chapter 2 examines the nature and scope of the FE student population and introduces the reader to some real students whose needs and expectations pose challenges for teachers and support staff. It also describes the different types of staff found in colleges and the multi-skilled nature of teachers. In Chapter 3, we discuss the rich diet that comprises the curricular and qualification offerings found in FE colleges, from basic skills workshops through to higher education courses.

Part II focuses on teaching and learning. Chapter 4 explores the relationship between teaching and learning, drawing on a number of theoretical approaches that can help teachers to reflect on their work and be used as a basis for examining the challenges they encounter. This underpinning theory is continued in Chapter 5, where we present a number of strategies for use in the different teaching situations found in a college. Part of the chapter highlights the increasing importance of e-learning and the use of information and communication learning technologies. In Chapter 6, we focus on assessment and recording achievement.

In Part III, we see that, as in all teaching, regardless of the sector, professional educators never stop learning about their work and spend a great deal of time reflecting on how to develop their competence and levels of creativity. In Chapter 7, we discuss the ways in which teachers (and their students) need to critically reflect on their practice, and the extent to which teachers can also function as researchers. As a result of the increased recognition of the importance of FE colleges to people's life chances and the UK economy, there is a growing body of FE-focused research. We discuss some of the findings of the latest research studies throughout the book and highlight the work of some key projects. The possibilities for continued professional development are discussed in Chapter 8, which also provides information about the organisations and resources upon which FE teachers can draw for support in their work. At the end of the book, we indicate further reading material for each chapter that will help you to extend your understanding of some of the complex learning and teaching concepts covered in the book.

In each chapter, we have included sets of questions and activities for you to consider. We have boxed these under the heading 'Reflections' and hope that you will find time to use them as catalysts for questioning your attitudes and approaches to your work in FE and for discussion with colleagues.

This book has been written in the spirit of sharing rather than preaching and, as such, reflects the philosophical basis of much of the teaching and learning that occurs in FE colleges. Our ideas come from our own experiences of teaching in colleges and, more recently, of working with FE professionals in a staff development and research capacity. We hope the book provides you with some useful and relevant information and ideas but equally we hope it provides enough challenging material to make you say, 'I think I would tackle that situation differently' or 'I can come up with a better way'.

Abbreviations

AAT	Association of Accounting Technicians
AELP	Association of Employment and Learning Providers
ALI	Adult Learning Inspectorate
AoC	Association of Colleges
APEL	accreditation of prior experiential learning
APL	accreditation of prior learning
AS	Advanced Subsidiary
ATL	Association of Teachers and Lecturers
ATLS	Associate Teacher Learning and Skills
AVCE	Advanced Vocational Certificate of Education
BERR	(Department for) Business, Enterprise and Regulatory Reform
BTEC	Business and Technology Education Council
CBI	Confederation of British Industry
CCEA	Council for the Curriculum, Examinations and Assessment (Northern Ireland)
CETTs	Centres for Excellence in Teacher Training
CIPD	Chartered Institute of Personnel Development
CoVE	Centre of Vocational Excellence
CPD	continuing professional development
CPE	continuing professional education
CPVE	Certificate of Pre-Vocational Education
CTLLS	Certificate for Teaching in the Lifelong Learning Sector
DBIS	Department for Business, Innovation and Skills
DCELLS	Department for Children, Education, Lifelong Learning and Skills (Wales)
DCSF	Department for Children, Schools and Families
DELLS	Department for Education, Lifelong Learning and Skills
Delni	Department for Employment and Learning Northern Ireland
DFE	Department for Education
DfEE	Department for Education and Employment
DfES	Department for Education and Skills
DIUS	Department for Innovation, Universities and Skills

DTI	Department of Trade and Industry
DTLLS	Diploma for Teaching in the Lifelong Learning Sector
EBP	education-business partnership
EC	European Commission
EFA	Education Funding Agency
EIS	Education Institute Scotland
ELLD	Enterprise and Lifelong Learning Department (Scotland)
ELWa	Education and Learning Wales
EMA	Education Maintenance Allowance
EPQ	Extended Project Qualification
EQF	European Qualifications Framework
ESF	European Social Fund
ESOL	English for Speakers of Other Languages
ETLLD	Enterprise, Transport and Lifelong Learning Department (Scotland)
FBU	Fire Brigades Union
FE	further education
FEDA	Further Education Development Agency
FEFC	Further Education Funding Council
FENTO	Further Education National Training Organisation
FESC	Further Education Staff College
FEU	Further Education Unit
FHEQ	Framework for Higher Education Qualification
GCE	General Certificate of Education
GCSE	General Certificate of Secondary Education
GFE	general further education
GLHs	guided learning hours
GLS	general and liberal studies
GNVQ	General National Vocational Qualifications
GTA	Group Training Association
HE	higher education
HEA	Higher Education Academy
HEFCE	Higher Education Funding Council (England)
HEFCW	Higher Education Funding Council for Wales
HEI	Higher Education Institution
HMI	Her Majesty's Inspectorate
HMIE	Her Majesty's Inspectorate of Education (Scotland)
HNC	Higher National Certificate
HND	Higher National Diploma
IB	International Baccalaureate
ICLT	Information and Communication Learning Technologies
IfL	Institute for Learning
IFP	Increased Flexibility Programme
IFS	Institute for Fiscal Studies

ILA	Individual Learning Account
ISR	Individualised Student Record
ITT	Initial Teacher Training
LEA	local education authority
LEC	local enterprise company
LEP	Local Enterprise Partnership
LLA	Lifelong Learning Account
LLSC	Local Learning and Skills Council
LLUK	Lifelong Learning UK
LSC	Learning and Skills Council
LSDA	Learning and Skills Development Agency
LSIS	Learning and Skills Improvement Service
LSRN	Learning and Skills Research Network
LSS	learning and skills sector
LSW	learning support worker
MSC	Manpower Services Commission
NAS	National Apprenticeship Service
NATFHE	National Association of Teachers in Further and Higher Education
NIACE	National Institute for Adult Continuing Education
NOS	National Occupational Standards
NQF	National Qualifications Framework
NTO	National Training Organisation
NVQ	National Vocational Qualification
Ofqual	Office of Qualifications and Examinations Regulation
Ofsted	Office for Standards in Education, Children's Services and Skills
OU	Open University
PGCE	Postgraduate Certificate of Education
PIU	Performance and Innovation Unit
PLTS	personal, learning and thinking skills
PRU	Pupil Referral Unit
PTLLS	Preparing to Teach in the Lifelong Learning Sector
QCA	Qualifications and Curriculum Authority
QCF	Qualifications and Credit Framework
QIA	Quality Improvement Agency
QTLS	Qualified Teacher Learning and Skills
RAC	Regional Advisory Council
RDA	regional development agency
RPA	Raising the Participation Age
SFA	Skills Funding Agency
SFC	Scottish Funding Council
SFEFC	Scottish Further Education Funding Council
SHA	Secondary Heads Association
S/NVQ	Scottish National Vocational Qualification

SQA	Scottish Qualifications Authority
SSC	Sector Skills Council
SSDA	Sector Skills Development Agency
STEM	Science, Technology, Engineering and Mathematics
TA	transactional analysis
TEC	Training and Enterprise Council
TS	teaching strategies
TSC	Training Standards Council
TVEI	Technical and Vocational Education Initiative
UCAC	Undeb Cenedlaethol Athrawon Cymru
UCU	University and College Union
UfI	University for Industry
UHI	University of the Highlands and Islands
UKCES	United Kingdom Commission for Employment and Skills
ULF	Union Learning Fund
ULR	Union Learning Representative
UTC	University Technical College
VLE	Virtual Learning Environment
WEA	Workers' Educational Association
WGA	Welsh Government Assembly
YPLA	Young People's Learning Agency

Part I

Further education in context

Chapter 1

Where will I teach?

Nature and scope of further education

This chapter describes the shape and scope of the complex and shifting landscape of further education (FE) in the UK. Part of the chapter presents a historical review of the structural changes imposed on FE by central government over the past 30 or so years. Teaching and learning are situated activities that are profoundly affected by the contexts in which they occur. At the same time, teachers and learners also shape and change the contexts in which they work and study. This chapter is intended to help you gain a better understanding of the nature of the context in which you teach in terms of how your college is being affected by internal and external pressures and the role colleges play in a broader educational landscape. In writing a book of this nature, we are faced with the challenge of trying to keep up to date with educational change in the UK, and particularly in England where government ministers seem to have an almost pathological desire to invent as many new policies as possible during their (often) very short term in office (see Fuller and Unwin, 2011). In the five years since we wrote the third edition of this book, the FE landscape has been changing, and we know that in the time that passes before someone reads this new edition, there will have been new policies invented and some agencies may have come and gone. Furthermore, the UK is currently dealing with the aftermath of the economic crisis that began in 2008. As a result, the coalition government, elected in May 2010, is administering a programme of substantial cuts to the public sector, including education. We want to stress, however, that while FE teachers work in a dynamic context, much of what they do still involves the age-old process of helping people to learn and achieve their ambitions.

FE colleges are now very much in the limelight in terms of public policy, having spent many years off the educational radar, unlike universities and schools, which have been much more successful in making sure both government and the general public understand the value of their activities. Of course, achieving greater visibility is not necessarily a good thing, particularly if colleges are expected, on the one hand, to play a major role in improving the nation's skills levels to help the UK get its economy back on track, while, on the other hand, providing a home for thousands of 14–18 year olds who the schools cannot or are disinclined to teach. Policymakers continue to believe that increasing the stocks of qualifications (which act as a proxy for skills) in the UK will benefit the economy (for critiques of this view and its impact on education, see, inter alia, Felstead et al., 2009; Coffield et al., 2008; Wolf et al., 2006; Wolf, 2002).

This book uses the term 'FE' to encompass colleges that provide education and training for learners from the age of 14 upwards. The lower age limit has dropped to 14 since 2002 when the then Department for Education and Skills (DfES) in England introduced the Increased Flexibility Programme (IFP) for 14–16 year olds. The IFP enabled school pupils to spend up to three days in a college so that they could access vocational learning opportunities (see Chapters 2 and 3 for more details). This raises issues related to teaching and learning in colleges, which we will examine in more detail throughout the book (see Orr, 2010; Lumby, 2007). The vast majority of students in FE colleges are still, however, over the age of 16, and colleges are the biggest providers of post-16 education in the UK.

A range of different types of institutions are designated as colleges. At the time of writing, there are 411 colleges in the UK. In England, there are 222 general further education (GFE) and tertiary colleges, 94 sixth-form colleges, 10 specialised designated colleges (mainly for adults and some with residential facilities), 16 land-based colleges, and 3 art, design and performing arts colleges. In Wales, there are 19 GFE colleges and 1 sixth-form college, while Scotland has 43 GFE colleges and Northern Ireland has 6 'super colleges' formed from the merger of 16 colleges over the past 5 years. These colleges form part of a complex landscape of public, private and voluntary education and training in the UK. The Association of Employment and Learning Providers (AELP) in England has some 600 members, including 50 FE colleges, spanning private, not-for-profit and 'third sector' organisations, while in Scotland, the Scottish Training Federation has some 100 members. In 2009, it was estimated that there were 12,300 private training providers in the UK, a figure that included organisations using the title 'college' (Simpson, 2009).

In the early 2000s in England and Wales, under the previous Labour government, the term, 'learning and skills sector' (LSS) emerged to incorporate all post-compulsory education and training, not including higher education in universities. The coalition government is now using the term 'further education and skills sector' in England. This shift in terminology may suggest a desire to distinguish colleges from other types of providers. Similarly, in Wales, Scotland and Northern Ireland, government websites make distinct references to FE colleges. Language is important here because, as we will see in Chapter 4, the labels that policymakers choose reflect their views on the purpose and status of education and training.

The figures quoted above for the numbers of colleges are subject to change because, much more so than in the case of schools and universities, colleges are subject to mergers and even closures. For example, in England, the current total number of 345 colleges has dropped from a figure of 429 in 2000, largely as result of mergers. The Scottish government has decided to bring its colleges within a regional structure to achieve economies of scale and to encourage much greater cooperation between institutions (Scottish Government, 2011). In 2011, there were some 3.3 million students in colleges in England and 347,336 in Scotland. In Wales, the figure is around 240,000 and for Northern Ireland, just under 90,000. The majority of FE students across the UK are over the age of 19 and studying part-time, but the full-time 16–19-year-old students outnumber those of the same age group found in schools.

Some FE colleges in England use the title 'tertiary college'. This was originally given to institutions providing both vocational and academic courses for the 16–19 age group, thus combining the functions of a further education college and a sixth-form college in areas where schools did not offer sixth-form (post-compulsory) provision. The existence of different types of college in England has been the subject of debate over many years, and their respective levels of achievement in terms of student outcomes and retention rates are regularly compared (see Simmons, 2009). The main debate tends to focus on whether 16–19-year-old full-time students following academic courses are better served by studying in schools, sixth-form colleges and tertiary colleges as opposed to general FE colleges. Sixth-form colleges focus mainly on 16–19 year olds studying A levels, though increasingly they also offer vocational courses, and in some areas they compete with both schools and other colleges for students.

Perry (2005: 1) has argued that 'colleges exist in a local infrastructure that is rarely designed, but more often the consequence of historical and organisational factors'. Some of the oldest of the FE colleges have their roots in the Mechanics' Institutes of the early nineteenth century, which were established to debate and provide courses related to the advancements in science. Mechanics' Institutes were established in Glasgow and London in 1823, with the latter eventually becoming Birbeck College in 1907 and subsequently part of the University of London. In the late nineteenth century, there was considerable concern that Britain was falling behind other industrialised countries such as Germany, France and the US. In 1890, the tax on beer and spirits was raised and the extra revenue, known as 'whisky money', was given to local councils to make arrangements for technical education (Bailey, 1983). As a result, colleges began to be established. For example, Huddersfield Technical College began as the Huddersfield Mechanics' Institute in the 1840s and became a technical college in 1896, whereas Lowestoft College, the most easterly college in Britain, traces its origins to evening art classes held in 1874, while courses in navigation for fishermen began in 1923. As Green and Lucas (1999: 11) note, the growth of the FE sector was 'part of the formation of the modern state in the late nineteenth century, reflecting one of the many aspects of a voluntarist relationship between education, training and the state' (see also Bailey, 2002).

The 1960s and 1970s saw a considerable expansion in the FE sector, not just within the area of technical and vocational education but also in the development of professional and academic courses. Some of these were on a full-time basis, often for those students who were looking for an alternative to education provided in the school sixth form. In the late 1970s and early 1980s, worldwide economic recession led to a sharp rise in the number of young people in the UK who could not find jobs. The Labour and Conservative governments of the day sought to alleviate youth unemployment by introducing a series of youth training and work experience schemes (see Unwin, 1997, 2010). Parallel programmes were also introduced for unemployed adults. Many colleges became involved in these schemes by providing off-the-job training and/or by acting as 'managing agents' working with local employers to give young people work placements.

FE colleges have worked hard to demonstrate an 'inclusive' approach. That is, they have provided mainly non-selective education for everyone who wished to benefit from extended education or vocational training. Most colleges also provide courses for young people and adults with learning difficulties and/or with disabilities. The 1996 Tomlinson Report (*Inclusive Learning*) had a major impact on colleges as it turned on its head the existing attitude to provision for learners with difficulties, including disabilities: 'Put simply, we want to avoid a viewpoint which locates the difficulty or deficit with the student and focus instead on the capacity of the education institution to understand and respond to the individual learner's requirement' (Tomlinson, 1996: 4). The 1998 Beattie Committee on inclusiveness in Scotland followed Tomlinson's lead. In 2002, the Disability Discrimination Act was extended to educational institutions, placing a duty on them not to discriminate against disabled learners and, where necessary, to provide them with personal support (for a report of a staff development initiative in Scottish colleges to support teachers in developing a more inclusive approach, see Doughty and Allan, 2008).

Selection does exist in parts of the sector. For example, sixth-form colleges are much more likely to specify entry qualifications for academic courses than GFE colleges. Colleges are multifaceted organisations, on the one hand providing for the needs of their local community, and on the other hand for a growing regional, national and, in some cases, international student clientele. In her 1997 seminal report on FE, Helena Kennedy declared that 'Defining further education exhaustively would be God's own challenge because it is such a large and fertile section of the education world' (Kennedy, 1997: 1). Felstead and Unwin (2001: 107), in an analysis of further education funding, argued that colleges in England were trying to fulfil four key aims:

- to respond to the government's economic agenda to improve basic and intermediate skill levels of young people and adults and increase their participation in education and training;
- to fulfil their role as the main provider of sub-degree post-compulsory education and training at local level;
- to continue to provide a wide-ranging curriculum that bridges the vocational/non-vocational divide; and
- to continue being a 'second-chance saloon' for young people and adults who want to return to learning.

In addition, the majority of colleges in the UK are increasingly engaged in higher education (HE) provision, often in partnership with local universities. Many of these students are studying for Higher National Certificates (HNCs) and Higher National Diplomas (HNDs), and, in England, for Foundation Degrees. Some colleges are also providing full honours degree programmes. Gallacher (2006: 45) argues that the substantial presence of HE in FE in Scotland has enhanced the status of FE colleges, which are now 'clearly viewed as key institutions in widening access, promoting social inclusion and providing opportunities for lifelong learning'. Field (2004), however, has agreed that deep inequalities still persist for adults who try to enter the more prestigious universities in Scotland via the FE route.

Despite the increasing closeness of the FE/HE interface, however, Parry (2005: 11) argues that, in England, 'higher education has still to be widely recognised and accepted as a normal or necessary activity in colleges'. These developments pose challenging questions about the nature of student and teacher identity, about the potential place of research in an FE teacher's portfolio and, ultimately, about the extent to which the traditional status boundaries between FE and HE will dissolve (see Pike and Harrison, 2011; Wilson and Wilson, 2011; Bathmaker and Thomas, 2009; Griffiths and Lloyd, 2009).

Since 2001, colleges in England, Wales and Northern Ireland have worked closely with higher education institutions (HEIs) and employers to introduce Foundation Degrees (see Chapter 3 for more details). Scotland is not delivering Foundation Degrees, preferring to stick with the existing HNCs and HNDs that have been available for many years in the UK, and have a high satisfaction rating with both students and, crucially, employers.

In August 2011, two GFE colleges in the North East of England (New College Durham and the Newcastle Colleges Group) were given the powers to award Foundation Degrees in their own right. The proposal to allow colleges this right was first aired in the Further Education and Training Bill in 2007. At that time, Universities UK, the membership organisation representing the majority of UK universities, warned that, by giving colleges degree-awarding powers, the 'UK HE brand' would be diminished, and the House of Lords blocked the proposal at the second reading of the bill. Others, however, including the Association of Colleges (AoC) in England, have argued that colleges have proved they can deliver good quality higher education and that they can respond more quickly to employer needs. Parry (2005: 14) has argued that in the light of the expansion of higher education, the concept of further education has 'become increasingly redundant' and that it should be abandoned 'in favour of an open system of colleges and universities'. The current coalition government has since declared its desire to allow more providers (public and private sector) into the higher education market and to expand the proportion of 'HE in FE' (DBIS, 2011a).

Since 1993, colleges in England have experienced a number of major changes to the way in which they are funded and their relationship with central government. Until April 1993, FE colleges were under the control of their local education authority (LEA) from whom they received the bulk of their funding (the rest coming from central government and other agencies). The 1988 Education Reform Act had given colleges and schools the power to manage their own budgets, thus beginning to loosen the control of the LEAs. In 1991, the White Paper *Education and Training for the 21st Century* announced that colleges were to be given the 'freedom' they needed to play a 'central part in providing more high-quality opportunities' and to enable them to 'respond to the demand from students and employers for high-quality further education' (DES/ED/WO, 1991: 58). In his foreword to the White Paper, the then Prime Minister, John Major, outlined his government's desire to 'knock down the barriers to opportunity', and for 'more choice', in order to 'give every one of Britain's young people the chance to make the most of his or her particular talents and to have the best possible start in life' (ibid.: foreword).

Under the terms of the 1992 Further and Higher Education Act, which followed the White Paper, all colleges, including sixth-form colleges, were removed from LEA control, just as polytechnics and higher education colleges had been in 1989. Colleges became independent, self-governing corporations with responsibility for their own budgets, staffing, marketing, course planning and provision. Two new national funding bodies were established for England and Wales: the Further Education Funding Council (FEFC) in England and the Welsh Funding Council in Wales. In Northern Ireland and Scotland, colleges were funded via the Northern Ireland Office and the Scottish Office respectively.

In 1999, the UK government embarked on a process of parliamentary devolution whereby power was transferred to the Scottish Parliament, the National Assembly for Wales and the National Assembly for Northern Ireland. As Gunning and Raffe (2011) explain, prior to devolution, education and training in the separate 'home countries' of the UK had always contained some differences (see also Bryce and Hume, 2009; Osborne, 2006). Scotland's schooling system was the most distinctive, having never been administered by the UK government, but complete separation only came when funding for its universities and for training was devolved. In 1999, the Scottish Further Education Funding Council (SFEFC) was established.

The removal of colleges from LEA control was part of the Conservative government's attempts to reduce the power of local authorities following the poll tax debacle. Gleeson (1996: 87) has argued that the 1988 and 1992 Acts and a further Education Act in 1994 led to post-16 policy being 'driven by market principles and deregulation' and a break with the 'municipal or public service view of school and further education which linked schools and colleges with LEAs within the spirit of the settlement which followed the 1944 Act'. Reference to the 1944 Education Act is important for it stated, for the first time, that it was a legal duty of LEAs to support FE provision and maintain colleges. The local political constraints on LEAs meant, however, that the funding available to colleges varied considerably from one part of the country to another. Simmons (2008: 368) reminds us that 'levels of service provided to students and the wider community were highly variable under local authority control and the deficiencies of that era need to be acknowledged'.

Though free from LEA control, colleges in England soon found that the FEFC was to impose a strict funding methodology that would determine the nature of the courses and qualifications they could offer. Lucas (1999: 54) has argued that 'few supporters of incorporation realised that a move away from the benign control of LEAs would mean so much FEFC regulation and downward pressure'. The creation of a national funding methodology was a central pillar of the FEFC's goal to forge FE into a coherent and more homogenised sector on a par with schools and higher education. What had often been referred to as the 'Cinderella' of the education sector was now expected, virtually overnight, to emerge from the shadows. The months and years following incorporation proved to be both an exhilarating and painful period for FE colleges. Taubman (2000: 82–3) records that following incorporation, 'further education had proportionally more days lost to strike action than any other sector of the British economy'. In their attempts to provide the 'choice' for students and employers laid out in the 1991 White Paper, and to maximise the funding on offer from the FEFC and other bodies, some colleges hit the media headlines for falsifying student numbers and other fraudulent practices (for a discussion of how this arose, see Shattock, 2000). Although it is fair to say that the vast majority of colleges managed incorporation without recourse to bad practice, the imposition, by government, of a market-driven approach across the public services in the mid-1990s encouraged educational institutions to compete in ways that did little to enhance the quality of education and training, nor to ensure that learners gained access to the most appropriate provision.

Just prior to the incorporation of colleges, the government had created a network of 100 Training and Enterprise Councils (TECs) in 1990 in England,

Wales and Scotland (where they were called Local Enterprise Companies). The TECs (and LECs in Scotland) were established as employer-led companies whose objectives were to fund, organise and manage work-based training programmes for young people and adults, but also to stimulate enterprise in their local areas. As many colleges acted as managing agents for government-supported training schemes and also as off-the-job training providers for employers and other managing agents, they found themselves in a paradoxical relationship with the TECs and LECs. On the one hand, they depended on the TECs and LECs for some of their funding, whereas on the other they competed with them for customers. Every young person who accepted a place on a youth training scheme was also a potential full-time FE student (see Unwin, 1999).

In 1997, the new Labour government, led by Prime Minister Tony Blair, announced that one of its first priorities would be to carry out a major review of post-compulsory education and training structures in England. This led to a White Paper in 1999, *Learning to Succeed*, in which the government spelt out its dissatisfaction with the current arrangements for the funding and planning of post-16 education and training. As you read the following quotation, you might hear echoes of recent policy documents:

> There is too much duplication, confusion and bureaucracy in the current system. Too little money actually reaches learners and employers, too much is tied up in bureaucracy. There is an absence of effective coordination or strategic planning. The system has insufficient focus on skill and employer needs at national, regional and local levels. The system lacks innovation and flexibility, and there needs to be more collaboration and cooperation to ensure higher standards and the right range of choices . . . the current system falls short.
>
> (DfEE, 1999: 21)

Just over a decade later, the current coalition government is still striving to achieve the same goals. Compare the quotation above with this one from a policy document on reforming post-compulsory education and training in England, which declares that the goal is:

> to create a simple transparent funding system that is both robust in ensuring funding goes only to high quality provision that delivers good value for money, while being innovative to respond to local circumstances.
>
> (DBIS, 2011b: 4)

The 1999 White Paper proposed a massive restructuring of the landscape in England. The responsibility and leadership of post-compulsory education and training (now post-14) would become overwhelmingly centralised, and delivery of programmes and services handed to agencies contracted to the state (for an earlier discussion on the 'contract state', see Ainley and Vickerstaff, 1993).

Using very similar language to the 1991 Conservative White Paper discussed above, *Learning to Succeed* based its reforms on the need for people to reach their potential by having access to as many learning opportunities as possible. Just as in a host of other policy documents dating back to 1976 when the then Prime Minister, James Callaghan, declared that the education system was failing the nation's economy, this new White Paper stressed the economic imperatives that should drive education and training provision. The FEFC would be abolished and replaced by the Learning and Skills Council (LSC) for England to oversee the 'learning and skills sector', covering FE colleges, private training providers, adult and community learning, prison education and the voluntary sector. The TECs (though not LECs, which continued until 2005) would be abolished and replaced by 47 local LSCs. The LSC's first chairman, Bryan Sanderson, who had previously been Chief Executive of BP Chemicals, was quick to impress on colleges that his new agency wanted them to operate within a tough business model. He expressed this in a lecture to the Royal Society of Arts soon after taking office in April 2001:

> Customers can be disaffected, there can be a high drop-out rate, there may be a mismatch between what the customer wants and what they get, there may be continuous rethinks on policy but none of those things seems ever to really matter because there's probably a belief that the money will come anyway. To be brutal, we in the Learning and Skills Council need to inject a little discomfort into this scenario – fear of the revenue streams suddenly drying up.
>
> (Sanderson, 2001: 23)

The abolition of the FEFC, which had inspected colleges as well as funding them, meant that new inspection procedures were required. The White Paper proposed, therefore, that the Office for Standards in Education (Ofsted) would extend its remit from just inspecting schools to inspecting college-based provision for 16–19 year olds, and that a new Adult Learning Inspectorate (ALI) would be created for work-based provision for 16–19 year olds as well as all college-based post-19 provision. The ALI replaced the Training Standards Council (TSC), which had been inspecting government-funded work-based training in colleges and other training providers. Finally, a new approach to careers advice and guidance was to be introduced. The White Paper announced that the existing careers services and organisations responsible for supporting young people more generally (for example, the Youth Service and the Probation Service) would work together under the umbrella of local agencies to be called Connexions. This latter reform had been recommended in a parallel report from the government's Social Exclusion Unit (see SEU, 1999).

The turbulent 2000s

In June 2001, the Labour government was re-elected and further reforms came into force. The DfEE was renamed the Department for Education and Skills (DfES). The significance of this was that responsibility for the Employment Service, which managed the New Deal programmes for unemployed people over the age of 18, passed to another new department, the Department for Work and Pensions. The regional development agencies (RDAs), responsible for raising the capability of the English regions to compete both nationally and internationally, remained under the remit of the Department for Trade and Industry (DTI). The Cabinet Office established the Performance and Innovation Unit (PIU), responsible for researching and policymaking in the area of workforce development and skills. The Cabinet Office also appointed an 'e-envoy' with responsibility for pushing forward Labour's policy to promote e-commerce and the use of new technologies, while the DTI appointed a new Minister for e-Commerce and Competitiveness. The important point here is that colleges in England, with their wide-ranging interests, were increasingly required to relate to all the government departments with influence over some aspect of post-14 education and training provision. Importantly, that influence was not confined to the government's education department. Keep (2006: 51) used a telling metaphor to capture the way policymakers in England seem to be fixated with 'reforming' education and training in England: he said they were playing with the biggest train set in the world. As a consequence:

> The centralisation of English E&T runs counter to trends elsewhere in Europe. Over the last decade in many other EU countries, such as the Netherlands, Italy, Sweden and Finland, E&T policy has been devolved to local social partnership arrangements, wherein the governmental role is taken up by elected local authorities or municipalities.

In contrast to England, there has been greater stability in Wales and Scotland. Gunning and Raffe (2011: 254) argue that, as a result:

> Providers such as college leaders feel closer to policy-makers than in England . . . And both countries have preserved a stronger role for local government and have not created a large number of schools directly accountable to central government as in England.

Finlay *et al.* (2006), in a study of the LSC, echo Ainley and Vickerstaff's (1993) earlier concern about the role of government agencies. They argue that, paradoxically, 'the apparent devolution of power to intermediary agencies', such as the LSC, was accompanied by 'a greater centralisation of power as the modernising state confines local public services to being the deliverers of central government priorities'. The pressure to deliver affects everyone involved and, ironically, the intermediary agencies found themselves subject to constant criticism and interference. Hence, despite having established the LSC, its parent department, the DfES, sought to restrict any sign of independence.

In June 2007, Gordon Brown replaced Tony Blair as Prime Minister. On his second day in office, he announced that the DfES was to be abolished and two new departments created to cover education and training: the Department for Innovation, Universities and Skills (DIUS) and the Department for Children, Schools and Families (DCSF). The DTI was also abolished and its innovation and skills remit absorbed by DIUS, while its other functions were taken over by the new Department for Business, Enterprise and Regulatory Reform (BERR). DIUS and BERR probably hold the record for the shortest-lived government departments, as they too were replaced in June 2009 by the Department for Business Innovation and Skills (DBIS).

Gordon Brown's government also signalled, through a White Paper, that responsibility for the funding and organisation of 16–18 education would revert back to LEAs, thus suggesting that the continued existence of the LSC was under review (DfES, 2007). This White Paper is also notable because it included the government's intention to make it mandatory, by 2015, for all young people in England to be in some form of government-supported education and training until the age of 18. The Coalition Government confirmed it would continue with this policy when it was elected in May 2010. The policy is referred to as Raising the Participation Age (RPA). The following year, in a follow-up to the 2007 White Paper, it was announced that the LSC would indeed be abolished (in April 2010) and replaced by the Skills Funding Agency (SFA) and the Young People's Learning Agency (YPLA). The former would be responsible for funding post-compulsory education and training for the 19+ age group, while the latter would manage the funding of provision for 16–18 year olds that was to be handed to the LEAs (DCSF/DIUS, 2008). The most significant effect of these changes was to cement a clear administrative divide between schooling up to the age of 18, and education and training for people aged 19 and over. The rearrangement of the patchwork quilt of government agencies in England under Labour was completed in April 2009 by the establishment of the National Apprenticeship Service (NAS) to work with the SFA.

In May 2010, the squares on the patchwork quilt were once more re-arranged. The media headlines at the time focused on what was dubbed a 'bonfire of the quangos' (quango is the acronym for quasi-autonomous non-governmental organisation) when government announced the abolition of 192 agencies in England, including the RDAs. As was noted earlier in this chapter, the DCSF was replaced with the Department for Education (DfE). DBIS was retained but, as we write, there is speculation that government oversight of HE might be transferred from DBIS to the DfE.

Another agency to fall under the axe was the YPLA, which was replaced in April 2012 by the Education Funding Agency (EFA) and has responsibility for the direct funding of 16–19 education and training in FE colleges and sixth-form colleges, as well as for schools. In a White Paper published soon after coming to power, the new Secretary of State for Education, Michael Gove, made it clear that he wanted schools to be free of LEA control. Thus, as more schools become 'academies' or 'free schools', the EFA will increasingly distribute funding directly to the schools themselves rather than via the LEAs. As Whitty (2012: 69) has argued, Gove is building on Tony Blair's agenda, which '. . . emphasised neo-liberal policies of parental choice and school diversity as the key to educational improvement and closing the social class attainment gap'. FE teachers in England who work with 14–19 year olds are affected by these changes as they are likely to disrupt collaborative arrangements between schools and colleges at the local level (see Hodgson and Spours, 2011).

Devolved government in Scotland, Wales and Northern Ireland also resulted in further structural change affecting FE colleges. In 2001, TECs and the FEFC were replaced in Wales by the National Council for Education and Training in Wales (known as ELWa, which stood for Education and Learning Wales). ELWa was responsible for all post-16 education and training, and incorporated both the Further and Higher Education Funding Councils for Wales (HEFCW). In 2006, ELWa was incorporated into the Department for Education, Lifelong Learning and Skills (DELLS) within the new National Assembly for Wales. DELLS also covered further and higher education funding. The Scottish Executive, which was established as the newly devolved government for Scotland in 1999, following the first elections to the Scottish Parliament, gave responsibility for FE to its Enterprise and Lifelong Learning Department (ELLD). This was then renamed the Enterprise, Transport and Lifelong Learning Department (ETLLD) and the Scottish Further and Higher Funding Councils were merged into the Scottish Funding Council (SFC). As the devolution process evolved, the parliamentary functions of the Welsh and Northern Ireland Assemblies were split from the administrative functions of what are now called the Welsh government and Northern Ireland Executive, and between the Scottish government (formerly Scottish Executive) and the Scottish Parliament.

In Northern Ireland, the Department for Employment and Learning (Delni) now has responsibility for further and higher education, while the Department of Education looks after schools, thus replicating the split in England. In the Scottish government, responsibility for schools, FE and HE sits with the Cabinet Minister for Education and Lifelong Learning, while in the Welsh government it sits with Education and Skills. The merger of the funding councils in Scotland, Wales and Northern Ireland marks a significant difference from the English context, where FE and HE are still funded separately despite the increasing closeness of their relationship described earlier in this chapter.

One area in which the devolved administrations showed divergence was in relation to careers advice and guidance. Northern Ireland (through Careers Service NI), Wales (through Careers Wales) and Scotland (through Skills Development Scotland) introduced an all-age model for careers education, advice and guidance well before the establishment of the National Careers Service (replacing Connexions) in England. Wales and Scotland have also been more active in setting up post-16 frameworks for credit accumulation and transfer encompassing all qualifications up to and including postgraduate and professional. Furthermore, a Welsh Baccalaureate qualification, initially trialled in 2003, has been available nationally since September 2007 (for more details, see Chapter 3). For the moment, however, we would argue that the similarities in the practice of teaching and learning in FE colleges in the 'home countries' still far outweigh their differences.

Finally, change has also affected the way that colleges are inspected. In April 2007, ALI was abolished and its responsibilities absorbed into Ofsted, whose acronym remained the same but now stands for Office for Standards in Education, Children's Services and Skills. In Scotland, the HM Inspectorate of Education (HMIE) became an executive agency of the Scottish Parliament in 2001 as part of devolution. Arrangements in Wales and Northern Ireland have, however, remained the same, with both retaining the titles of Her Majesty's Inspectorates, though in Wales this is referred to as Estyn.

FE funding

The way in which educational institutions are funded has a major impact on their character. Allocating funding is a highly charged political process, and government and its agencies are constantly reviewing their formulae. As shown above, the establishment of the further education funding councils in 1992 was designed to rationalise a system of funding that was highly localised. In 1993, the Audit Commission and Ofsted produced a highly critical report on 'drop-out' rates for 16–19 year olds on full-time courses in English colleges. The report, which was titled *Unfinished Business*, highlighted, for the first time, the large numbers of students who were leaving courses before completion (30–40 per cent) and condemned this as a huge waste of public money, as well as a waste of students' time and effort (Audit Commission/Ofsted, 1993). The new funding councils were, therefore, charged with designing a more efficient funding regime that would improve retention and achievement rates.

Under this new funding methodology, every student enrolled at a college would attract funding units – the precise number of which depended on the course they were following, the progress made and whether they achieved the intended outcome. This introduced the principle that funding should follow the learner. The FEFC also drew up a list of those qualifications it would fund (known as Schedule 2) and those it would not. Colleges could, of course, provide courses leading to non-Schedule 2 qualifications but they would have to charge students fees for these or get them funded from somewhere else. A further ploy was to repackage existing non-Schedule 2 provision to bring it within the Schedule 2 framework. As Unwin (1999: 79) discovered, this relied on the creativity of college lecturers and curriculum managers. For example, one college lecturer explained that 'flower arranging is off, but floristry is on because we can get that accredited', whereas another described how popular classes in interior design techniques such as stenciling were reclassified under the heading 'Decorative Paint Techniques' (ibid.). Colleges were awarded their funding allocation annually after submitting a strategic plan in which they set out a target number of units for that year (see Felstead and Unwin, 2001). To assist colleges with their funding plans, the funding councils introduced the Individualised Student Record (ISR).

Opinions differ as to the effectiveness of the FEFC funding methodology. Jaquette (2009) argues that incorporation improved achievement rates by linking funding directly to student success, but that this came at the expense of centralisation, and a loss of local accountability as colleges were forced to pursue national economic interests rather than local ones. Lucas (1999), while acknowledging some positive outcomes, argues that the FEFC model led colleges to put financial considerations above the quality of learning. Felstead and Unwin (2001) highlighted the way in which the need to amass funding units encouraged colleges to recruit full-time students to courses that were inexpensive to run. This, in turn, meant colleges were less concerned about local labour market needs.

The FEFC model is important in that it established the government's control over what was eligible for funding. In each of the 'home countries', FE colleges are subject to differing funding arrangements, but, in the current climate of economic austerity, policymakers have stepped up their calls for 'better value for money'. Between 1999/2000 and 2009/2010, public spending on education in the UK grew by 5.1 per cent in real terms, which, according to the Institute for Fiscal Studies (IFS), was the fastest growth for any decade since the mid-1970s (Chowdry and Sibieta, 2011). In contrast, the IFS estimates that from 2010/2011 to 2014/2015, education funding will fall by 3.5 per cent, representing the largest cut over any four-year period since at least the 1950s (ibid.).

While schools face the smallest cuts (about 1 per cent in total), some of the heaviest burdens will fall on colleges. From the 2010 Comprehensive Spending Review to 2014–2015, the SFA's budget for education and training for individuals aged 19 and over in England will be cut by 25 per cent, while Scottish colleges face cuts in the region of 11 per cent. This means that funding agencies as well as the institutions they fund are under intense pressure. In a letter to the Chief Executive of the SFA in March 2011, the Secretary of State at DBIS, Vince Cable, wrote:

> it is vital that public funding is used as effectively as possible, and that the Agency controls unit costs and retains sufficient flexibility to meet any cost pressures that may arise . . . It is our joint expectation that the (SFA) will reduce its administration costs by 2014–15 by 33%, with savings over 24%

being released into front-line participation. I recognise that this is a challenging goal, and that the achievement of savings beyond 24% will be subject to managing effectively a number of risks.

(Cable, 2011: 3)

Along with the long-standing desire to simplify post-16 funding, the coalition government is keen to get employers and individuals to share more of the cost of education and training. This is clearly set out in a DBIS strategy document published in 2010, which states:

The main driver in this new system is empowered learners and businesses. We expect that by giving learners and employers a good range of information about the curriculum and the quality and value of different learning opportunities . . . they will be better informed to make choices about where and what to learn. This will drive a step change in the quality of learning and establish clear accountability of providers to their customers rather than of providers to government.

(DBIS, 2010: 53–4)

Similar rhetoric can also be found in the *Review of Post-16 Education and Vocational Training in Scotland* (Roe, 2011). Some readers of this book may at this point be shouting, 'We've heard all this before!' They might be able to cite a DfES report from 2006 that declared:

Funding will be targeted on priority areas and follow the needs of learners and employers – with young people's choices funded in full and increasing amounts of funding for adult learning flowing through demand-led mechanisms – Learner Accounts and Train to Gain.

(DfES, 2006b: 65)

Here again, we see the obsession with 'choice' and 'demand' as being the drivers that will 'modernise' the public services. The reference to Learner Accounts and Train to Gain is also significant. The former was the previous government's attempt to recreate the Individual Learning Account (ILA) initiative, which it had launched in September 2000 and quickly closed in October 2001 after it led to fraudulent practice by a number of training providers who were claiming money for non-existent learners and/or for delivering non-existent courses.

The concept of Learner Accounts (later called Skills Accounts) and Train to Gain are closely related. In 2002, a series of regional Employer Training Pilots was set up, funded through local LSCs and the Business Link network, to encourage employees without a Level 2 qualification to seek training. In 2006, the initiative was renamed Train to Gain, and became available on a national basis with a massive budget of some £1 billion. Under Train to Gain, money was available (in the form of Learner Accounts) to fund individuals so they could obtain their first Level 2 qualification (either NVQ or GCSE equivalents) and to compensate employers (with less than 50 employees) while their employees engaged in training, although larger employers could also take part. A skills broker was also funded by the LSC to help the employer and employee decide on their training needs and arrange suitable training. The Train to Gain initiative was heavily criticised for wasting public money on training that employers would normally have paid for (often referred to as the 'deadweight problem') and also for funding the accreditation of employees' existing skills rather than paying for retraining or upskilling (for critical evaluation, see Keep, 2008; Hillage *et al.*, 2006). Prior to the 2010 general election, the Conservative Party announced that, if elected, it would end Train to Gain and plough the funding into the expansion of apprenticeships. Many FE colleges in England benefitted from Train to Gain funding, which in some cases amounted to one third of a college's overall budget. When it became clear that it was going to end, many colleges refocused their attention on apprenticeships.

In her passionate polemic about FE, Alison Wolf (2009) called for 'an adult approach' to the funding of post-19 education and training. By this, she meant that governments and providers should stop deciding what types of courses and qualifications should receive public funding and allow the market to decide (see also Banks, 2010). Adults would shape the market by paying for what they wanted, with some of the fee being subsidised by government. In 2010, the UK Commission for Employment and Skills (UKCES) proposed the intro-duction of what it called Personal Learning Accounts to provide a financial incentive for individuals and a 'mobilising effect on the population' (UKCES, 2010: 2). Scotland, Wales and Northern Ireland all continue to experiment with various forms of learning accounts.

In England, the latest version is the online Lifelong Learning Account (LLA), administered by the National Careers Service. The LLA is a curious beast as it lacks the one element that was central to the design of earlier versions – an actual amount of money made up of a contribution from government and from the individual, which the individual could then spend. The LLA has two functions: (a) to provide a place where adults can record their education and training achievements, CV, and so on; and (b) it records the cost of the government-funded course they are attending.

The LLA has been introduced at the same time as the highly controversial decision to abolish the Education Maintenance Allowance (EMA) in England. When the Labour government came to power in 1997, it was concerned that the numbers of 16 year olds staying on in full-time education in the UK had plateaued at around 70 per cent of the cohort. In 1999, the EMA was introduced as a system of financial support (administered by LEAs in England) in the form of a means-tested weekly allowance for 16–19 year olds from low-income households. Maguire and Thompson (2006: 64), in a review of the evaluation studies of the EMA, discuss the difficulties in trying to assess whether this type of social policy initiative can be said to have worked. They argue that, 'What is indisputable is that the introduction of EMA removed the inequities and unpredictability which surrounded the system of student support for young people in post-16 education that previously existed'. However, they also report that while the evaluation evidence shows increasing participation and retention rates in post-16 education, in particular among young men, it is less clear about the impact on achievement rates: 'This raises alarm bells about young people being "warehoused" in education' (ibid.). Despite a huge outcry, the coalition government announced that it was replacing the EMA in England from the autumn of 2011 with a smaller initiative targetted at 16–19 year olds in care, care leavers and those on income support. Scotland and Wales have continued with the EMA and it is under review in Northern Ireland. As an FE teacher, you will be aware that the financial circumstances of all your students (regardless of age) will have an effect on their capacity to continue with their studies and achieve their potential (see Thompson, 2011).

Colleges vary in size and scope and, hence, their funding differs considerably. A small college in England might receive funding in the region of £8 million from government, while one of the very large ones might receive in excess of £50 million. We could ask: Does size matter? Perry (2005) suggests that, as far as England is concerned, it does, and cites the fact that the larger colleges have a better inspection record. He notes, however, that they face the same problems as smaller colleges when it comes to maximising their resources. He argues that a move towards what he calls a 'national brand' might be a creative way forward. This might involve organising colleges in a federated system with one chancellor in a similar way to some of the community colleges in the US or some universities, such as London, in the UK. Colleges could then pool the costs of human resource management, IT infrastructure, publicity and, crucially, the development of teaching resources and curriculum design. In the current economic climate, some colleges are actively seeking ways to share resources.

Colleges have always built their income from a range of activities, including charging fees to some adult learners and some employers, from funding for higher education students, and from the European Social Fund (ESF) for projects related to deprivation or to increase diversity. The acute dilemma for college managers is how to balance the time they and their colleagues need to spend meeting government demands and targets with the need to chase and develop other income streams. Too often, the national and the local are in conflict. Stoten (2011: 300) argues that college principals have to operate at three levels:

- macro – dealing with government departments and agencies and FE employer and lobby groups such as the Association of Colleges, the Sixth Form Colleges Forum and the 157 Group;

- meso – dealing with stakeholders in their local education and training market; and
- micro – dealing with the management of their own institutions.

Some principals also operate at the global level as their colleges recruit international students and may have links with institutions in other countries.

Responsiveness, collaboration and the curriculum

Anyone who has worked in or carried out research on FE over the years will have witnessed the dynamism that characterises much of the sector. Colleges are constantly changing and adapting to new demands and circumstances. A major part of being responsive involves collaboration with a whole host of organisations and communities, some of whom, particularly local and regional government agencies, are also in a continuing state of flux. In July 2001, the then Secretary of State for Education and Skills, Estelle Morris, announced that 16 colleges in England could establish Centres of Vocational Excellence (CoVEs). By January 2006, 400 CoVEs had been established, including, for example: Accrington and Rossendale College – Construction Crafts; Canterbury College – Travel and Tourism; Cornwall College – ICT Networking Skills; Lough-borough College – Sports Science, Exercise and Fitness; and South Birmingham College – Childcare Training (see Wahlberg, 2007).

The CoVE concept recognised that amid the great diversity of provision within one institution, there will be one or more core subject areas for which it has particular expertise. The initiative also indicated a policy decision to retain a sectoral approach to the development and management of vocational education and training that had been developing since the 1960s. In 2002, the Sector Skills Development Agency (SSDA) was launched to lead a 'Skills for Business Network' of Sector Skills Councils (SSCs) to cover the whole of the UK. The 25 SSCs replaced the existing National Training Organisations (NTOs) and were given increased funding by government to deliver an ambitious remit. This would involve identifying the skill needs of their sectors, working with education and training providers to devise new qualifications, collaborating with local and regional agencies, championing the work of their sectors, and raising the levels of skills among the population.

Post-school education and training providers were covered by their own SSC, Lifelong Learning UK (LLUK), which replaced the Further Education National Training Organisation (FENTO) in 2005. As a result of the 2006 Leitch Review of Skills (Leitch Review, 2006), the SSCs were given even stronger powers and responsibility, and the SSDA was replaced in 2008 with the more powerful UKCES. For colleges in England, the most significant shift was the decision to place SSCs in the lead role with regard to the design of new diplomas for 14–19 year olds and the recommendation that only those vocational qualifications approved by SSCs should be eligible for government funding. As we shall see later in this chapter, however, under the coalition government, LLUK was abolished as part of the 'bonfire of the quangos'.

The SSCs represent a now dominant policy theme that post-16 education and training should be 'employer-led' (for critiques, see Keep, 2005; Unwin, 2004). In 2006, yet another initiative was announced: National Skills Academies (for an evaluation, see Chowdry and Sibieta, 2011). There are currently 19 academies covering sectors such as retail, social care, IT, and creative and cultural. They are expected to reshape and coordinate education and training provision at the local and regional levels to ensure it meets employer needs. Some have physical premises, while others are 'virtual' in that they are shopfronts for provision found in existing institutions such a colleges, private training providers and Group Training Associations (GTAs).

The phrase 'employer-led' permeates government documents and ministerial speeches. Given the origins of many colleges, as described earlier in this chapter, it could be argued that such an approach poses no problem for the FE sector. The reality, however, is that many employers do not want to 'lead' the design of qualifications and many struggle to define their training needs. Some employers take a very short-term approach to training and would like to abandon qualifications, while others regard training as equating to a few hours of induction on the job. At the other end of the spectrum are employers with long and proud histories of close cooperation with education through their professional bodies or local arrangements.

College staff

From the above description of the nature and scope of FE, it is clear that staff in colleges are faced with many competing demands on their time and energies. Those who manage the system are responsible for multimillion-pound businesses. They are accountable to different funding bodies, to local and national employers and to the external inspectorates for the quality of education and training provision. These pressures may appear contradictory at times (for example, the need to provide excellence in vocational education and training at the same time as driving down costs and increasing student numbers). As one FE lecturer we spoke to put it, 'It is impossible to put a financial value on people's learning needs and achievements'.

Employment patterns within the sector have changed in recent years, with an increase in part-time staff, more flexible contracts and the introduction of non-traditional teaching hours (for example, at weekends). New contracts issued by colleges outline very different terms and conditions of service from what one might expect for a teacher in a primary or secondary school. Edwards (1993: 48) has suggested that 'the trends towards multi-skilling and flexibility elsewhere in the economy are also to be found in institutions of post-compulsory education and training'. Hill (2000) reminds us, however, that the 'flexible firm' model has characterised the FE sector for many years due to the need for colleges to supplement their core staff with part-timers as they respond to the changing student market and to government initiatives. The following extract from the employment contract of a main grade lecturer in one of the largest FE colleges in England illustrates the extraordinary range of duties she will be expected to undertake:

> Formal schedule teaching, tutorials, student assessment, management of learning programmes and curriculum development, student admissions, educational guidance, counselling, preparation of learning materials and student assignments, marking student work, marking examinations, management and supervision of student visit programmes, research and other forms of scholarly activity, marketing activities, consultancy, leadership, supervisory, administration and personal professional development.

The reference to 'research and other forms of scholarly activity' signals an interesting extension to the workload of FE teachers – one that is discussed in detail in Chapter 7.

Although many staff in colleges belong to trade unions, national terms and conditions no longer exist. This means that colleges differ as to how many teaching hours they expect lecturers and support staff to deliver. Colleges in Wales and Scotland appear to be more uniform than those in England. Overall, pay rates for lecturers in GFE colleges fall below those for teachers in schools and sixth-form colleges. Colleges also vary in terms of their staff profiles. In England, FE has an ageing and gendered staff profile: 36.5 per cent of all college staff were aged over 50 in 2009/2010, compared to the average of 24 per cent for all sectors of the economy; and two thirds of college staff were female, though the ratio of male to female in relation to full-time staff is 50:50 (LSIS, 2011). Senior managers and 'technical' staff are the two areas where men still outnumber women. Scotland has a slightly higher percentage (57 per cent) of women working full-time, while colleges in Northern Ireland have a higher percentage of male employees, whereas Welsh colleges have a similar profile to those in England.

A new or established teacher in the FE sector may be working on a number of part-time contracts in different institutions. The future workforce could comprise freelance professionals moving between colleges in response to demand for their expertise. This unpredictability in employment reflects the way in which the organisation of work in wider society is being restructured, but it must be stressed that the FE sector has been particularly affected by uncertainty since the mid-1990s. Avis (1999: 251), building on the work of a number of commentators (for example, Ainley and Bailey, 1997; Hodkinson, 1997; Randle and Brady, 1997; Elliott, 1996) on the increasing problems faced by FE staff as a result of marketisation and managerialism, highlights the following areas for concern, which, over a decade after his article was written, still remain:

- loss of control;
- intensification of labour;
- increase in administration;
- perceived marginalisation of teaching; and
- stress on measurable performance indicators.

Gleeson and Shain (1999: 558), however, argue that 'the influence of markets and managerialism is as much a contested as a controlling one', and that 'While there is evidence of deprofessionalisation and casualisation in FE ... here also exists competing forms of resistance and response from lecturers and senior managers which challenge the hegemony of managerialism at college level'. As in any other profession, FE teachers are subject to the controlling tendencies of managers and to the restrictions placed on their actions by external agencies. The extent to which FE teachers are able to exert their professional identities will differ from college to college and will also be influenced by the status of their subject area, their level of confidence in their ability, and the degree of support they receive from colleagues and managers. It is worth remembering that FE teachers still spend much of their time with students and, as Bloomer (1997) argues, 'it is an individual matter as to how far teachers decide to exert agency and thus take control of their work situation'.

In their study of staff satisfaction in 80 colleges in England, Davies and Owen (2001: 8) found that staff were much more likely to feel valued within a college that had 'an embedded culture of continuous improvement – rather than one of blame – which encouraged bottom-up initiatives within a clearly understood framework'. Such colleges might be said to have embraced the characteristics of what Fuller and Unwin (2004) have referred to as an 'expansive workplace learning environment' (for more details, see Chapter 8).

Teachers in FE colleges come from a diverse set of backgrounds. Some will have academic qualifications and others with professional qualifications will have perhaps become teachers after a substantial career in business or industry. There will be those who have qualified through a craft or technician route, who have spent a considerable time on the shop floor or training apprentices. In addition, there is a range of support staff: kitchen assistants, laboratory technicians, audio-visual technicians and learning support. There will also be clerical and administrative staff and those responsible for student services. Robson (1998: 588) argues that 'the very diversity of entry routes into FE teaching . . . creates, in sociological terms, a weak professional boundary' and thus weakens the profession's overall standing (see also Avis and Bathmaker, 2006; Robson et al., 2006). She adds that most FE teachers who deliver technical and vocational subjects retain strong allegiances to their first occupational identity (as formed in industry or commerce). Moving into a college can, therefore, be a stressful experience if those preformed occupational identities are threatened or disregarded.

The growth in staff with responsibility for 'learning support' reflects a number of issues: the increasing emphasis in colleges on flexible and student-centred learning; the need to improve retention and attainment levels; and the recognition that lecturers need help in the classroom to support students with very mixed abilities. Colleges also have to make provision for students with disabilities and learning difficulties. In their investigation of the nature and scale of learning support in colleges in England, Robson et al. (2006) adopted the following definition for the role of the learning support worker (LSW):

> The definition of a learning support worker that was adopted for this investigation is any member of staff employed in an educational context who is not on a teaching or training contract but who provides support to learners through direct and regular contact with them. We do not include staff that hold other designated roles (such as librarians, technicians, careers advisers or sign language interpreters).

Robson et al. (ibid.) found that in addition to providing support to students with disabilities or learning difficulties, LSWs were supporting: learners to improve their basic skills; those on English for Speakers of Other Languages (ESOL) courses; learners with histories of non-attendance at school; learners whose behaviour is deemed to challenge the system; and learners who have particular blocks in learning. Colleges differ in the way they utilise LSWs. Robson et al. found that some colleges employed no LSWs, while others employed them in significant numbers. In terms of profile, they found that 80 per cent of LSWs were women and the vast majority were employed on full-time contracts. Unlike classroom assistants in schools, who tend to have comparable terms and conditions across the country, the pay rates of LSWs range from just above the minimum wage to approaching a basic lecturer's salary. The range of duties undertaken by LSWs also varied from college to college. LSWs are clearly providing a very valuable service, but their presence in colleges raises challenging questions about the boundaries between their interaction with students and that of the lecturers.

In a follow-up study of LSWs, Robson and Bailey (2009: 113–15) argued that serious thought needs to be given to their impact on the identity and role of FE teachers:

> Clearly, they are now systematically sharing this work with others, and though this is perceived in many instances as a benefit and a relief, a fundamental change to the FE teacher's role may be under way as a consequence. The teacher's key role and work would then be to plan the

teaching and learning activities, including the contribution of the LSW, to meet the identified needs of the students. In other words, a more collective approach to care and support for FE students would involve moving away from the allocation of the LSW to specific individual or named students to a model where teachers and LSWs work flexibly and collaboratively in supporting their students' needs . . . There are clear implications of such a move for the training and development of both groups of staff but it can be argued that the standing of both groups would be enhanced. Political rhetoric currently stresses the need to 'professionalize the FE workforce' but it is clear that this agenda cannot focus on teachers alone.

Getting qualified

Since September 2001, all new teachers employed to teach in an FE college in the UK have had to possess a recognised teaching qualification based on national occupational standards controlled by the SSC, LLUK, until its responsibilities were taken over by the Learning and Skills Improvement Service (LSIS) in 2010. The qualifications are delivered in a variety of ways through partnerships between colleges and universities. In September 2007, LLUK introduced a new compulsory introductory qualification for all new entrants teaching publicly funded programmes in the post-school 'learning and skills' sector to give them a 'threshold status' to teach. This is known as Preparing to Teach in the Lifelong Learning Sector (PTLLS). Staff for whom teaching will be their main role were required to progress to a full teaching qualification known as the Diploma for Teaching in the Lifelong Learning Sector (DTLLS). To be granted the status of 'Qualified Teacher Learning and Skills' (QTLS), a Postgraduate Certificate of Education (PGCE) is required. To be granted the status of Associate Teacher Learning and Skills (ATLS), teachers have to acquire either the DTLLS or a Certificate for Teaching in the Lifelong Learning Sector (CTLLS). They also have to undergo a period of reflective practice, termed 'professional formation', monitored by the Institute for Learning (IfL), which was set up in 2007 to manage the register of qualified teachers and trainers, to confer QTLS and ATLS status, and to log the 30 hours of continuing professional development (CPD) that all teachers and trainers have to complete annually.

As we write, the Lingfield Review is underway with a remit from government to review the current arrangements to regulate and facilitate the professionalism of the Further Education and Skills workforce in England (for a comparative study of teacher training in England and Scotland, see Avis et al., 2011). In its controversial interim report, published in March 2012, the Lingfield Review recommended that the 2007 regulations be revoked, and that FE employers be given the discretion to decide on the appropriate qualifications for their staff and the level of continuous professional development (Lingfield, 2012). So far, in response, government has taken away the

IfL's regulatory function, reducing it to the status of a voluntary membership organisation.

The introduction of a compulsory teacher training certificate for FE teachers based on competence-based occupational standards has been highly contested by many people, including FE teachers themselves and academics researching the sector (for a review of the history, see Lucas and Nasta, 2010). The arguments about the suitability of the approach connect to much broader debates about the appropriateness of the competence- and standards-based model introduced in the UK in the 1980s (for a history, see Raggatt and Williams, 1999). Lucas (2004: 15), while welcoming the introduction of compulsory qualifications for FE teachers and a more coherent approach to teacher training, has questioned whether the standards-based model is adequate for a profession that operates across distinctly different learning contexts servicing the needs of a very heterogeneous population of learners.

The standards are based around the QTLS and ATLS boundaries: teacher and teacher-related. The latter role covers LSWs and also people who act as assessors for competence-based qualifications, but do not teach. The standards are organised into six overarching domains:

Domain A   Professional values and practice
Domain B   Learning and teaching
Domain C   Specialist learning and teaching
Domain D   Planning for learning
Domain E   Assessment for learning
Domain F   Access and progression

The UK is very different from many other European countries in the way it approaches vocational teacher training, in that people wanting to teach vocational specialisms have to attend the same generic training courses as teachers of general education. The reasoning is that whether one is teaching bricklaying or French, the principles are the same. In some other countries, notably Germany and Finland, the concept of vocational pedagogy is regarded as having distinctive characteristics. In 2012, a Commission on Adult Vocational Teaching and Learning was established by DBIS to explore these issues, and it will report in April 2013.

Inspection and governance

Colleges face increasing pressures in terms of funding, accommodation and resources in a climate of increased student enrolments and output-related performance indicators. In Scotland, colleges are inspected by Her Majesty's Inspectorate of Education (HMI) on behalf of the SFC. In Wales, HMI (known there as Estyn) inspects colleges on behalf of ELWA, and in Northern Ireland, HMI inspects colleges on behalf of the Department of Education. Since

April 2007 in England, colleges have been inspected by Ofsted against the following themes: effectiveness of provision; capacity to improve; achievement and strategy; quality of provision; and leadership and management. Colleges have been graded as follows:

Grade 1   Outstanding
Grade 2   Good
Grade 3   Satisfactory
Grade 4   Inadequate

Colleges have to address the following questions:

1   How effective and efficient are provision and related services in meeting the full range of learners' needs and why?
2   What steps need to be taken to improve provision further?
3   How well do learners achieve?
4   How effective are teaching, training and learning?
5   How well do the programmes and courses meet the needs and interests of learners?
6   How well are learners guided and supported?
7   How effective are leadership and management in raising achievement and supporting all learners?

From September 2012, Ofsted is replacing the 'satisfactory' grade with 'requires improvement', and colleges will have to achieve an 'outstanding' grade for teaching, learning and assessment to be judged 'outstanding' overall.

As well as publishing information on completion rates for all courses, colleges are required to publish the actual destinations of all their students who achieved qualifications in the previous teaching year. Colleges are encouraged to use these destination data to spot patterns and trends and as a basis for evaluating student experience.

In 1992, when the Conservative government took colleges out of LEA control and made them corporate bodies, it meant that 'Governing bodies and college principals were required to change their modus operandi almost overnight' as they switched from a 'service philosophy' to 'one akin to entre-preneurialism' (Shattock, 2000: 89). Colleges were now required to recruit the majority of members of their governing bodies from the private sector, as these people were expected 'to impose a proactive market orientation on colleges that had previously been reactive and bureaucratic' (ibid.: 91). This policy has since been questioned following a series of financial and mis-management scandals that were widely reported in the national media from the mid-1990s onwards. In 1999, the Labour government changed the regula-tions on college governance to create governing bodies that had a better balance of representation from business and the community. Under the reign of the

er, greater centralisation occurred. In 2006, government asked the
develop proposals for self-regulation as part of a broader strategy
lernisation' of management across the public services (see Collinson,
governance regulations were introduced in 2008 and were further
auap.   2010.

Gleeson *et al.* (2011: 792) provide the following periodisation to show how college governance in England has evolved since incorporation:

> *1993–1997*: de-regulation, whereby business governors dominated the culture of governing bodies and operated boards on business lines, moving away from local authority control to marketplace freedoms;
>
> *1997–2000*: re-regulation, when community dominated governors and stakeholders returned to the boards of colleges;
>
> *2000–2008*: centralised-regulation and marginalisation, whereby the planning role of the board was replaced by the LSC;
>
> *2008+*: self-regulation and single voice, whereby boards are encouraged to operate in a multi-agency framework (sector- and employer-led) involving stakeholder partners/competitors represented on the board.

A review of college governance commissioned by LSIS and the AoC in 2009 reported that 'no single dominant approach to governance and strategic leadership' had emerged in the FE sector and that this was a result of its history, 'with its multiple and changing influences' (Schofield Review, 2009: 13).

In an earlier study, Gleeson and Shain (1999: 553) argue that it is impossible to separate the problems of FE governance from wider debates about democracy, inclusive management styles, deregulation and, crucially, the role of FE itself. For FE teachers, however, the nature and style of their college's governing body will affect their professional lives, and having some knowledge and understanding of the way in which their college is governed could be helpful.

Conclusion

This chapter has stressed that FE colleges are large, complex and heterogeneous organisations. They operate at the global, national, regional and local levels, with some involved across all four. They are busy, dynamic places of learning with shifting populations composed of students of all ages, and they are constantly called upon to respond to the demands and ideas of government. The Sharp Commission (2011: 4) on the role of colleges in local communities stated that:

> The Commission's vision is of colleges as a 'dynamic nucleus' at the heart of their communities, promoting a shared agenda of activities which both

fulfil their central role of providing learning and skills training to young people and adults, but also reach out into their communities, catalysing a whole range of further activities. We see the college as the central player in a network of partnerships, dynamic in the sense of developing and engaging with other partners. This enables the network itself to become part of the dynamic, with colleges at its heart.

The men and women who fought hard to create education and training opportunities for local people back in the nineteenth century would probably share this vision, and feel proud that their pioneering efforts were bearing fruit in the twenty-first century.

Chapter 2

The student body

Who will I teach?

Diverse student body

One of the distinguishing features of the FE sector has always been the diversity of its student population. Since FE is essentially 'education for all', this is reflected in its student body in terms of age, gender, ability, attainment, economic, social class and cultural background and differing learning needs. Teaching in FE presents a set of challenges that are quite different from those presented in primary or secondary education.

The following vignettes illustrate the way in which FE colleges in England, Scotland and Wales serve a wide range of student communities and offer increasingly diverse provision. Such provision will also change over time as a result of college mergers, changing occupational and demographic profiles, new qualifications and funding regimes.

College 1: Birmingham Metropolitan College

The college is a major provider of further and higher education across the West Midlands, operating across six sites as well as providing in-company training for employers and employees. In 2008, it was awarded an RIBA Further Education Design Excellence Award for its new city centre campus. The principal and two students were selected as Olympic torchbearers for the 2012 Games. It caters for part-time, full-time, distance and open learning students and has a large international programme with students from over 50 different countries. The college offers a wide range of programmes from entry level to higher education and professional courses, including business, engineering, travel and tourism, podiatry, health and social care, IT, media, and performing arts. It has recently made a substantial investment, in partnership with Kidderminster College, in the development of an academy in Kidderminster to provide education and training for up to 1000 young people (16–18) and adults to enable them to progress to further education, training or higher education. In line with Local Enterprise Partnership (LEP) priorities, its focus will be upon developing skills required by local employers and encouraging local jobs growth. The academy will work in partnership with national and local companies to develop training programmes specifically designed for their needs. An example of this partnership approach is the proposed Samsung Experience Academy, where students will learn about new 'smart' products and gain qualifications for the creative and technological industries.

College 2: Orkney College

Once one of Scotland's smallest colleges, Orkney College is now a constituent college of the University of the Highlands and Islands (UHI), which is Scotland's newest university. It serves a dispersed rural community, with a main campus in Kirkwall and an annex in Stromness for maritime studies. Traditionally, it has focused on agricultural education and training, but more recently it has diversified its provision to include hospitality, catering, business, health and social care. Students can also access modules offered through other UHI partners, including a range of degree and postgraduate programmes. Although the majority (80 per cent) of the population lives on the Orkney mainland, the rest of the population is scattered across the outlying islands. For them, the college provides courses through a network of outreach centres, mainly located in schools. The UHI network also enables online study, as well as access to specialist research centres.

College 3: Coleg Morgannwg

This is a large GFE college with four main campuses across Rhondda Cynon Taff, South Wales. It also offers programmes at 80 outreach and community venues throughout the area. A new collaborative venture is currently (2012) under development through a strategic alliance with two local schools to provide a 'new build' post-16 learning centre, capable of offering a wide range of post-16 opportunities (including over 24 A levels and the Welsh Baccalaureate). The Rhondda campus is in an area with high levels of social and economic deprivation, and the college sees its mission as contributing to the economic regeneration of this part of Wales. This includes provision for adults returning to work and for those with poor levels of basic skills.

College 4: Warwickshire College, Moreton Morrell

Moreton Morrell, formerly an independent agricultural college, is now part of the larger Warwickshire College (six campuses over two counties). It is located on a 750-acre site in rural Warwickshire and offers a wide range of land-based provision from pre-entry/entry level supported learning in art and horticulture to BSc in equine science. It has a full working farm, an indoor and outdoor riding school, a riding arena and a purpose-built farriery teaching unit. Residential accommodation is provided on site for 200 students. Several small, former specialist colleges, such as Moreton Morrell, have been merged with larger GFEs during the past 10 years because of the significant costs involved in maintaining land-based provision. Mergers have facilitated pooled use of sites for a wider range of provision and extended opportunities for the use of attractive locations for public functions (for example, equine events, conferencing, restaurants).

As these vignettes illustrate, there are many different kinds of teachers within the same college from those teaching literacy and numeracy at one end of the spectrum and undergraduate or even postgraduate courses at the other. Colleges also prepare students for professional examinations (for example, in accountancy, banking or personnel management). These students are likely to be employed and attend college on a day-release or evening basis. Students may range from age 14 to 65 and beyond. As we mentioned in Chapter 1, 14–16 year olds have been attending colleges since 2002 under the IFP initiative (see Harkin, 2006). Following the 2010 general election, the new government signalled it would pursue a different education agenda to its predecessors. One of its first actions was to relabel the DfES as the Department for Education (DfE) and also to relabel the IFP (in England) as 'alternative provision'. The DfE's website states that:

> School is the best place for most children to learn, but for some children, an education outside of school can be the most appropriate option.
>
> (DfE, 2011)

This statement clearly indicates that the coalition government regards schools and colleges as having different purposes.

The inclusion of school pupils in colleges is organised and delivered by partnerships of schools, colleges and training providers at local level. Scotland, Wales and Northern Ireland have all introduced similar programmes. The introduction of 14–19 Diplomas in England in 2008 also enabled schools and colleges to deliver joint programmes for students focusing upon practical activities related to particular areas of vocational interest (for example, hairdressing, catering and construction) and allowing for more active and experiential learning approaches (see Chapter 3). Some of the 14–16 year olds in colleges arrive there from Pupil Referral Units (PRUs). They may include teenage mothers, pupils excluded from schools for behavioural reasons, children who are 'school phobic', and pupils who are awaiting the results of special needs assessments (Attwood et al., 2004; Culham, 2003). These different age ranges are not confined to particular programmes of study. An A-level group, for example, will not necessarily include only 16–18 year olds as would be the case within a school sixth form; many adults study A levels at evening classes in colleges.

Students in FE represent an enormous range of different circumstances and any one class or group of students will be heterogeneous in nature. In this sense, the work is real mixed-ability teaching. It is not only the ability of the students that differs, however, but also their motivation, prior experience, expectations and the way in which they are funded. They may also have very different social class and cultural backgrounds and their domestic circumstances may be widely different. Some of the students may be returning to learning after a long break, others may be continuing their education but in a different environment. Many will be attempting to combine full-time employment with part-time study, or full-time study with a part-time job. They may be juggling the competing demands of family commitments and study requirements. Some students may have been 'sent' by their employers, or required to undertake training as a consequence of receiving state benefit. Some students may have physical disabilities; others may have emotional and behavioural challenges. The teacher in FE has to be sensitive to this diversity in the planning, preparation and delivery of programmes.

The patterns of attendance will vary between full-time and part-time, day or evening, employment release, block release or attendance at individually designed short courses. An increasing number of students are registering as distance or open learners. Some students may be attending college solely to have prior learning accredited for the purpose of acquiring an occupational qualification. Others may never attend the college but will be assessed by college staff at their place of employment. Students who attend college on a day-release basis from work, or 14 year olds who attend both school and college, may face challenges in adjusting to the different environments and different personnel. As a group of pre-16 students recently noted, 'At school we have to call teachers Miss, or Sir, here (in college) we just call him (the lecturer) Adam'. One student remarked, 'There's more respect here, they treat you as adults'.

Attempts to develop more flexible provision for 14–16 year olds have increased during recent years. An important aspect of this has been the con-tribution made by FE colleges in providing opportunities for young people, to engage in vocational and work-related courses more attuned to their interests and learning preferences. One East Midlands college, which has been running school partnership programmes since 1999, currently offers eight individual programmes across ten different subject sectors from entry Level 1 to full Level 2 qualifications to pupils from local schools. Evaluation of this type of provision (McCrone et al., 2007: v) reported that, 'teaching 14–16 year olds in colleges was becoming increasingly embedded and an expected element of the lecturers' role'. Staff in the five colleges participating in the research also noted, '. . . the positive impact of young people attending college between 14 and 16 years old on progression post-16' (ibid.: vi). Nevertheless, the selection of teaching staff was also seen as significant, as it is important for 14–16 year olds to be 'taught by lecturers who were committed to and enjoyed teaching them' (ibid.: vi).

There are now more opportunities to access higher education (HE) via the FE route through access programmes, Foundation Degrees, franchised provision from HEIs, and 'two plus two' degrees. According to Higher Education Funding Council England (HEFCE), in 2007–2008, 113,000 students (based on full-person equivalents) undertook HEFCE-funded programmes in FE:

> Fifty-two colleges taught one-half of the higher education students in the further education sector. Each of these colleges had over 1000 higher education students, with over 4000 at the largest providers. At other end of the sector, there were 43 FECs (mostly sixth-form colleges) with less than 100 higher education students.
>
> (Parry et al., 2012: 12)

In 2010, two GFEs were granted degree-awarding status, a sign of the changing higher education landscape outlined in the higher education White Paper (DBIS, 2011a). There are even colleges that focus mainly on provision at Level 3 and above (for a fuller discussion of qualification levels, see Chapter 3). On the other hand, many programmes are aimed at encouraging people of all ages, employed as well as unemployed, to improve their basic literacy, numeracy and ICT skills; you may see these referred to as skills for life or basic skills. The coalition government has affirmed its commitment to raising the basic skill levels of young people and adults to at least Level 2 wherever possible, and qualifications are available at entry level, and Levels 1 and 2. Many colleges will be supporting learners in achieving basic skills, either as standalone qualifications, or as part of larger programmes, and preparing them to take national tests.

The need for FE colleges to market their services more actively both at home and abroad has led to an increasing number of international students in British colleges. Some colleges have established overseas offices or agents to market their courses and to attract international students; others send staff abroad to teach on college programmes. Some colleges are involved in vocational education and training research and development programmes sponsored by the European Commission or by the British Council. These may involve student or staff exchanges and study tours. International students may be studying courses to improve their English language competence; others will be pursuing vocational qualifications. One college, situated in the north of England, for example, has established a residential facility for overseas students seeking to study business, and promotes it internationally as a business school.

From what has been outlined so far, it is clear that colleges have to provide for a diverse student population, some of whom have specific learning needs and disabilities. There are also a small number of specialist colleges, the majority of them private and some residential, that cater for those with particular disabilities and who may need more intensive support. The 1996 report of the

Tomlinson Committee's review of FE's provision for students with learning difficulties and disabilities, *Inclusive Learning*, highlighted the need for the sector to make further improvements and to embrace the concept of inclusive learning (Tomlinson, 1996). As Dee (1999: 141) explains, Tomlinson sought to reject the stereotyping of people with learning difficulties and/or physical disabilities. The Beattie Committee in Scotland was established to 'review the range of needs among young people who require additional support to participate in post school education, training and employment; the assessment of need; and the quality and effectiveness of provision in improving skills and employability'.

The Kennedy Report (Kennedy, 1997), *Learning Works*, went further in highlighting the need for colleges to widen participation to include under-represented groups in their communities. Since then, the duty of colleges to embrace the inclusion agenda has been more explicitly addressed in the Equality Act 2010. However, many colleges had addressed the need for supported learning through their provision of specialist courses for those requiring more intensive support at entry and pre-entry levels long before this recent legislation. An example of how colleges are trying to be more inclusive is illustrated by the following list of groups of people found in one English college's student magazine and who are encouraged to join courses:

- homeless;
- ex-offenders;
- people with mental health difficulties;
- people from ethnic minorities;
- full-time carers;
- women in refuge centres;
- travellers;
- care leavers;
- single parents on low incomes;
- long-term unemployed; and
- people overcoming drug or alcohol dependency.

We are very aware that this brief discussion of the FE sector's response to the needs of people with learning difficulties and/or physical disabilities raises far more questions than can be dealt with here. Clough and Barton (1995: 2) point out that people with what were once, and sometimes still are, called 'special needs' are the 'recipients of powerful professional categories' that 'envelop their identities'. There is also considerable debate about whether their needs are best met in specialist provision, and the case for integration is by no means fully accepted. Corbett (1997: 171), writing about young people, notes:

> The tensions within the inclusive ideology are evident. At one level, concepts of 'entitlement for all' and quality assurance measures suggest that

the most vulnerable young people are no longer to be offered a second-rate education and training diet but are to be assessed and guided in a way that equates with the treatment given to their peers. At another level, they are no longer seen as 'special' or in need of additional protective care, which can open up opportunities for real progression into mainstream developments but can also mean that they become casualties of a market culture in which the weakest go to the wall. If they are included, this means inclusion into a harsh and uncaring economy where there are no favours given, only deals bargained for.

Despite cuts in funding, many FE colleges still offer some provision for adults wishing to pursue leisure or recreational programmes. Examples recently noted in a range of prospectuses include: 'Mature Movers'; 'Get into IT'; 'Spanish for Beginners'; 'Sugarcraft'; and 'Researching Your Family'. This adds another dimension to the work of colleges and to the student profile. Many of these students may be studying at outreach centres or in premises away from the main college site. It should also be remembered that there are eight residential adult education colleges in the UK: six in England, one in Wales and one in Scotland.

The FE teacher will be faced with more changes and challenges as colleges address the key priorities of widening participation, inclusion and raising standards. The inclusive college is one that caters for the widest possible student population with an enormous diversity of learning needs, where programmes may be delivered through a range of techniques. The inclusive college has to serve community needs, as well as respond to a commercial market.

Student identity, disposition and motivation

The dispositions and motivations of such a diverse range of students will obviously be widely different, and the ways in which students learn will vary in pace and-style. This requires a flexible teaching approach from FE teachers in order to provide for the needs of individual learners (see Chapter 5). The teacher will also have a central role to play in other aspects of learning support (for example, through guidance and counselling, both on entry to a programme and throughout its duration). Returning learners may also need support not just in the subject being studied, but in how to study it. These competing pressures on the FE teacher's time are not easy to balance when the substantial managerial and administrative loads that are inherent in most vocational programmes are added to them.

The call for a more 'personalised learning' approach, coupled with an evolving Qualifications and Credit Framework (QCF), are likely to have a significant impact on the way in which provision in colleges is organised. Teachers are required not only to tailor learning programmes more directly to individual learner needs, but also, we are told, to the needs of employers. Key aspects of the personalisation agenda include: 'responding to the needs of the whole person'; 'seeking and responding to the needs of the learners'; 'responding to the needs of the local community and employers'; 'raising the ambition of all learners'; 'supporting every learner to become expert'; 'encouraging individuals to take responsibility'; and 'fostering openness and trust' (DfES, 2006a: 25). This implies a wide-ranging and complex role for teachers and trainers, many of whom will be doing the job on a part-time basis.

Every learner and teacher has an individual identity, and some would argue that we all have multiple identities – as we weave in and out of the different areas of our lives, we take on the identity that is most appropriate for the spaces and places in which we find ourselves. There is now a large body of research exploring the relationship between identity, personal biography, individual dispositions and learning (see, inter alia, Billett and Somerville, 2004; Evans *et al.*, 2004; Bloomer and Hodkinson, 2000). The concept of disposition comes from the work of the French sociologist Pierre Bourdieu, and relates to the way in which individuals have subconscious (or tacit) attitudes to and ways of approaching life (see Bourdieu and Wacquant, 1992). Our 'dispositions' develop and change as we grow and are affected by a whole range of life experiences. Understanding something of the personal biography of students can be helpful to teachers, though, in reality, there is often little time to garner this information, and, in some circumstances, it would not be ethical or even advisable to enquire too deeply. Being empathetic to our students' circumstances is, however, an important part of being an effective teacher. Just as we might hope our students realise we have lives outside college and that they will have an impact on our life in college, so too should teachers remind themselves that students are only students for part of their waking hours.

REFLECTION

We now present a series of vignettes of typical students to be found in any college. We would like you to read each one and consider the following questions:

1   As a teacher, what perceptions do you have of each of these students and of their learning needs and dispositions?
2   What steps would you take to ensure the students were being adequately supported?
3   How does your disposition towards being a teacher change from week to week, and how has it changed over time?

Mark

Mark is 18 years old and is taking a BTEC Level 3 National in Music Technology as a full-time student at his local college. His school experience was rather negative, although he achieved seven GCSE subjects with grades A*–C. He is an accomplished musician. His parents were not enthusiastic about his transfer to the local college at 16 and would have preferred him to remain in the sixth form at school, as his sister had done, and to study what they regard as 'proper A levels'. His school, however, did not offer programmes in music technology but wanted Mark to take an A-level programme, including music and mathematics.

Since transferring to college, Mark has enjoyed the freedom of being allowed to organise his own time, although he has found it difficult to meet coursework submission deadlines. He has taken an active part in college concerts, composing music for dance performances. Much of his time outside college is spent rehearsing with a local band and doing occasional 'gigs'.

He is now starting to think about 'next steps' and has asked his tutor about possible options. She has suggested that Mark considers applying for a degree programme in music technology at a London college. His sister, now a medical student, thinks the idea 'ridiculous' and suggests that Mark should think about something more 'realistic'. Mark's parents have already indicated that they would not be willing to pay fees for such a course, nor to support him in London. They are unhappy about the influence that the college tutors appear to have had on their son's decision to pursue a career in what they regard as a precarious field.

Scott

Scott is on a full-time Level 2 programme in Sport. He left school last year with four GCSEs, grades D–E. He had no idea what he wanted to do and there was very little on offer at his school for those who had failed to achieve good GCSE grades. His mother insisted that he find some further course of study because she did not want him 'hanging around the house'. Scott is very interested in football and thought that the course might be a reasonable way of spending the time. The course also provides an opportunity to gain a coaching certificate.

The course has proved to be a disappointment, mainly because it is not what he expected it would be. He enjoys the practical work, particularly playing football and spending time in the gymnasium. He dislikes the theoretical aspects of the course (for example, physiology and psychology) and finds the assignments very difficult. He cannot keep up with the volume of work and is constantly late in handing in assignments. He feels that he is falling further and further behind and is unable to manage his time to do anything about it.

He has two part-time jobs; one of them is in a sports retail outlet, the other in a local restaurant, usually washing up and preparing vegetables. This takes up all his time at weekends. Sometimes he feels so tired in the week that he does not want to attend college, but he knows that his mother would be very annoyed if he withdrew and he has no idea what else he might do. If he were offered more hours at the sports retailer, he would definitely give up the college course, but at the moment this is unlikely because the store has seen a decline in trade recently.

Corinne

Corinne is 42 and a student on a Foundation Degree in early years at a large college servicing a dispersed rural catchment. She has worked for over 10 years in several early years settings, including day nurseries, play groups and nursery classes. Her current employer was keen for her to study for the degree, which involves combining workplace experience with taught sessions at college. Over the two-year programme, students are expected to undertake a substantial amount of independent study and to submit written assignments. The course is validated by a local university and allows opportunities for progression to a bachelor's degree.

Although Corinne left school at 16, she attended college and gained a qualification in nursery nursing before she began a career in the sector. Since then, she has kept abreast of developments within her professional field and attended relevant training courses. When her two daughters started their secondary education, Corinne felt she would like to have the opportunity of pursuing further study without having to give up her job. She was delighted when her employer mentioned the possibility of the Foundation Degree.

She approached the return to study with trepidation and found the demands of extended writing challenging. The volume of assignments was at first difficult to manage alongside her full-time job and the care of her two teenage daughters. Although she found she could cope with the content of the work (after all, she had been doing the job for years), writing about it was a different matter. She is always anxious about the expectations of staff and about the adequacy of her performance, particularly her writing skills.

She has successfully completed the first year of the programme and gained in confidence as a result. She has come to realise that most of the other 23 students in the group felt the same as she did initially. They have all recognised that they have been greatly helped by their tutor, who has supported them 'all the way' and really 'gone the extra mile'. They also recognise that they have gained a lot from each other and from the cohesion of the group; this has been cemented by group social outings. Corinne says that she 'can't wait for her graduation and having all the family there for the ceremony and photographs'.

Gary

Gary is 16 and has been in college for six weeks on a Level 1 course designed for young people who have an interest in catering but who have not yet fully committed to a career path and who have left school with few qualifications and poor basic skills. The course is essentially practical and provides the opportunity to acquire a Level I certificate in Introduction to the Hospitality Industry, as well as a Level I award in Work Skills. Basic numeracy and communication skills are also included in the course.

Although keen at the beginning of term, Gary's enthusiasm began to wane after three weeks. He started to miss theory classes and, by the fifth week, he was turning up late for practical sessions. Staff noticed that he was not wearing correct kitchen uniform despite being repeatedly told about it. He appeared to resent any criticism from the staff.

The quality of his practical work is good when he is left on his own to complete a task. He is aggressive when asked to work with other students and takes extended breaks, which delay the completion of any joint activities. Other students have begun to resent this and have mentioned it to the lecturer in charge. The lecturer has discussed this with Gary, who has given assurances about his future conduct. Gary has been told that he will not be allowed to participate in the work experience placement unless his behaviour improves.

During a practical session, Gary became involved in an argument with another student who had suggested that Gary could not weigh or add up quantities correctly. Gary became abusive and threatened the student. He also used offensive language to the kitchen assistant, who has lodged a formal complaint. The catering lecturer has intervened and asked Gary to discuss the matter with him fully.

Arpinder

Arpinder works for a firm of accountants and attends, one day a week, an accountancy course offered by his local college. He is one of Carol's students (see Chapter 4). He is 32 and decided to study for accounting qualifications because he has friends who run a successful accountancy practice. He sees the course as the first step towards achieving a full professional qualification. He realises, however, that it will take him up to three years to qualify. Before starting his present job he worked for a retail chain as an assistant store manager, but he did not like the long and irregular hours of work.

The company he works for is reasonably supportive of Arpinder's attendance at college and allows him time off work to attend. However, they are not prepared to pay his fees. So far, he has been able to meet the cost himself.

He is very keen to progress as quickly as possible and has found the course helpful, although he has been irritated by the repeated changes in the teaching staff. During a recent busy period, his firm asked him to remain at work on college days with the promise of making up the time later when he needs some exam revision time. He cannot envisage the situation improving in the foreseeable future. In addition, his father has recently been seriously ill and he has had to spend a considerable amount of time supporting his family.

He is becoming anxious about the effect this is having on his course and the possible outcome for his test results. He feels he has invested heavily in the course in terms of financial, personal and emotional commitment. He is becoming increasingly dispirited and depressed about the possibility of not meeting the goals that he has set for himself.

Grace

For three mornings a week, Grace attends a Skills for Life programme run by the FE college at a local community hall. She is a single parent, aged 28, and has three children, aged 6, 8 and 10. She had an extremely negative and disrupted school experience, having attended four different schools in a period of six years. She left school at the earliest possible opportunity without any formal qualifications. She did not expect, nor want, to have any further contact with the education system. On leaving school, she took a series of low-paid, unskilled jobs – none of which lasted for very long. She has had no paid employment since the birth of her first child.

When her children started school, she began to take an interest in their work and in some of the activities in which the school sought parental involvement. She was interested in helping in a practical way but when approached about the possibility of 'listening to readers' she became very anxious. She was reluctant to become involved in case her own deficiencies were exposed.

When her husband left, Grace decided to try to find some part-time employment but soon realised that it was virtually impossible to find any work unless she improved her reading and writing skills. She also wanted to improve her basic numeracy skills. She found that there were a series of classes being held in her local community hall, just 10 minutes' walk from home. The college delivers a range of flexible Skills for Life courses at a range of community venues throughout the borough. All students undertake an initial needs assessment with a personal tutor before embarking on a course. There are no fees because Grace has no formal qualifications in English or mathematics.

Grace was extremely nervous about returning to study. For the first few weeks, she attempted to disguise the nature of the course when talking to friends and neighbours. However, after a short time, she began to gain confidence and discovered a new group of friends among the class members. The atmosphere was extremely supportive and the lecturers were friendly. She began to look forward to the mornings spent improving her writing skills and started to enjoy reading. This new-found confidence tended to spill over into other areas of her life. She was approached about standing as a parent governor at her daughter's school.

Grace now wants to continue her studies, with the intention of gaining some vocational qualifications. She has discovered that the next stage of the programme will be held in the college and not in the local hall. She is reluctant to travel the five miles (eight kilometres) to the college but she is even more reluctant to become a student there. The prospect of entering a formal education institution is threatening; she is concerned about her ability to cope with the work.

George

At 35, George has been unemployed for the past 15 months. Prior to that, he was employed as a storeman at a manufacturing company. The company was forced to close, resulting in some 350 job losses. Some of the skilled workers eventually managed to find alternative employment but the large number of unskilled workers, like George, found it virtually impossible to find work.

George and several of his former workmates now attend college as part of a government-funded programme designed to help the long-term unemployed. This scheme is open to those, over 25, who have been unemployed for more than 12 months and who are claiming Jobseeker's Allowance. The college George attends provides a range of sector-specific practical training courses as well as help with wider employability skills development (for example, preparing CVs, online job search, interview techniques). Employment mentors support students with their job searches and in building their skills. The college also has an employer engagement team, which works with local employers to try to secure work placements for students. Trainees are paid a weekly rate, the receipt of which is dependent upon attendance at the programme. Colleges receive payment for the trainees, part of which is related to successful outcomes.

George is attending a painting and decorating course. He is hoping that even if he does not secure employment in a company, he may be able to become self-employed. Having already suffered 15 months of unemployment, George is unsure about the value of some parts of the programme in helping him to secure a job.

Tom

Tom is a Year 11 pupil at a large, inner city comprehensive school. He attends the local FE college one day a week as part of a school-college link programme (see Chapter 3) that the college runs in partnership with a number of local secondary schools. In addition to his day at college, Tom spends another day on a placement at a local agricultural showground. The remaining time he spends at school following core curriculum subjects including English and mathematics. On his college days, he is working towards a Level 1 qualification in Horticulture as well as an award in skills for working life.

Tom enjoys the day at the college, but prefers the time he spends at the showground doing practical landscaping work. He dislikes the time he spends in school, but has come to terms with the fact that he will have to attend if he is to be allowed to continue with the college and work experience. He has a poor school attendance record, but he has not missed one day at college or on his work placement. He is concerned about the behaviour of some of the students who are in his college group, especially the ones from a 'rival' school; there have been two incidents in the car park at break times and a 'flashpoint' during a workshop.

He hopes to be able to continue with this type of work when he leaves school. He is aware that there are opportunities in this area; his uncle already has a flourishing business. He describes himself as being 'well set up' as a result of his college and work experience. His school form tutor says that he is a 'changed person' since joining the programme and she is pleased with the relationship she has developed with the college's link tutor. The high point in his year was when his photograph appeared in the local newspaper showing him at work during the county agricultural show.

Vicky

Vicky is 22 and has moderate learning difficulties (MLD). She attends her local FE college on a full-time basis and has done so since she left her special school at 19. She is in a group of 10 young people with similar learning needs, although the nature of these needs is diverse and some group members have specific physical needs as well. The programme is wide and varied, and includes a range of different modules geared to the students' individual needs and preferences. There is a strong core of basic skills work as well as modules on 'managing myself'; 'money management'; and 'keeping safe and healthy'. So far, Vicky has taken modules in 'small animal care'; 'horticulture'; and 'art and design'. In addition, she has gained a grade D in art and design GCSE, the first formal qualification she has ever achieved and of which she is extremely proud. She has also participated in the Duke of Edinburgh's Award scheme, attending an awards ceremony at Holyrood House.

She enjoys her time at college and has met new friends with whom she has developed strong relationships. She is also very fond of her tutor, Mrs Baines, and particularly enjoys the special events that Mrs Baines organises for the group. Recently, these have included a bowling evening, a meal at the local pizza restaurant and a fancy dress Valentine's disco.

Vicky's parents are extremely pleased with the way in which Vicky has developed during her time at college. They notice in particular her increased independence and her willingness to join in conversations. Previously, she had been very withdrawn. She is now able to travel independently to and from college on public transport. Their only concern is about Vicky's future and what will happen when she is no longer eligible to attend college. She has successfully completed two periods of sheltered work experience during her college course, and they are hoping that one of these employers may offer her a part-time job.

Hussein

Hussein has recently arrived from the Middle East and has joined an intensive English language course at his local college before beginning a degree in engineering at a nearby university. He realises that he will have to work extremely hard in order to pass the English language competence test set by the university. This is a condition of entry on to the degree programme. He is concerned because there are 20 students on the English programme, from many different parts of the world and with a very wide range of English language competence. He is concerned that the weaker students will hold him back.

About half the students work as au pairs with English families and seem, as far as Hussein is concerned, to be using the classes as an opportunity to socialise. They do not hand in required pieces of homework and are reluctant to join in with some of the 'speaking' exercises. He feels that he is working hard and trying his best and finds the behaviour of the young au pairs a distraction and an irritation. He wonders if he should transfer to a small private language school where he knows the fees are higher but where, perhaps, he will receive more individual attention.

Najma

Najma is 19 and on the advanced apprenticeship in hairdressing. She spends four days a week working as a hair stylist in a big city salon and one day at college working towards an S/NVQ Level 3 and key skills. Najma started doing Highers in her Scottish school, but left after one year to try to find a job. She had always been interested in hairdressing and applied for the apprenticeship with a salon in her home town. Unfortunately, she did not get on with the salon owner and so left after six months. She then applied for her current apprenticeship. Her current salon is much more upmarket than the previous one, and Najma enjoys the hectic pace and competitive atmosphere. Her work is judged closely by her supervisor and by her tutors at college, and they have identified her as a potential competitor for the regional trials of the 'Skills Challenge Competitions' organised by Skills UK.

Najma is a very confident and articulate young woman who finds it hard to keep her opinions to herself. At college, she can cause problems for her tutors when she criticises the work of other students. Recently, she was particularly critical of a fellow apprentice during an open day for the public. This resulted in the customer complaining to the tutor as she was worried that her hair was being done by an incompetent student. The tutor had to deal with three people: the tearful customer, the tearful apprentice and Najma.

Conclusion

All of these students will have developed their own perspective on learning and will communicate that perspective through their behaviour in the classroom, workshop, tutorial, seminar group and so on. Their prior experience of education will have shaped their attitudes to learning, to teachers and to their fellow students. These issues are explored in detail in Chapters 5 and 6, where we return to these vignettes and consider what teaching and assessment strategies might be most appropriate for helping students such as these to learn most effectively.

It will be clear from some of the vignettes that some form of inter-agency collaboration will be necessary to ensure that the students' needs are catered for and that the different 'stakeholders' who have an interest in the students' progress are kept informed and, where necessary, involved. In the case of Najma, for example, the college tutors and the salon supervisor need to review how they can each help Najma adjust her behaviour, while in the case of Tom, the college, employer and school need to find ways to share their ideas in order to support him. Vicky's parents will also be keen to talk to Mrs Baines about possible next steps for their daughter.

Chapter 3

Diverse curricula and qualifications

What will I teach?

Introduction

Numerous curricular traditions (academic and vocational, liberal and radical) and forms are to be found in colleges, providing a range of learning opportunities for their diverse student body. The curriculum principles guiding the organisation of teaching and learning in different areas of the college will reflect the parameters within which they have to work. Some teachers will have more freedom to experiment with the curriculum than others, but many will be constrained by the requirements of regulatory bodies. Rogers (2002: 207) provides a helpful model for thinking about what the concept embraces. He proposes that a curriculum comprises five elements:

1   *Philosophical framework*: This reflects the assumptions that lie behind the way the curriculum has been designed. Hence, 'Woodwork may be seen as a series of techniques or as part of a concern for good design and good living . . . Natural history may be taught as a leisure pursuit or as part of socially concerned issues . . . In particular, it (the framework) will reflect our assumptions as to whether the education we are engaged in is designed to reproduce or transform existing social systems, whether it is aimed to lead to conformity or to liberation' (ibid.: 207). Within the context of FE there is also concern about the conflation of educational and economic goals. Colleges are servants of several masters: funding bodies, employers, but most importantly learners. It is not axiomatic that the needs of these constituencies are convergent.

2   *Context*: This reflects the way that learning is organised in terms of the quality of the 'setting' (for example, lighting and heating, levels of noise) and the 'climate' (that is, the nature of the social relationship between teacher and learner, and learner and learner).

3   *Content*: This relates to the subject matter to be covered (sometimes laid down in a syllabus, or qualification specification), the sequence in which it is handled, and the 'conditions' attached to the learning (for example,

what is required of the learner, the pace of the learning and the resources required).

4   *Events*: This relates to the planned activities through which learning is facilitated (for example, lectures, discussions, group work, practical activities, the use of technology) and the unplanned events (for example, disruptions or changes of direction stimulated by new insights).

5   *Processes of evaluation*: This relates to the ways in which learner achievement and experience are evaluated (for example, from formal tests through to learner feedback on student satisfaction surveys).

The idea of a curriculum is often seen, simplistically, as a framing device for the topics (or subjects) and ideas that a teacher might cover throughout a course of study. Lawrence Stenhouse, a much celebrated English educationalist, argued, however, that a curriculum should not be seen in 'product' terms, but as a dynamic space in which teachers constantly experimented with new ideas for supporting the learning of their students (see Elliott, 1983). Young (1998), however, criticises both the 'curriculum as fact' and 'curriculum as practice' models. He argues that the first is underpinned by the 'view of knowledge as external to knowers, both teachers and students, and embodied in syllabi and text books' (ibid.: 25). The model of 'curriculum as practice' appears to reverse the assumptions of the 'curriculum as fact' model, but, says Young, it 'gives teachers a spurious sense of their power, autonomy and independence from the wider contexts of which their work is part' (ibid.: 28). The problem for many teachers in colleges is that the space, time and freedom for experimentation appear to have been squeezed out as the pressure to achieve qualification targets has come to dominate their daily life. Bloomer (1997: 188) has argued that:

> In policy, planning and, to some extent, practitioner circles it (the curriculum) has come to mean little more than a prescription of 'content' coupled with a series of checks for its successful implementation. 'Objectives', 'outcomes' and 'quality assurance' now cover all, while 'delivery' is the metaphor to describe the process.

This might seem a pessimistic view, but qualifications now frame much of what happens within colleges. The response to cries for educational reform over the past 30 years or more has been a tendency to increase the number of qualifications rather than to look at the broader aspects of the curriculum.

The quest then becomes one of trying to find ways to exert some agency as a teacher and think through the ways in which the demands of a qualification can be translated into teaching and learning strategies that will stimulate both student and teacher. Carr (1993: 7) reminds us that:

The way in which the curriculum is made and remade – the process of curriculum change – is essentially a process of contestation and struggle between individuals and social groups whose different views about the curriculum reflect their different views about the good society and how it may be created.

It has been argued that 'vocational learning brings together teaching and learning within specific contexts which often have wider developmental concerns, for example lifelong learning, but also seek to develop other generic, or transversal skills, as well as sector-specific knowledge and skills'. (Huddleston, 2011: 43). It may seem that some of this has been forgotten when we look at the pace and extent of qualification reform over recent time, in particular the drive to an 'outcomes-based' approach in the design of qualifications. What teachers need to keep in mind is that the qualification specification is only one element of a complex mix of interrelated factors that constitute the curriculum (see Rogers, 2002). In planning our schemes of work, we have to ensure that we cover the content of the specification, but the process, context, events and evaluation that we build into our planning are as much a part of the holistic curriculum experience of our students as simply 'covering the spec' or 'passing the test'. In short, most vocational learning involves a range of opportunities, both formal and informal, and will have multiple outcomes.

As a result of government pressure for a more 'personalised' approach, many of the colleges we visit talk about the need to develop more 'individualised learning programmes' for students. The following quotation is worth reading as it reflects how policymakers back in 2004 tried to 'sell' personalisation:

> The central characteristic of such a new system will be personalisation – so that the system fits to the individual rather than the individual having to fit to the system. This is not a vague liberal notion about letting people have what they want. It is about having a system which will genuinely give high standards for all . . . And the corollary of this is that the system must be both freer and more diverse – with more flexibility to help meet individual needs; and more choices between courses and types of provider, so that there really are different and personalised opportunities available.
>
> (DfES, 2004a: foreword)

The current strategic plan for a large college situated in the North East of England identifies one if its strategic aims as being to 'Provide personalised learning opportunities for all learners', with a target to ensure that, '100% full-time 16–18 year olds in college will undertake some enrichment activities as part of their programme' (for further information about this college's strategic plan, see www.citysun.ac.uk/about-us/strategic-plan). However, it is also recognised within the plan that funding for such activities is challenging given the current economic climate.

Recent pronouncements by the coalition government in outlining its plans for FE in England return to the theme of 'personalisation', but are often couched in terms of marketisation and customer choice:

> Under our new system, learners will select training and qualifications valued by business and available through a broad range of autonomous providers who will attract learners depending upon the quality of their offer.
>
> (DBIS, 2010: 5)

You may wish to reflect upon what is being offered here in terms of a curriculum and also note the use of the term 'offer'. Is this simply allowing access to a diverse range of training providers and thus access to qualifications, under 'quasi-market' conditions, or is something more implied? For example, such proposals suggest that students should be able to access learning programmes as and when they wish and in whatever location, including perhaps remotely from home, in the workplace, or on the journey to work. They also imply that students should have access to reliable, independent information about what is on offer and what the benefits might be. For many students, such decisions may already have been made (for example, by their employers or by funding agencies who have decided where to place training contracts and what courses will attract funding). Local infrastructure may simply restrict the type of provision available and, hence, choice may be illusory.

The appropriateness of the individualised/personalised style of curriculum design is hotly contested. It should be remembered that many students value the opportunity of learning with others and of working cooperatively, and that learning within a community can challenge the prejudices and limited horizons of learners that can easily remain unchallenged when learning becomes an entirely individual affair, or simply a matter of passing a test online.

The concept of curriculum also embraces the notion of the 'hidden curriculum', which refers to the way in which all teachers, usually sub-consciously, act to socialise their students into the rules and behaviours expected of a particular educational setting, or, within the vocational sense, a community of practice. In the same way, employees learn the 'hidden curriculum' of the workplace. Indeed, in any setting where people come together, even in the home, there are norms of behaviour that lie invisible, but exert a profound influence. In her research on courses for nursery nurses in colleges, Colley (2003), building on Hochschild's (1983) concept of 'emotional labour', has shown how, during their work placements, student nurses have to learn a substantial hidden curriculum of working in a nursery (that is, how to manage their feelings when confronted with the day-to-day realities of looking after small children):

> In a group tutorial discussion soon after the start of the course, following the students' first few days in placement, there were many expressions of

delight at being with children. But the session also revealed events they experienced as far from pleasant: taking little boys to the toilet; finding oneself covered in children's 'puke' and 'wee'; and being hit by children.

(Colley, 2003: 15)

What is 'taught' and 'learned' might, therefore, diverge, depending on where students apply their learning and what they take from it.

Just as the range of students in FE colleges is too wide to enable it to be described in tidy categorisations, to talk about an FE curriculum as if it were a homogeneous entity would be totally misleading. FE's curricular traditions derive from a range of complex origins and prepare students for different destinations. Squires (1987: 96) has suggested that 'It is at this point that the "radical monopoly", to use Illich's phrase, of the education system breaks down, and a plethora of institutions and interests become involved'. Although written over 20 years ago, the observation is perhaps even more apposite today, as Figure 3.1 illustrates. The balance of influences depicted in Figure 3.1 will shift in response to changes in government policy, economic conditions, the numbers and types of students enrolling, the variations in funding mechanisms and so on.

The range of courses on offer will also be dependent upon the size of the institution and upon its location. Traditionally, colleges have served their local communities and have been dependent upon local companies sending their employees on day-release programmes, usually at a craft apprentice or technician level. Notable examples were the colleges in some parts of South Yorkshire and Nottinghamshire, which were almost entirely dependent on the local mining industry for their students. Pit closures meant that these colleges had to diversify, and to seek and exploit new markets. Similarly, many large engineering departments contracted or were closed.

Against this background, new courses catering for the burgeoning demands of the information technology and creative and cultural sectors and for the service industries were developed. In 2012, policymakers are putting a great deal of emphasis on what is referred to as the STEM (science, technology, engineering and mathematics) agenda and the need to grow the number of technicians in the British workforce to meet the needs of sectors such as oil, gas and electricity, and chemicals and pharmaceuticals. This is also linked to the desire to 'rebalance' the economy in the light of the 2008 banking crisis and the realisation that the UK needs to invest more in manufacturing. The illustrations given at the beginning of Chapter 2 make it clear that boundaries are shifting. Some colleges have been subject to mergers and others have developed geographically dispersed outreach centres (in the case of one college in East Anglia, at a distance of 40 miles from the main site). All of this will affect the curriculum offerings of a college and, of course, its staff who have been required to adapt to new programmes, changing subject content, methods of assessment and different groups of learners (we meet some of these staff in Chapter 4).

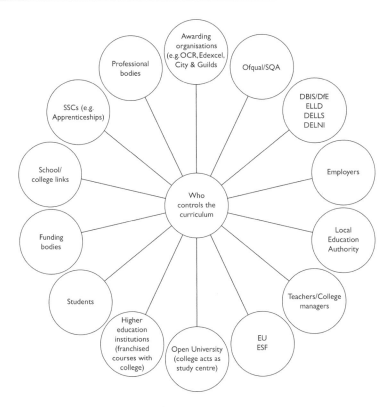

Figure 3.1 Influences on curriculum design

REFLECTION

The diversity of curriculum provision is revealed in these titles from the classified pages of the educational press. What type of curriculum do you think is offered in these faculties/departments or divisions?

Faculty of the Built Environment
Department of Hospitality and Tourism
Department of Health and Social Care
School of Science
Division of Sport, Leisure and Tourism
Faculty of Business, Management and Humanities
Faculty of Visual Communication
Faculty of General Education and Student Services

You might also want to consider how these different aspects of a college's provision relate to each other.

Funding is often tied to the ways in which courses meet the needs of the local community. However, local labour markets can be volatile and predicting future training requirements is not an exact science. There is also a further consideration in that the demand from students may not match the supply of jobs within local, regional or even national labour markets. Pressures for increased student numbers and, hence, increased funding, may persuade colleges to offer those courses that are popular irrespective of job opportunities.

Programmes of study will, of course, have a syllabus, sometimes called a specification, that teachers follow and this might be devised by them or imposed by an awarding organisation (for example, City and Guilds or Edexcel). (Note that the term has recently changed from 'awarding body' – you may see the two terms still used interchangeably.) This sets out the content of the programme and usually includes guidance on assessment. Remember, this is not the same as the curriculum, although the two are often used as if they were. Most courses in colleges lead to nationally recognised qualifications because it is often the achievement of qualifications that triggers funding. The ways in which the content of these courses is specified will differ in style according to the nature of the qualification. Competence-based qualifications are derived from occupational standards and so do not, as such, include much information regarding the wider aspects of the curriculum (for example, processes and philosophical underpinnings), although they are likely to say something about contexts and assessment. They are designed to be assessment-led and achievable without the need to attend a programme of learning, though, of course, most individuals working towards such qualifications need to acquire new skills and knowledge and, hence, teachers have to design a curriculum in order to support their students.

The dominance of qualifications in the UK education and training system has been heavily criticised (see Nuffield Review, 2008; Unwin et al., 2004). Since the 1980s, public funding has been more and more closely tied to the delivery and attainment of qualifications, which, in turn, form the basis of numerous government targets. Towler et al. (2011: 504), in a study of teachers' and learners' perceptions of learning in two FE colleges found that teachers were concerned about how students came to college with low expectations of their responsibilities as learners. In addition, teachers felt constrained by the demands of qualifications and the attitude of students that learning was associated with passing tests. They argue that:

> Instrumentalism of the curriculum . . . is in danger of disenfranchising teaching professionals from the deeper aspects of learning processes (e.g. creativity, critical thinking) that are essential if students are to acquire a genuine 'learner voice'.

To break this cycle, they argue, teachers need to 'scaffold learning' in order to start building students' confidence and ability to critically reflect on their learning from the start of a course.

At the time of writing, reforms are ongoing. You will need to keep abreast of changes by constant reference to relevant government agency websites.

Levels and frameworks

Many countries now have a National Qualifications Framework (NQF) that arranges nationally recognised qualifications in a level-based system so that people can see how different qualifications equate to each other. Young (2003: 3), in a review of frameworks round the world, argues that they are driven by powerful political and economic forces. He states that 'Not surprisingly the idea of an NQF is also invariably linked to that of a learning society which is contrasted with societies of the past in which learning, at least recognised and accredited learning, was largely restricted to initial education and training'. Young has found that frameworks tend to share the following goals:

- to be transparent to all users in terms of what they signify and what learners have to achieve;
- to minimise barriers to progression, both vertical and horizontal; and
- to maximise access, flexibility and portability between different sectors of education and work and different sites of learning.

While these goals are certainly laudable, frameworks can exert a malign influence over education and training systems in that they require qualifications to follow an outcomes-based model so that everything can be shaped to fit the framework. As shown later in this chapter, the outcomes-based approach has proved to be controversial in recent years because of the danger of subjugating the learning process to simply achieving outcomes.

Figure 3.2 illustrates the way in which qualifications in England, Wales and Northern Ireland are classified, and attempts to suggest equivalences between qualifications that may be regarded as 'general' or 'academic' (for example, GCSEs/A levels/Highers) with those that are vocational or occupational in orientation (for example, BTECs/NVQs/SVQs). This classification is regulated by Ofqual in England. Scotland has its own Scottish Credit and Qualifications Framework, which encompasses all levels, including higher education (for a critique, see Raffe, 2003). In Wales, the regulatory function is carried out by DCELLS and in Northern Ireland by CCEA (Council for the Curriculum, Examinations and Assessment). HE qualifications in England, Wales and Northern Ireland (from certificates of HE at Level 4 through to doctorates at Level 8) are included in the Framework for Higher Education Qualifications (FHEQ), which is regulated by the Quality Assurance Agency.

Attempting to locate all qualifications within a common overarching framework, and to assign equivalences to them, is a major challenge (see Young, 2008). As Stasz (2011: 4) has argued, 'The development and awarding of qualifications in Britain is a complicated system involving multiple government departments, public and private organisations and elaborate and detailed rules and specifications'. Since qualifications differ in their type, composition and purpose, it is difficult to make the necessary comparisons in order to assign levels. Qualifications frameworks need to be adapted as new ideas about the meaning of 'levels' and the relationship between different curricular areas emerge and, of course, as new occupations develop within sectors.

The move towards qualifications frameworks has been influenced by policy at European level and the desire to identify and locate qualifications across member states through the European Qualification Framework (EQF). Member states are encouraged to relate their qualifications to the EQF with the intention that, from 2012, all new qualifications issued will carry a reference to an EQF level.

Within the QCF, qualifications are made up of units with associated credits. This allows learners to build up units and credits over time, in contrast to academic qualifications, for example, where the outcome is often determined by the result of a terminal examination. The QCF allows for accumulation and credit transfer; each unit has a credit and level value (1–8 indicating level of difficulty, see Figure 3.2). The title of the qualification indicates its size (for example, award = 1–12 credits; certificate = 13–36 credits; diploma = 37+ credits). One credit is equivalent to 10 hours of 'notional' learning time (that is, the amount of time in which a learner could be expected to achieve all the learning outcomes for the unit).

Here is an example of the way in which a qualification on the QCF is titled: City and Guilds (Level 3) Certificate in Retail Skills. Note it describes the awarding organisation offering the qualification (City and Guilds); the level or complexity of challenge (Level 3); the size (Certificate) and the subject (Retail Skills).

You should be aware that at the time of writing there is considerable discussion surrounding frameworks. While the NQF and QCF are both still operational, the plan is to develop a single framework in response to the Wolf Review of 14–19 vocational education in England (Wolf, 2011) and the government's subsequent request for further reform of vocational qualifications.

Bridging the academic/vocational divide

> The Government is committed to raising the status of vocational education and training.
>
> (DBIS, 2011b: 21)

> It is my view that the single most important purpose of A level qualifications is to prepare young people for further study at university, whether in the specific subject studied at A level or in a related subject area . . . Qualifications that command the confidence of our best universities will also command the confidence of teachers, parents, students and employers.
>
> (Gove, 2012)

Level	Examples of NQF qualifications	Examples of QCF qualifications
Entry	- Entry level certificates - English for Speakers of Other Languages (ESOL) - Skills for Life - Functional Skills at entry level (English, maths and ICT)	- Awards, Certificates and Diplomas at entry level - Foundation Learning at entry level - Functional Skills at entry level
Level 1	- GCSEs grades D-G - BTEC Introductory Diplomas and Certificates - OCR Nationals - Key Skills at Level 1 - Skills for Life - Functional Skills at Level 1	- BTEC Awards, Certificates and Diplomas at Level 1 - Functional Skills at Level 1 - Foundation Learning pathways - NVQs at Level 1
Level 2	- GCSEs grades A*-C - Key Skills Level 2 - Skills for Life - Functional Skills at Level 2	- BTEC Awards, Certificates and Diplomas at Level 2 - Functional Skills at Level 2 - OCR Nationals - NVQs at Level 2
Level 3	- A levels - GCE in applied subjects - International Baccalaureate - Key Skills Level 3	- BTEC Awards, Certificates and Diplomas at Level 3 - BTEC Nationals - OCR Nationals - NVQs at Level 3
Level 4	- Certificates of Higher Education	- BTEC Professional Diplomas Certificates and Awards - HNCs - NVQs at Level 4
Level 5	- HNCs and HNDs - Other higher diplomas	- HNDs - BTEC Professional Diplomas, Certificates and Awards
Level 6	- National Diploma in Professional Production Skills - BTEC Advanced Professional Diplomas, Certificates and Awards	- BTEC Advanced Professional Diplomas, Certificates and Awards
Level 7	- Diploma in Translation - BTEC Advanced Professional Diplomas, Certificates and Awards	- BTEC Advanced Professional Diplomas, Certificates and Awards - NVQs at Level 5 (in the QCF framework)
Level 8	- Specialist awards	- Award, Certificate and Diploma in strategic direction

Figure 3.2 Qualifications by level across the NQF and QCF

Source: www.qca.org.uk/493.html

These two recent statements, from different government departments in England, reflect long-standing tensions within post-16 education and training concerning the perceived value, status, currency, parity and economic benefits of 'academic', or general, and vocational education, particularly within the 14–19 phase. Scotland has attempted to do this by allowing the combination of general and vocational options within an overarching framework. Wales, through the Welsh Baccalaureate qualification and its 'Learning Pathways 14–19', has attempted to develop a more broadly based curriculum that permits a combination of general and vocational qualifications and is underpinned by wider curricular aims (for example, choice, flexibility and a learning core that includes knowledge, skills, attitudes, values and experiences that all learners require in order to progress).

The Scottish government recognises the importance of the totality of the curriculum experience, including informal as well as formal learning, which extends beyond simply subject learning: 'The curriculum includes the totality of experiences which are planned for children and young people through their education, wherever they are being educated.' These experiences are grouped into four categories:

- curriculum areas and subjects;
- interdisciplinary learning;
- ethos and life of the school (college);
- opportunities for personal achievement.

(see www.educationscotland.gov.uk/thecurriculum, n.d.)

In England, such a fundamental and inclusive reform of 14–19 education provision has yet to be achieved; although many attempts have been made, the results have been described as 'tinkering and tailoring' rather than wholesale reform (Jephcote and Abbott, 2005). Much of the difficulty derives from a system that at 14–19, within general education:

> . . . is selective, particularly post 16, casting a shadow over 'alternative' vocational provision, which is populated with 'refugees' from GCSEs and A levels. The focus on preparation for GCSE and A level examinations encourages mechanical and instrumental learning habits in young people also fails to support a broad and coherent curriculum.
>
> (Nuffield Review, 2008: 1)

Similar concerns had been voiced by Young (1993: 220), previously categorising the English and Welsh 16–19 curriculum as representing 'divisive specialisation', with:

- sharp academic/vocational division;
- insulated subjects; and
- absence of any concept of the curriculum as a whole.

In 2004, a review of the 14–19 curriculum in England was conducted by the Working Group on 14–19 Reform, known as the Tomlinson Review (DfES, 2004b). This proposed a unified diploma system for all 14–19 year olds to replace all other qualifications available to that age group. The proposals attracted a considerable groundswell of support from across the political parties, the worlds of education (public and private) and business, trade unions and the media. There was enormous disappointment, therefore, when Tony Blair announced that the government would not support the replacement of GCSEs (General Certificate of Secondary Education) and A levels, but would pursue a version of the diploma for vocational education (see DfES, 2006b).

There had been criticism of Tomlinson's proposals. Some argued that the fundamental principle of trying to 'unify' the academic and the vocational actually served to further devalue vocational education. Others argued that the proposals were overly complex and did not pay enough attention to how young people in apprenticeships would be covered (see Huddleston *et al.*, 2005). The key breakthrough, however, was that Tomlinson drew nationwide attention to the divisive and inadequate nature of the current arrangements. In contrast to England, Scotland has been moving towards a more unified 16–19 curriculum since the mid-1980s. Since devolution, Wales has signalled its desire to break away from England. It has combined elements of the Tomlinson diploma and the International Baccalaureate to create the Welsh Baccalaureate. This is available nationally at foundation, intermediate and advanced levels. The qualification includes existing A levels and GCSEs, as well as vocational qualifications, but they form 'options' to be taken alongside a 'core' programme consisting of four components: key skills; Wales, Europe and the world; work-related education; and personal and social education.

There is a distinct sense of déjà vu in much of this since, in 1996, just prior to winning the 1997 general election, the Labour Party in England published *Aiming Higher*, which called for the broadening of A-level programmes, improvements to vocational programmes, and the merger of all 16–19 qualifications within a single credit-based framework (see Hodgson and Spours, 1999). This drew on the 1996 Dearing Review, which examined the complex system of regulation governing award-bearing courses for 16–19 year olds in England, Wales and Northern Ireland. Dearing's concern, probably shared by thousands of teachers and managers in the post-compulsory sector, was for greater coherence in the system. One outcome of the Dearing Review was the reduction in the number of awarding bodies, mainly as a result of the merger of boards previously responsible for the award of vocational and academic qualifications. For example, BTEC merged with the University of London Examinations and Assessment Council (ULEAC) to form Edexcel. Once in government, Labour watered down its earlier proposals and published *Qualifying for Success* (DfEE, 1997). This caused Hodgson and Spours (1999: 124) to conclude that 'New Labour's evolutionary approach to qualifications reform is practical but piecemeal and somewhat backward looking' and 'essentially reactive to the Conservative legacy', reflecting 'a historical preoccupation with academic learning'.

You might wish to reflect upon the extent to which current provision for 14–19 year olds shares these characteristics. In September 2000, steps were taken along the road of reform in England with the introduction of vocational A levels (AVCEs), which replaced GNVQ Advanced, and the modularisation of A levels into groups of three and six units (since revised to two and four units and now about to undergo further reform). This reform was intended to pave the way for greater flexibility post-16, thus affording students the opportunity of mixing vocational and academic qualifications. The AVCE was revised and re-specified in 2005 as an Applied GCE (General Certificate of Education), a qualification more akin to its A-level cousin.

The reforms, commonly referred to as Curriculum 2000, also introduced 'key skills' as a component of all vocational and academic programmes, including government-supported apprenticeships. At this point, it might be helpful to include some analysis of the development of key skills. The idea that young people should develop generic skills that go beyond and underpin subject-specific knowledge or practical skills has been debated by educationalists, employers and policymakers for at least 40 years in the UK (see Canning, 2007; Green, 1997). These 'skills' have been variously labelled 'generic', 'core', 'inter-personal', 'transferable', 'employability' and 'life skills'. In 1979, the then Further Education Unit (FEU) published a landmark report, *A Basis for Choice* (FEU, 1979), which called for a 'core skills' curriculum, an idea that was forcibly promoted by the Confederation of British Industry (CBI) in its 1989 report, *Towards a Skills Revolution*. The proposition, strongly supported by policy-makers, employer organisations and more recently higher education, is that there is a definable set of core or key 'skills' that are essential for employability, for transferring learning from one context to another, and for 'learning to learn'. Over the years, various lists and categorisations of these skills have been produced (see Fettes, 2012).

Most notoriously, the Manpower Services Commission (MSC) produced a list of 103 core skills to be acquired by trainees on the Youth Training Scheme in the 1980s. The six key skills that appeared in 2000 comprised: 'communication'; 'application of number'; 'information technology'; 'improving own learning and performance'; 'problem solving'; and 'working with others' (the last three are referred to as 'wider key skills'). In 2010, functional skills (English, mathematics and IT) were introduced and will take the place of key skills in the autumn of 2012. The wider key skills are now covered by personal, learning and thinking skills (PLTS). The UKCES (2009: 10) argues that:

> We take employability skills to be the skills almost everyone needs to do almost any job. They are the skills that must be present to enable an individual to use the more specific knowledge and technical skills that their workplace will require.

Green (1997), however, argues that this fixation with key skills 'represents an impoverished form of general education' that has always been missing from the UK's approach to vocational education (see also Unwin and Wellington, 2001). There are complex philosophical and educational debates about whether such skills can be neatly categorised and whether they can be separated from the actual context of the subject that is being studied or, indeed, the workplace.

The Wolf Review (Wolf, 2011) reprised concerns about functional literacy and numeracy within the 14–19 age group, and government in England has accepted its recommendation that all vocational programmes, including apprenticeships, should ensure young people achieve at least Level 2 in mathematics and English by the age of 19 if they are not at that level when they start.

REFLECTION

Consider the following:

> The academic-vocational divide is not just about whether people learn welding or economics. It is about esteem and status. This means that colleges of further education which deliver vocational provision have an especially tricky mission. Many of their students have had a highly unsatisfactory experience of education.
>
> Their enthusiasm for learning may be low. They are often ill-prepared for big choices about their future working lives or about the education they may need to achieve it. They have already experienced failure by comparison with other people of the same age.
>
> (ESRC, 2007: 58)

- How far does this compare with your experience in college so far?
- How, if at all, might reforms to 14–19 education and training (such as those proposed in the Wolf Review) ameliorate this situation?
- Are the issues highlighted here so deep-seated as to require a multi-agency, cross-sector approach beyond the remit of the FE sector?

General education and qualifications

GCE Advanced and Advanced Subsidiary (AS) levels

Most of the provision within the general education category in England, Wales and Northern Ireland includes GCE A/AS level, GCE Applied A levels, and GCSEs. A levels were first introduced in 1951. As Young and Leney (1997: 53) note, 'A levels represent a highly insulated form of subject specialisation which directs learners' attention entirely to individual subjects treated separately'. During the past 15 years or so, there has been increasing criticism of the narrowness of A levels, particularly since young people are forced to make choices at 16 that effectively limit their opportunities to pursue a broader-based curriculum. In addition, Young and Leney (ibid.) remind us that, 'knowledge is more and more being produced at the interface of subjects and disciplines, not in subjects in isolation from each other' (see also Guile, 2006).

For those who have an interest in these issues, there is an extensive literature on the subject, which we do not have the space to fully consider here (see, for example, Pring et al., 2009; Raffe et al., 1998; Edwards et al., 1997; Hodgson and Spours, 1997; Dearing, 1996; Finegold et al., 1990; DES/WO, 1988).

The current A level is divided into four units, each of which is assessed through examination and coursework, though the latter is being progressively reduced and is likely to disappear as part of current reforms. The first two units of the A level form the Advanced Subsidiary (AS) level. This is both a qualification in its own right and the first half of the full A level. To achieve a full A level, candidates must complete a further two units, known as A2. Both the AS levels and A levels are qualifications in their own right; the A2 units are not a qualification. Currently, examinations may be retaken, either at the unit level (once) or for the whole qualification. Again, this may change in the future. The applied A level has replaced the former AVCE, which in turn replaced the Advanced GNVQ. This qualification has been substantially revised to make it more comparable with other A levels. This in itself tells us much about the perceived status of 'general' and 'vocational' qualifications (see Wilkins and Walker, 2011).

It could be argued that the advanced level curriculum is merely a collection of subjects, and only gains coherence at individual student level, even if then. In this model, a teacher's attention is naturally focused on achieving the desired number of student passes, and at acceptable grades. There may be a danger of 'teaching to the test' rather than considering the development of the whole individual. This situation may be exacerbated by the fact that a proportion of students taking A levels in colleges may be resitting examinations in which they have previously been unsuccessful. Since entry to HE is normally dependent upon achieving specified grades at A level, there is pressure on students and teaching staff to concentrate on 'getting through'. As a teacher, your lesson planning will be informed not only by the subject specifications, but also by the content of past examination papers and by examiners' reports.

Every summer, when the A level results are published, there is an outcry from certain sections of society who claim the exams must be getting easier as each year the pass rate improves. The elite English universities (such as Oxford, Cambridge, Durham and Bristol) also complain that it is becoming harder to distinguish between the best A level candidates.

As part of the drive to increase the 'stretch and challenge' of post-16 study, the Extended Project Qualification (EPQ) was introduced in 2008. This is an optional Level 3 qualification requiring a high degree of planning, preparation and independent research. It is about the size of an AS qualification in terms of teaching and learning time. Its introduction has been popular with teachers, learners and HE (Ipsos Mori/Social Research Institute, 2012). At the same time, a new A⋆ grade was made available at A level.

A final consideration within this section is the gradual extension of the International Baccalaureate (IB) to more sixth form and FE colleges. It is a broad two-year programme of study in which students have to follow six subjects, including their own language, a second language, an arts subject and a science subject, as well as some compulsory elements, which include theory of knowledge, community service and an extended project. Other 'academic', more broadly based, post-16 qualifications, including the Cambridge Pre-U and the AQA Baccalaureate, have also been developed, perhaps suggesting that the narrow three A-level diet is inadequate in terms of providing a broad and balanced curriculum for post-16 learners.

GCSEs

Another major area of general education provision within the FE sector in England, Wales and Northern Ireland is that of covering courses leading to GCSE. There was a long tradition in FE for students to enrol in order to resit GCSE examinations in which they were unsuccessful at school, very often in English and maths. These numbers have dropped considerably over the years, however, as it was seen to be better for young people to make a fresh start by enrolling on different types of programme, very often vocational in orientation. Adult students may, however, be tackling GCSE subjects for the first time, perhaps combining one or two of these with other qualifications. Adults on 'access to HE' programmes, for example, may need to achieve a pass in GCSE maths and English in order to access an HE course. You will realise that these learners have particular needs that go far beyond simply teaching to the specification.

For those teaching on general education programmes leading to nationally recognised qualifications, accredited by awarding organisations, the subject content is prescribed. The flexibility comes in the way in which teachers interpret the content and in the manner in which they seek to deliver it. The question of teaching style is considered more fully in Chapter 5. The starting point will be the specifications issued by the awarding organisation with whom your candidates are registered. It is from these that you will need to plan a coherent scheme of work. This will then be broken down further into individual lesson plans. You may already have recognised that there can be a danger in over-emphasising an input-output model: an emphasis on input, or knowledge to be imparted, to achieve a particular outcome (that is, success in the examination – we discuss this further in Chapter 6). However, as teachers, you should always be mindful of your students' wider developmental needs as learners. These may include: help with study skills; additional or specific learning support; and personal and interpersonal skills development. As Dimbleby and Cooke (2000: 78) argue, 'A curriculum model based on developing the broad talents of each individual leads to a range of learning models'. Chapter 4 will help you to think about students' different learning preferences.

Provision for pre-16 learners

The coalition government in England has stated its commitment to the policy of the previous Labour government to 'raise the participation age'. This means that young people will have to remain in some form of education and/or training, either part-time or full-time, to the age of 17 (by 2013) and to 18 (by 2015). This means that appropriate provision will need to be identified and developed. Some of the approaches already adopted within 14–16 school/college partnerships could provide useful models in terms of curriculum development.

There are, however, challenges for FE staff, who may have had no training, or experience, of teaching younger students. We met one of these students, Tom, in Chapter 2.

In addition to the subject content that may be delivered to this age range, other factors are critical to the development of a holistic curriculum model. These include: appropriate recruitment and selection procedures (not simply for students whom schools wish to direct elsewhere); school/college liaison to ensure that there is clarity about how the interests of the young person are best served; providing appropriate contexts for learning; ensuring staff are trained and committed to teaching this age group; tutorial and pastoral support; and attention to inclusion, health and safeguarding issues.

In summary, this type of integrated provision requires securely founded and adequately resourced partnerships of providers, who have a commitment to learners' entitlement to high-quality, applied learning delivered by those with recent and relevant sector experience and within realistic learning environments. We now turn to look at the type of provision they might access.

Vocational education and qualifications

The FE sector has always been the main provider of vocational education in the UK. During the 1980s, there were some developments within schools in both pre-vocational and vocational education through initiatives such as the Certificate of Pre-Vocational Education (CPVE) and the Technical and Vocational Education Initiative (TVEI) (for a discussion, see Pring, 1997). However, since the introduction in 1993 of GNVQs, the involvement of schools in this area of work has increased substantially. The fact that points garnered from the achievement of these qualifications could be used to boost school league table performance (sometimes with a tariff of four GCSE equivalence) provided further incentives. Wolf (2011) drew attention to such practices and their 'perverse incentives'.

Unlike schools, however, colleges offer many types of vocational programmes. One large FE/HE college advertises its provision thus:

> The college offers a vast number of courses spanning an unrivalled breadth of subjects, both academic and vocational, covering the following areas: AS and A levels, Applied and Sports Science; Creative and Performing Arts; Information and Communication Technology; Medical, Healthcare and Vocational Science; Skills for Life; Teacher Training; Technology.

Some specialist awarding organisations offer a small number of highly specific qualifications (for example, those offered within the land-based sector for game keeping and farriery). Many professional bodies also award vocational qualifications (for example, the Association of Accounting Technicians (AAT), and the Chartered Institute of Personnel Development (CIPD)), as do some multinational companies such as Microsoft.

Vocational qualifications also form part of the framework requirements for government-supported apprenticeships. In England and Northern Ireland, intermediate apprenticeship requires the achievement of a competence-based element at Level 2 (usually an NVQ or similar attesting to performance in the workplace); a knowledge-based element (either contained within the NVQ or a separate qualification such as a BTEC certificate); and functional skills. For an advanced apprenticeship, the requirements are set at Level 3 and for higher apprenticeship at Level 4. In Scotland, the modern apprenticeship requires the achievement of Level 3 or Level 4 qualifications, while the Skillseekers programme is at Level 2. In Wales, foundation apprenticeship is at Level 2 and apprenticeship at Level 3.

Following the Wolf Review (Wolf, 2011), all government-funded vocational qualifications for 14–19 year olds in England must conform to seven criteria:

- be as large as a GCSE in terms of guided learning hours (GLHs);
- include at least 20 per cent external assessment (externally set and marked test under controlled conditions);
- contain synoptic assessment that involves making connections and bringing together different units of the course;
- be graded pass, merit, distinction and distinction*;
- contain appropriate content for 14–16 year olds (although the qualification is available to older learners);
- enable progression to further study at the next level in the same subject or to broader study at the next level; and

- have a proven track record (demonstrate significant take up in terms of numbers of candidates and centres).

You should bear in mind that, as these are new regulations, most qualifications will be in the process of transition. Also, these regulations only apply to qualifications offered to pre-16 students, to bring them into line with GCSE criteria ('Section 96' qualifications – those eligible for funding). There are similar regulations covering qualifications for post-19 learners (known as 'Section 97'

Unit title: Gives a broad indication of the content to be covered, for example: 'Working to Quality Practice in Care Settings.' (OCR National)

Level: Identifies the level on the NQF or QCF, for example: Level 3.

Unit type: Indicates if the unit is 'core', 'specialist' or 'generic'.

Guided learning hours: Time required for teacher input working specifically on unit content.

Type of assessment: States how the unit is assessed, for example: internal, external, by portfolio.

Learning outcomes: Describes what a learner should be able to 'know, understand or be able to do' upon completion of the unit. It may appear as Unit introduction in some specifications, giving the learner 'a snapshot of the purpose of the unit' (Source: Edexcel, 2012).

Unit content: This may look to you more like a 'syllabus'; it identifies the knowledge, understanding and skills required to meet the assessment objectives and points to the teaching, learning and assessment that is required in order to underpin this.

Assessment objectives: States what evidence is required to demonstrate that the candidate has met the learning aims for the unit; all AOs should be covered for successful achievement of the unit.

Grading criteria/grading grid: Show what evidence students have to produce in order to meet the grading criteria for each level - Pass, Merit etc.

Teacher guidance: This section is particularly addressed to tutors and provides further advice on approaches to delivery, assessment, links to other units within the qualification, to other qualifications, and to National Occupational Standards (NOS), essential resources and indicative reading for learners.

Signposting to key skills/functional skills and PLTS: Opportunities for development of generic skills are signposted within unit specifications, where appropriate, and in some cases mapping to National Occupational Standards. For example, when candidates are presenting findings on business performance they may be able to compare data from their selected case study businesses and compare them with national data (Functional Skills: maths). Similarly, students may be able to present data in the form of charts and tables (Functional Skills: ICT).

Figure 3.3 Example of unit specification

REFLECTION

You might wish to consider the ways in which you could incorporate opportunities for functional skills (English, maths and ICT) development in some of the following assignments. There may also be opportunities for the development of personal learning and thinking skills (PLTS) – independent enquirer; self-manager; effective participator; team worker; creative thinker; reflective learner.

1   Prepare a plan of the layout of the workshop (drawn to scale and showing all dimensions) indicating options for optimising use of space. Remember to consider the health and safety implications of your choices (engineering).

2   Provide a monthly breakdown of the numbers of customers using the college restaurant; the most popular choices from the menu; the average spend per customer; the percentage of waste (hotel and catering).

3   Together with other members of your group, prepare a presentation for the steering committee on the feasibility of offering access to the college's sports facilities to local residents on a paying basis (leisure and recreation).

qualifications). There is an important point to be made here in terms of the concept of a curriculum. While the content of the qualification may be the same, or very similar, students who are following the programmes may be very different. We have seen already that learners could be full-time, part-time, in employment, seeking work, pre-16, post-16, post-19, with differing personal, social and economic circumstances. What should the entitlement be for these different groups of learners beyond access to the subject content? Remember that at the beginning of this chapter we said that the concept of curriculum went beyond simply defining the content to be covered.

Let us look now at the general features of the specifications for vocational qualifications. At this point, it would be helpful for you to select the awarding organisation's specification for any of the programmes on which you teach, or are preparing to teach. If you are new to teaching, you will probably be perplexed as to how this might be transformed into a scheme of work, or into individual classes, especially if your own experience has been on academic programmes. Each specification comprises a number of sections. Figure 3.3 is for illustrative purposes only and draws from a range of specifications and awarding organizations to provide a general overview.

In the majority of vocational programmes, the emphasis is on developing the skills of the learner within a particular context so that he or she is able to apply the knowledge and skills learned in the classroom to the workplace and vice versa; to enable him or her to become more self-reliant. The responsibility has to shift from the teacher to the learner but these are skills that have to be cultivated. It may be difficult for teachers who have been accustomed to 'leading from the front' to change to a more student-centred approach; as a teacher recently said to us, 'It's scary to let go'. Equally, it may be difficult for students to come to terms with a more flexible approach.

Here are some students' responses to group work while studying Unit 4 'Principles of customer service' in the Level 2 First Award in Business. The tutor had decided to use role play in order to allow learners the opportunity to practise their customer service skills. Note the assessment guidance provided by the awarding organisation concerning the use of such approaches states:

> learners should demonstrate effective communication skills to meet customer needs when dealing with three different customer types in different situations. Evidence will be through records of how these skills have been applied (through role play, part-time work or a work place-ment). Centres must ensure that learners record a personal statement from evidence they have gathered to show how they demonstrated the skills (e.g. in a log or diary if they have demonstrated these skills during a work placement or part-time job.
>
> (Edexcel, 2012)

> 'I really enjoyed this, it was a laugh. Lee was really going over the top, acting up and everything. Still, it's better than taking notes. There should be more classes like this.'
>
> (Student A)

> 'Roy (the tutor) should give us more idea what to do, I felt stupid, I don't like working in groups because I don't get on with other people and I've had some trouble with that. It's worse when you have to do this acting stuff.'
>
> (Student B)

> 'I thought it was OK because Roy explained what we had to do and we had some time to prepare first. Also, he said how we could use this for evidence in our log books, which is always good because we are always stressing about getting assignments and stuff in on time.'
>
> (Student C)

The 14–19 Diploma

From September 2008, a new qualification, the 14–19 Diploma, became available to young people in schools and colleges in England (for a critique, see Ertl and Stasz, 2010). This is a composite qualification available at three levels (foundation, higher and advanced), incorporating three elements: principal learning; additional specialist learning; and generic learning (functional

The Model

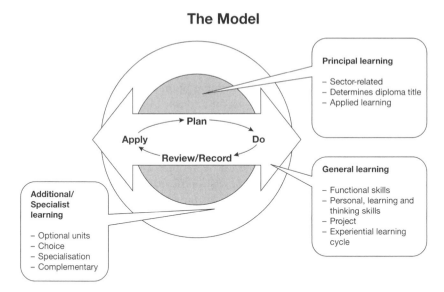

Figure 3.4 Diploma model

skills, and personal and thinking skills). In addition, they require the completion of a project, allowing independent study and research at the appropriate level for the qualification (at the advanced level, the Extended Project Qualification (EPQ) fulfils the requirement), and 10 days' work experience. The model is represented in Figure 3.4.

The content of the diplomas was developed by Diploma Development Partnerships (DDPs), led by the SSCs (for example, Semta for engineering) and included representation from employers, education (schools and colleges), awarding organisations and training providers. The principal learning includes the core diploma subject (for example, creative and media). This gives the diploma its title and is supposed to be aligned closely with industry standards and requirements. Content should be properly contextualised and related to current sector practice, including access to workplaces and practitioners.

The generic element of the diploma includes functional skills, English, ICT and maths (at the appropriate level), as well as the opportunity for independent learning through completion of a project, allowing for in-depth study. The additional specialist learning is intended to complement the principal learning and might include, for example, a GCSE in a related subject for foundation- and higher-level diplomas, or an A level for an advanced-level diploma. A student working towards a diploma in society, health and development might wish to include a GCSE in science. A student taking an advanced diploma in creative and media might wish to include an A level in art and design. The model was designed for flexibility, to enable learners to combine a learning programme matching their needs and aspirations.

Crucial to the successful delivery of these diplomas are partnerships between schools, colleges, training providers and employers. It is very difficult for any one institution to deliver diplomas on its own, although some schools have tried to do so.

Plans to develop diplomas in science, humanities and modern languages were cancelled by the coalition government upon taking office in 2010. The coalition government's lukewarm response to the 14–19 Diplomas in general, together with proposed reductions in funding, sounded alarm bells for those already committed to their implementation and to learners already embarked upon them. In summer 2010, around 4400 students had completed diplomas, with increased enrolments expected for September 2010. The first advanced-level diploma holders were gaining access to HE. It was estimated that around 40,000 had started diplomas since their introduction. However, the future of the diploma was hit by further body blows from the new government. These included: the abandonment of the entitlement for every 14–19 year old in England to study one of the 14 diploma lines at all 3 levels if they so wished; downgrading of the tariff for diplomas following the Wolf Review (previously a full foundation diploma equated to 5 GCSEs, grades D–G; intermediate diploma to 7 GCSEs, grades A*–C; and an advanced diploma 3.5 A levels); reduction in available development funding; increased competition between and across institutions for 14–19 provision; a requirement to pass functional skills in addition to the achievement of the full diploma; and the insistence that the 'royal route' of 'academic' A levels would remain.

Admittedly, the diploma design was complex and their administration was bureaucratic, but there was a real attempt, involving employers, SSCs, teachers,

---

REFLECTION

The students combine hand and mind to learn in a very practical way, integrating national curriculum requirements with the technical and vocational elements. The UTC ethos and curriculum is heavily influenced by local and national employers who also provide support and work experience for students.

(www.utcolleges.org/about/about/)

This statement outlines the mission of University Technical Colleges (UTCs) in England.

■ How far do you think that the diploma qualification is seeking to serve the same purpose?
■ How do you feel it can endure outside the special institution of the UTC?
■ What is distinctive about the diploma qualification in terms of its curricular design?

trainers, HEIs, and, it has to be said, a considerable amount of public funding to develop a holistic programme of study combining practical and general education located within sector contexts that, with further refinement, could have spoken to the needs and aspirations of young people and allowed for progression. For the engineering sector, there has been particular disappointment about the downgrading of the diploma, as it is the qualification of choice for students enrolled in the new University Technical Colleges (UTCs) in England.

At the time of writing, 14–19 Diplomas are still available in schools and colleges but their future is uncertain. However, the content of the principal learning within some diplomas may prove fruitful for further development, especially since for some sectors (for example, engineering) it has been welcomed.

Competence-based qualifications

FE has a long tradition of providing job-specific training for both young people and adults, covering a wide range of occupational sectors. The provision of occupational training was the *raison d'être* of many early technical colleges and much of this provision was on a day-release basis. In the 1980s, there was a radical shift away from the existing model of curriculum and qualification design to an assessment-led, competence-based approach (see Unwin *et al.*, 2004; Raggatt and Williams, 1999). The new National Vocational Qualifications (NVQs) and Scottish Vocational Qualifications (SVQs) had a major impact on colleges because they were deliberately designed to be independent of programmes of study. By setting out lists of job-specific competences, it became possible for an individual to be assessed in order to see if they required any further training. If they were able to provide evidence of their competence, then they could, in theory, be accredited with a full qualification without having to attend a course. This process is known as the accreditation of prior learning (APL) or the accreditation of prior experiential learning (APEL). A further implication of this new approach was that colleges and other providers could employ people purely as 'assessors'. Ecclestone and Hayes (2008: 11) have argued that 'Assessment has replaced learning as the major function of vocational education. As a result, students are "achieving" more but learning less' (for a critique of APEL, see also Scott, 2010).

Assessment of candidates for the award of an NVQ/SVQ must be done through a centre approved by an awarding organisation. This might be a workplace, a college, a training provider or a voluntary organisation. Colleges now employ staff who are qualified assessors, but who are not involved in any teaching or training. For example, one college located within a popular tourist town offers local guesthouses the opportunity of NVQ assessment for their housekeeping staff within the workplace.

There is a considerable literature on the introduction of competence-based qualifications in the UK, much of it highly critical (see, inter alia, Brockmann *et al.*, 2011; Young, 2008; Hodkinson and Issitt, 1995; Wolf, 1995; Hyland, 1994). At the heart of the criticism is the concern that by separating qualifications from learning, the competence-based model takes us back to a Taylorist model of work-based training in which workers were only allowed to acquire the minimum skills and knowledge required to do an immediate job. This sense of a highly restricted approach to vocational education and training is further compounded by the associated assessment regime as a candidate's performance is not graded: you are either judged to be competent or not – if the latter, you do not 'fail' in the traditional sense, but are expected to return for further assessment when you are ready. Debates about the efficacy of not grading competence-based qualifications have raged since their introduction in the late 1980s (for a discussion, see Johnson, 2008).

Concerns have been expressed that the manner in which the competences (or 'learning outcomes') are written will have a negative effect on teaching and learning. There is a danger that where there is a high degree of granularity in the outcomes, teachers will be concerned solely with the generation of evidence to meet each criterion rather than with the development of competence in the wider sense (Cort, 2009, 2010). A learning outcome may be defined by several assessment criteria; the larger the number, the greater the danger of atomising the learning without paying attention to the interrelatedness of the units of the qualification as a whole.

At the time of writing, the QCF in England is being populated with occupational qualifications that conform to specific standards and rules, in terms of size, credit value, guided learning hours and level of difficulty. This is despite the warnings about granularity discussed above. In some cases, NVQs have been transferred directly on to the QCF; in other cases, occupational qualifications have been re-specified to align more closely with the occupational standards (usually referred to as national occupational standards) for the sector. For example, within the care sector, the SSC 'Skills for Care' has phased out NVQs and replaced them with a new range of skills qualifications based on QCF principles and informed by the perceived training requirements of the sector following wide consultation. At such a time of transition, you will need to ensure that you are aware of what is happening within your sector.

In order to help you think about the implications for curriculum design, we provide an example (see Box 3.1), by way of illustration, of a qualification and its associated assessment criteria taken from the catering sector: the Level 2 award in the Principles of Practical Food Safety for Catering. All QCF accredited qualifications are unit-based. The number of units required for each qualification is set out within the specification and will vary according to the occupation and level. In order to gain the qualification, a candidate must complete all the units necessary for the award.

Box 3.1 QUALIFICATION OVERVIEW

Title of Award: Level 2 Award in Practical Food Safety for Catering

Awarding organisation: NCFE

QCF Level: 2

GLH: 40

Credit value: 4

Assessment requirements: Internally assessed and externally moderated portfolio

Source: NCFE Level 2 Award in Practical Food Safety for Catering: Section I, Qualification Overview, July 2011.

The specification for this qualification outlines: (a) the *qualification aims* ('to take personal responsibility for themselves and food safety; develop knowledge and skills to be able to store, prepare, cook, hold and serve food safely in line with good practice and food safety legislation'); (b) *for whom it is intended* (for example, young people who wish to progress to further qualifications within the sector or those already working in the sector, either full-time or part-time); and (c) *entry requirements* (for example, if any prior learning or qualification is required, such as if a Level 1 qualification is required before commencing Level 2).

The assessor confirms, through evidence in the learner's portfolio, that the learner has achieved the learning outcomes for the unit by meeting all the assessment criteria. For each learning outcome, there will be a number of assessment criteria, as in the example in Box 3.2 taken from the mandatory unit for the Level 2 Food Safety Award.

**Box 3.2 LEARNING OUTCOME AND
ASSESSMENT CRITERIA**

The Learner will (Learning outcome)

2. 'Understand the importance of keeping him/herself clean and hygienic.'

The Learner can (Assessment criteria)

2.1 'Explain the importance of personal hygiene in food safety including its role in reducing the risk of contamination.'

2.2 'Demonstrate effective personal hygiene practices, for example use of protective clothing, hand washing, dealing with personal illnesses, cuts and wounds.' (p. 15)

Types of evidence

Candidates may draw upon a range of evidence (for example, witness statements provided by workplace supervisors, observation records of candidates' performance in the workplace (signed and dated), products, design drawings, worksheets, photographs, peer reviews) depending upon the nature of the award being sought. In all cases, assessors must ensure that all the learning outcomes and associated assessment criteria have been achieved before signing that the candidate has been successful. The assessor is also supposed to support learners through the assessment process. Assessment decisions will be moderated by an internal moderator (within the college, training organisation or company) and then by an external moderator (from the awarding organisation). Its purpose is to ensure that decisions have been made by 'competent and qualified Assessors, the product of sound and fair assessment practice, recorded accurately and appropriately' (NCFE, 2010: 15).

Since candidates are required to demonstrate competence in the workplace, colleges have had to find suitable work placements for full-time students, and for trainees not in employment. This can be challenging for colleges since employers face many competing demands to provide work placements. Some colleges are able to provide realistic learning environments (for example, in college restaurants, motor vehicle workshops, offices and reception areas, or hairdressing salons).

In summary, competence-based qualifications and the 'personalised learning' agenda have put pressure on colleges to:

- develop more flexible and responsive provision that can accommodate individual student needs;
- develop learning support materials and learning resource centres that students can access individually according to their own needs, with or without the help of a lecturer;
- modularise their programmes (although this is by no means universal) to enable students to 'pick and mix' units rather than having to follow a complete programme;
- develop partnerships with employers in order to ensure an adequate supply of work placements for students;
- design simulated work environments to allow students to demonstrate competence under the same conditions and pressures as they would in employment;
- develop adequate systems of guidance, advice and counselling to enable students to access the appropriate parts of the curriculum; and
- develop support structures to enable students to build portfolios of evidence and to identify learning opportunities within the workplace and within the college.

> **REFLECTION**
>
> ■ How does the teacher juggle these possibly competing demands?
> ■ How can potential learners seek impartial and informed advice?
> ■ What are the implications for teachers, and teaching, of modularised (or unitised) programmes?
> ■ If students are allowed to 'pick and mix' units, how can they build a coherent programme of study?
> ■ Is it possible to talk about a curriculum within the 'learning outcomes approach' outlined in this section?

Higher education in further education

Although some FE colleges have always provided a certain amount of advanced work (for example, through HND and HNC programmes), the provision of degree-level courses is relatively recent (see, inter alia, Griffiths and Lloyd, 2009). In some cases, colleges are delivering the first two years of a degree programme, with the third and fourth years being delivered in the university. In other cases, colleges may deliver the whole of an undergraduate programme. There may be franchising arrangements in place or colleges may have their own programmes accredited by an HE institution. Sometimes, the HE institution may not be local to the college. There are further examples where colleges may be running whole, or parts of, degree programmes from several different HE institutions.

Where FE colleges are delivering programmes through franchising arrangements, the subject content will be prescribed by the HE institution. There will be quality assurance protocols covering staffing, assessment and resources. Standards of assessment will be monitored, moderated and verified, and examinations will be set by the university. Those involved in teaching such programmes may be located within a separate department or unit within the college specialising in HE provision. However, HE courses may fall within the remit of a department of general education or within a curriculum area (for example, Business and Management).

As we mentioned in Chapter 1, the introduction of Foundation Degrees in 2001 provided a major opportunity to expand what is often referred to as 'HE in FE' provision (see, inter alia Guile, 2011; Evans et al., 2009). As a teacher of 'HE in FE', you may find there are tensions between how you are expected to work and your own identity. Gale et al. (2011) argue, for example, that lecturers may not be given the space and time to pursue scholarly activities, including research. Similarly, Wilson and Wilson (2011) argue the need for a research culture to be developed in FE and a shift away from relying on 'reflective practice' as the sole approach to professionalism (for a further discussion, see Chapter 7).

As a teacher, you will need to consider these factors in developing your teaching strategy. If you return to Corrine, the HE student described in Chapter 2, you will see that she has particular learning needs, some of which derive from a lack of confidence. Pike and Harrison (2011) argue that colleges and universities need to make more effort to support students in the transition from FE to HE, particularly in relation to helping them overcome anxieties about their academic ability (see also Bathmaker and Thomas, 2009). Useful resources and support groups are being developed (for example, those provided by the Higher Education Academy (HEA), which has a dedicated 'HE in FE' newsletter and termly briefing).

REFLECTION

■   What are the challenges for you as an FE teacher in providing a quality learning experience for non-traditional HE students?
■   What opportunity do you have to engage in research and scholarly activity to enhance teaching and learning?

General adult education

> In adult learning, colleges are the giants who have learned to dance, but they have not yet written the music or the choreography. The success of a new adult and lifelong learning culture in the future will depend on the extent of their powers to create, produce and direct new and better learning, as much as it will depend on performing and delivering it.
>
> (Howard, 2009: 7)

The term 'adult' as applied to education is not easy to define. For some, adult education refers to any provision beyond compulsory schooling, while for others the term denotes a particular type of provision sometimes referred to as 'liberal adult education'. For funding purposes, UK governments divide post-compulsory education and training into three phases: 16–18; 19–24; and 25+. Age 19 has become the official point at which someone is treated as an 'adult'.

The scope of adult education has always been, and is, extremely wide. There are some institutions that exist primarily to teach adults (for example, the Workers' Educational Association (WEA), the Open University (OU), and adult and community education services – where they still exist – provided by local authorities). (For a more detailed discussion of the history of adult education provision, see Field, 2006; Fieldhouse and Associates, 1996.) Adult education may also be engaged in through a whole range of informal mechanisms, including, for example, the University of the Third Age (U3A), faith-based groups and voluntary organisations. The number of places available for adults who want to learn for pleasure is, however, being constantly eroded, mainly because of funding cutbacks. In addition, as we noted in Chapter 1, funding requirements mean that many courses now have to lead to a qualification. A retired architect, reflecting on his part-time Spanish language course, commented to us: 'I thought I was going to study Spanish language and literature, not learn how to answer A level questions designed for teenagers.'

Since the 1990s, the term 'adult education' began to be replaced by the term 'lifelong learning'. The concept of lifelong learning came to public attention in 1994 when it formed a major part of Jacques Delors' European Commission (EC) paper on competitiveness and economic growth and the EC declared 1996 the European Year of Lifelong Learning. Since then, governments around the world have urged their citizens to become lifelong learners. Field (2000: viii–ix), in a detailed critique of lifelong learning, bemoans the way in which 'lifelong learning has been used by policymakers as little more than a modish repackaging of rather conventional policies for post-16 education and training, with little that is new or innovative'. He continues:

> This tendency to wrap up existing practice in a more colourful phrase can also be seen in the rush by providers to claim their adherence to lifelong learning: and even professorial titles have all been subjected to this rebranding. The educational result is a kind of linguistic hyperinflation, in which the term is constantly devalued.
>
> (ibid.)

Field goes on to argue that although politicians have largely promoted lifelong learning as being essential for economic prosperity, the 'silent explosion in informal and self-directed learning' has 'only partly been driven by economic changes' and has equally as much to do with 'transformations in people's lives and identities' (ibid.). (See also Schuller and Watson, 2009.)

One way in which the previous Labour government responded to the lifelong learning agenda was through the creation of learndirect, which was used as the operating name of the University for Industry (UfI). The vision was for a UK-wide network of learning centres, many of which would be based in colleges, public libraries, schools and other existing sites of learning linked to a central database that could be accessed through a call centre and a website. The initiative attracted criticism for:

- using the name 'university';
- using the term 'industry', which suggested its function was purely economic; and
- setting up yet another quango that would take money away from existing providers.

An example of the media reaction to the UfI name was the following extract from an editorial column in the *Times Higher Education Supplement* in April 1998:

> The first obvious thing about it is that it is no university. It is designed to trawl the highways and byways, using all the modern means of public persuasion, to draw in those who have learned little and like it less. Only very much second and later is it to help people who are already skilled but seek retraining . . . Tackling educational failure and skill shortages is admirable, but calling the project a university risks debasing the currency which the government has said it wishes to defend.
>
> (THES, 1998: 11)

The tone of the THES's comments does, of course, say a great deal about the academic vocational divide in the UK and social class. Although they were made over a decade ago, they are worth reflecting on in the light of the current government's desire for more institutions to apply to use the name 'university' and also the expansion of programmes at the HE/FE interface. In response to criticisms about the name, the government relaunched UfI as learndirect.

Today, learndirect boasts, '10,000 people log on and learn with learndirect everyday' and, '93% of our learners say that learning with us has given them skills to help them in their future working life' (for further information about how learndirect operates, see http://learndirect.co.uk/about/). The emphasis is very much upon online skills tests, including English, maths and IT, jobseekers and employability skills, rather than upon the wider developmental aspects of learning. Learners may access some courses freely; for others there is a charge.

Other notable government responses to lifelong learning have been the introduction of ILAs (discussed in Chapter 1) and the Union Learning Fund (ULF). The ULF has a much more positive history than ILAs. Established in 1998 by the then DfEE, the fund has enabled trade unions to train learning representatives (ULPs) who provide advice and guidance to employees in the workplace, and to develop a range of collaborative projects to stimulate participation in education and training. It is managed by Union Learn, the learning and skills organisation of the Trades Union Congress (TUC). The Fire Brigades Union (FBU), for example, has used ULF monies to improve employees' literacy and numeracy where necessary, before they embark on the NVQ Firefighter Level 3. Working with Northumberland Fire and Rescue, the FBU has instituted an English and maths assessment process carried out by the FBU learndirect learning centres (for further information about the Union Learning Fund, see www.unionlearningfund.org.uk/case-studies/fbu-nvqs.cfm).

It will be clear from this diverse picture that it is quite impossible to talk about a single adult education curriculum. It is perhaps more useful to think about the ways in which adults learn and the strategies that we as teachers might develop in order to help them learn more effectively. These themes are returned to in Chapters 5 and 6. As Howard (2009: 8) suggests, 'Colleges should be the institutional backbone of the lifelong learning system (their) values and missions should be inclusive and pluralistic, offering a comprehensive and diverse curriculum for a diverse adult population.'

Conclusion

There are many different curriculum models in use in FE colleges and, as a teacher, you may be involved in more than one. As we have seen, curriculum design has become very much shaped by qualifications requirements. The challenge, then, is to find ways to take back some control over the content of what you actually teach and to enjoy sharing your subject expertise with your students. Williams (2008: 159) has cautioned against FE being driven by an economic agenda: 'What is lost from education is any sense of purpose beyond the instrumental: there is no space for education for enjoyment, for personal development or simply for its own sake'. Halpin (2008: 60), in a call that challenges the narrow concept of 'employability skills', has called for teachers to create opportunities for learning that actively stimulate their students' imaginations: 'These qualities of the life of the imagination contribute positively to the growth of personal adaptability and autonomy, resulting in people being less reliant on others to help them to make sense of experience and their lives generally'.

As we write, there is a renewed interest in seeing vocational education as a vehicle for the teaching and learning of aesthetics and the importance of the material and sensual aspects of our lives, of the history of societies and their artefacts, and for re-enaging people with the concept of 'craftsmanship' (see Unwin, 2009; Sennett, 2008). In Chapter 1, we argued that it was important for FE teachers to have some understanding of the history of their profession and the organisations in which they work. An intriguing aspect of that history, in the light of this discussion about curriculum and qualifications, is the period from 1957 to the late 1970s when all day-release students were required to spend one hour on general/liberal studies (GLS) in order to foster the 'habits of reflection, independent study and free inquiry' (Ministry of Education Circular 323, quoted in Bailey and Unwin, 2008). In 1961, the Association of Liberal Education (ALE) was formed, with the primary purpose 'to encourage the extension of liberal education in an industrial society that increasingly demands specialisation' (ibid.: 66). Underpinning this purpose were 'four beliefs':

1   The student's right to be regarded as an individual human being, not merely as a potential worker, and, as such, should be offered full educational opportunity to develop his [*sic*] powers of thought and personality.
2   The student should be encouraged to understand and question his [*sic*] place in society, his [*sic*] rights and duties.

3   Education in the schools, colleges and universities of the country should not be confined by narrowly vocational or over-specialised curricula.
4   It is the duty of teachers periodically to examine and revise the subject-matter and methods of their teaching.

While much has changed since the days of GLS, these ideas are still worth debating. You might wish to reflect on the extent to which your own teaching and the programmes of study you cover enable students to 'foster habits of reflection, independent study and free inquiry'.

Part II

Teaching and learning

Chapter 4

The process of learning

Introduction

We begin this chapter with four comments on teaching and learning:

> When adults teach and learn in one another's company, they find themselves engaging in a challenging, passionate, and creative activity. The acts of teaching and learning – the creation and alteration of our beliefs, values, actions, relationships, and social forms that result from this – are ways in which we realise our humanity.
>
> (Brookfield, 1986: 1)

> The constructs a learner brings to the learning environment are interwoven with personal meaning and value, are frequently implicit and deeply embedded. Any acquisition of new knowledge will entail adjustments to this system and if personal horizons of understanding are to be extended, new learning must be assimilated with what is already known.
>
> (Harkin et al., 2001: 37)

> . . . teaching and learning are primarily social and cultural rather than individual and technical activities; they should therefore be studied in authentic settings; this in turn means addressing their complexity, through a cultural perspective on the interrelationships between individual dispositions and agency, and institutional and structural contexts.
>
> (Colley et al., 2003: 3)

> In the aftermath of the tsunami disaster of 2004 in South East Asia a radio journalist interpreted the reopening of a school as the first sign of a return to a 'normal life'. He observed: 'the children can start to learn again'. His comment was a stark reminder of the received assumptions that surround the concept of learning.
>
> (Fuller, 2007: 17)

In order to meet the challenge of teaching in the FE sector, it is essential to have some knowledge of the different theories that help us to understand how people learn. We began Chapter 1 with the statement that 'teaching and learning are situated activities' and, hence, any discussion of teaching and learning must always pay attention to the nature of the context in which it takes place and the wider context of which it forms a part. At the same time, teachers much take account of the contexts within which students live and work, their personal biographies, and their dispositions towards learning. As with any space in which people gather together, colleges are sites of conflict, power and control. Teachers wield considerable power over their students, but are themselves subjected to powerful controlling mechanisms that reflect the ethos and values of the college in which they work. Students too can exert power, particularly if they are paying substantial fees for their courses, and some may choose to create problems for particular teachers if they regard themselves as being unfairly treated.

Before we continue, we need to say something about terminology. The terms 'teaching' and 'learning' are used in everyday parlance, but the terms 'learning' and 'learner' have come to have much more prominence over the past few years due to a recognition that a great deal of learning takes place outside formal education and training settings and that individuals continue to learn throughout life. The historical narrative that has led us from the notion that education was the preserve of the privileged classes learning in a small number of exclusive institutions to the concept of learning as a socially situated, ever-present process in which everyone participates is perceived to be one of empowerment and progression (see Unwin *et al.*, 2004: x). While we would agree that a much more inclusive concept of learning is to be welcomed, we have to be careful that we remain alert to the potential pitfalls. A key concern is that if the term 'learning' is substituted for the word 'education', then people will focus much more on process and give less attention to the nature of what is being learned. Second, while, of course, individuals do a great deal of learning without the aid of a teacher (in the formal sense of that role), teachers are crucially important in helping and pushing learners to go beyond their immediate comfort zones. Throughout this book, we have tended to use the word 'student' rather than 'learner' to signify that most of what we are concerned with here is the relationship between teachers and their students. You will have your own views on these issues and might reflect on the terms you and your colleagues use.

Another term that requires attention is 'pedagogy'. This term is often used interchangeably with teaching and comes from the Ancient Greek word 'paidagogas', which relates to the 'leading' (agogas) and 'instruction' of children by slaves (pais). The term has come to encompass the complexities of the teaching/learning relationship. Miriam Zukas (2006: 71), who with Janice Malcolm has examined pedagogical approaches in relation to lifelong learning, argues that pedagogy is much more than the restricted notion that teaching consists of a bag of techniques and tricks:

> Instead of conceptualizing pedagogy as teachers' actions inside classrooms to bring about learning, such that teaching is a decontextualised transfer of knowledge, skills and practice to the acquisitive learner, we have tried to escape this teaching/learning polarization by conceiving of pedagogy as encompassing 'a critical understanding of the social, policy and institutional context, as well as a critical approach to content and process of the educational/training transaction.
>
> (Zukas and Malcolm, 2002: 215)

The quotation refers to 'a critical approach to content and process'. A major figure in the promotion of the concept of 'critical pedagogy' was the Brazilian educator Paolo Freire (1974), who identified three stages of learning:

- task-related;
- learning about personal relationships; and
- 'praxis'.

Praxis relates to Freire's belief that learning should develop individuals' capacity to examine their surroundings critically and, hence, lead to some form of action. Others have argued for pedagogical approaches and 'democratic practices' that take account of student diversity in terms of social class, gender, ethnicity, sexual orientation and age (see, inter alia, Roberts 2012; Clarke, 2002; McLeod et al., 1994; Giroux, 1991). Bathmaker and Avis's (2005: 16) research into the experiences of trainee FE teachers led them to argue for a more realistic and pragmatic approach – one that sees critical pedagogy as an aspiration that recognises the 'complexity, contradictions and messiness of classroom practices'.

The following comment from Mary Hamilton (2006: 136), who writes from the perspective of the way adults acquire and use literacy, brings some of these ideas together and poses a challenge to all teachers. She argues that we need:

> pedagogies that keep in touch with change, that are responsive, exploratory, that ask questions, that are prepared to constantly challenge the institutional walls we build around learning, not just inviting others in but going out, barefoot into the everyday world.

This discussion of the complexities that lie behind the creation and use of pedagogical approaches poses considerable challenges to attempts by governments and others to reduce teaching to a simplified list of 'skills' or techniques (see Edwards, 2001). As we saw in Chapter 1, the government's standards-based approach to FE teacher training was initially seen by many in the sector as inadequate. Gleeson (2005: 242), drawing on evidence from the Economic and Social Research Council's (ESRC) Learning Cultures in Further Education project (see James and Biesta, 2007), stresses that individual teachers should be treated as professionals and, hence, encouraged to pursue their own ways of working with students.

The study and development of pedagogy has a troubled history in the UK, whereas in many other European countries it is given much greater importance. A leading historian of education, Brian Simon (1999), traces this back to the view in English public schools in the nineteenth century that teachers were there to socialise their upper- and middle-class pupils. The teachers came from the same backgrounds as the pupils and this, accompanied by a degree from Oxford or Cambridge, was sufficient qualification for the role. In terms of FE, as shown in Chapter 1, the relatively recent requirement for all teachers in colleges to have a teaching qualification is currently under threat in England. The approach to teacher training for FE in the UK also differs from that of some other European countries where closer attention is paid to developing pedagogical approaches that are appropriate for specific disciplines, including vocational and practical subjects. Regardless of whether you are training to teach catering or hairdressing in the UK as opposed to, say, mathematics or English literature, you will study on the same generic course. Clearly, all teachers, regardless of their field of expertise, need to share a common core of pedagogical expertise, but there has been concern for some time that FE teacher training does not pay enough attention to what might be termed 'practical learning'.

In their study of community colleges in the US, Grubb and Associates (1999: 98) also found a neglect of what they refer to as 'occupational teaching', other than cursory references to 'hands-on learning and project-based instruction'. They argue that such teaching is 'rich and complex' with many competencies to master, including 'manual and visual abilities, problem solving, and inter-personal skills as well as conventional linguistic and mathematical abilities' (ibid.: 99). In the best examples, Grubb and Associates (ibid.) found that vocational (or occupational) teachers used a much more holistic approach than their academic colleagues, drawing on students' own experience, varying the types of task and making connections between what was being learned and the workplace.

The characteristics of learning

As discussed in Chapter 2, you could be teaching students whose ages range from as young as 14 to those in advanced old age, all of whom will have spent some years being taught in other educational institutions and learning in informal settings, and in their places of work. You will, therefore, be confronted with people who have a great deal of experience as learners, and that experience will be of a particularly personal nature. For some of your students, their learning experiences may have been entirely pleasurable, whereas for others learning may be equated with anxiety and even pain. You will meet students who lack confidence as learners and many who find it difficult to know how to learn for themselves without being totally dependent on a teacher. The nature of a person's prior learning experience has a profound effect on their approach and attitude to further learning activity. As such, teachers do not start with a clean sheet. It may seem unnecessary to point out that people, whether they are teenagers or adults, learn in different ways, but it is a truism whose implications can be lost in the hectic whirl of the average teaching day. Just as your students will approach their learning in different ways, you too will have developed your own strategies for acquiring knowledge and understanding and for learning new tasks. Your own very personal approach to learning will influence your approach to, and style of, teaching.

REFLECTION

Give some thought to the following questions and try to answer them as honestly as possible. You could also try them out on a friend, partner or member of your family.

1   What was the last thing you learned?
2   Do you attend a regular class of any kind (for example, keep-fit, camera club, local history)? If you do, why do you attend and how did you get started?
3   Do you enjoy learning? Do you, for example, enjoy learning from books, listening to lectures, watching experts, finding out answers for yourself?
4   Do you consider yourself to be a good learner? How would you define a good learner?
5   Given your answer to question 4, were you a good learner at school? Have you improved as a learner since leaving school?
6   Is there anything that prevents you from learning?

In answering the questions above, you may have revealed aspects of your persona as an adult learner that even you find surprising. The last question, for example, may have brought forward a certain personal barrier to learning that you have not articulated before.

Your answers may also reveal something about your own personal definition of what learning means. You might, for example, agree with the 'behaviourists' who say that in order to claim learning has taken place, a person's behaviour has to change (see Skinner, 1968). The 'behaviourist' school of thought was pre-eminent in the 1950s and 1960s, particularly in the US through the work of B.F. Skinner, and had a great influence on workplace training and the pro-grammed learning approach adopted in correspondence courses. Indeed, the competence-based approach (discussed in Chapters 3 and 6) has been criticised as being a return to the techniques of behaviourism. What the 'behaviourists' overlooked (as a result of which, they are now seen to be the 'bad guys' of learning theory) is the contribution and agency of the learner.

Kolb, whose work has been influential in adult education and workplace training, defines learning as 'the process whereby knowledge is created through the transformation of experience' (Kolb, 1984: 41). His 'learning cycle' claims that learners progress through four stages:

- observation and reflection;
- generalisation and abstract conceptualisation;
- active experimentation; and
- concrete experience.

Each of these stages can be entered first during an individual's learning journey. Although praised for its contribution to the development of learning theory, Kolb's model has also been criticised for being too simplistic. For example, Jarvis (1987: 18) has pointed out:

> consider the situation where a person is reading a complex mathematical tome and is involved in abstract conceptualisation from the outset: the next stage of the learning process might be reflection rather than active experimentation and so the arrows would need to point in both directions. In addition, Schön (1983: 49–69) discusses the idea of reflection-in-action in which they occur almost simultaneously. Hence there may be stages of Kolb's cycle that are not sequential.

Despite the flaws in his model, however, Kolb's key contribution is his emphasis on the central importance of learning from experience. There is a general consensus among adult learning theorists that the experiences that adults gain during their lives play an important part in any learning activity on which they embark. Those experiences can have both a positive and negative effect. They can help adults to contextualise and conceptualise new information, but experience can also hinder learning by reminding adults of past failures. The recognition that adults learn in different ways and that each adult comes to learning with a unique set of experiences has contributed to the development of the theory of 'experiential learning', echoes of which are to be found in the work of the French psychologist Jean Piaget and the American philosopher John Dewey (see Piaget, 1970; Dewey, 1966, 1938). In its simplest form, experiential learning recognises that adults approach any learning activity with some preconceived idea about what it is they are about to try and learn. This is because of the wide range of experience they already have, so they do not approach learning with a totally blank mind. A great deal of teaching, in all sectors of education, undervalues this prior experience in learners, and tends to follow what Freire called the 'banking' concept of education:

Education thus becomes an act of depositing, in which the stt
the depositories and the teacher is the depositer. Instead of commɪ.
the teacher issues the communiques and makes deposits which the students
patiently receive, memorise, and repeat.

(Freire, 1974: 58)

Although the role of the teacher in FE may be constrained by the prescriptive
nature of much of the curriculum, and, particularly, by the emphasis on the
assessment of predetermined outcomes, a recognition that learning is a highly
personalised activity should guide the teaching and learning process. Indeed,
it could be argued that many of the developments in the FE world, such as
the modularisation of courses, competence-based qualifications, open and
flexible learning, and the redefinition of the student as a 'consumer' of learning
necessitate teaching styles that are largely learner-centred and experiential in
emphasis. The danger in treating students as consumers, however, is that the
'product' (for example, a module or a qualification) they are 'buying' becomes
more important than the learning process. Whether they are learning on their
own or in groups, students should not be seen as, or even allowed to be, simply
passive participants.

A question of age: the concept of adulthood

You may be surprised by the references to adult learners and adult learning
when we began this chapter by acknowledging the fact that you could be
teaching people as young as 14. If you were teaching in a school, you
might regard all students up to the age of 18 as children and would probably,
therefore, turn to theories of how children learn for some insight before preparing to teach. People mature differently, and there are some 12 year olds
who demonstrate greater sophistication as learners than many twice or even
three times as old. Colleges of FE have always seen themselves as being
different from schools in a number of ways, but a key difference is in their
attitude to students. The vast majority of students in colleges have left
the compulsory stage of education and entered the non-compulsory world in
which they will be required to take responsibility for their own learning.
Although, in reality, significant numbers of students in the 16–19 age bracket
may have been persuaded to attend college by their parents, from the
college's point of view they have chosen to attend as opposed to being obliged
to attend by the state. The following quotations from college prospectuses
illustrate this:

We treat our students as adults who want to take responsibility for their
own lives and who will thrive in the supportive and lively atmosphere of
the college.

(Sixth-form college)

The college prides itself on creating an adult atmosphere in which all students are treated with respect and seen as individuals with individual needs and aspirations. In return, we ask our students to behave responsibly and make the most of their opportunities at college.

(College of art and technology)

That colleges actively promote themselves as being 'adult oriented' reflects their appreciation of the fact that young people in the 16–19 age bracket, who could continue their post-16 education in schools, are attracted to FE colleges precisely because they want to get away from the 'child-oriented' ethos of their secondary education. As they enter the second half of their teenage years, these young people will be developing a sense of self that, according to Rory Kidd (an influential writer on adult learning), 'is essential to all learning' (Kidd, 1973: 127). Attending college offers young people the chance to develop this sense of self within a context that allows social interaction with people of all ages. It is not surprising, then, that colleges devote considerable resources to ensuring that the social and student support facilities they provide are of a high enough standard to encourage social interaction in addition to that which takes place in the formal learning situation. For the more mature students in a college, development of a sense of self may also be a central feature of their college experience, particularly if they are returning to learning and studying for the first time in a number of years. In their research with American women mature students in HE, Belenky et al. (1986: 31) asked these women to try to describe how they saw themselves. One woman said, 'I don't know . . . No one has told me yet what they thought of me'.

REFLECTION

It might be useful at this point to revisit the vignettes in Chapter 2 and consider the ways in which the development of a sense of self applies to those students. Consider these questions:

1   How might Mark's parents affect his personal development?
2   What strategies could the college use to enable Gary to develop a more constructive attitude?
3   How could Grace be helped to transfer with confidence to the college?
4   To what extent will Tom's experiences at college affect his attitudes towards school?

In Chinese culture, there is a tradition that says people cannot be classed as adults until they are married. In the UK, the legal system has a curiously confused approach to adulthood. For example, a 16 year old can marry but cannot vote, drive a car or be served with alcohol in a public place. Employers, too, often display somewhat illogical attitudes to age in their recruitment strategies. For example, some employers advertise for experienced and skilled people yet only consider applicants under the age of 35, whereas others categorise all 16–19 year olds as lacking enough maturity. Given the spread of student age in an FE college, you could find you are teaching people a great deal older than yourself one day, followed by a day when your students are very close to your own age or the same age as your children.

Younger and older students: differences and similarities

As explained in Chapter 1, colleges in England are now having to make provision for students as young as 14. There are dangers in separating out 'young learners' for special attention. As Griffin (1993: 23) explains, 'Youth/adolescence remains a powerful cultural and ideological category through which adult society constructs a specific age stage as simultaneously strange and familiar'. Adults criticise young people for behaving badly while, at the same time, reminding themselves that they probably behaved in the same way when they were teenagers; though the media headlines that followed the riots in English cities in the summer of 2011 would suggest that some adults have short memories. In the 1950s and 1960s, radical forces in society, including the civil rights movement in America, the student riots in Paris, the huge growth in youth consumerism, and the close links between music and drug taking led to young people being defined as a social problem (for a detailed discussion, see Furlong and Cartmel, 1997). Economic prosperity gave young people the financial means to indulge their interests and greater leisure time than had been enjoyed by their parents. Although the economic crisis of the late 1970s and early 1980s put a stop to the relatively smooth transition from school to work that teenagers had been enjoying in the previous two decades, the importance of identifying oneself as part of a youth culture had been firmly established. We see this continuing today with the importance young people place on having the right make of mobile phone and designer clothes, and the means to go clubbing, even if that means getting into serious financial debt. Furlong and Cartmel (ibid.: 61) explain that, 'In late modernity, the visual styles adopted by young people through the consumption of clothing are regarded as having become increasingly central to the establishment of identity and to peer relations'. They stress, however, that although this consumerism is evident across all social classes, not everyone has the financial means to keep up with the latest fashions, resulting in a pattern of both financial and cultural exclusion. As we write, around one million young adults are unemployed in the UK as a result of the continuing economic crisis.

The way in which many teenage students in full-time education service their consumer needs is by working on a part-time basis, sometimes as much as

20 hours per week. We know from research that many 16–19 year olds work part-time, and many have some work experience from the age of 14, so that 'earning and learning' has become the common experience for young people (Hodgson and Spours, 2001: 386). The massive growth of the service sector in the UK has benefited from a willing army of young, part-time workers whose identity shifts, often on a daily basis, between student, employee and consumer. Service sector employers can offer flexible hours, the possibility of working long shifts to earn extra money, and employment close to home. And employers will often demand little in the way of prior experience or qualifications.

For teenagers concerned to earn just enough money to cover their social life and mobile phone bills, such jobs are very attractive. The implications of this shift in the meaning of the term 'full-time student' are considerable. Teachers in schools and colleges alike are finding that they cannot assume that young people will devote their time outside the classroom to homework or that they will be alert enough to pay attention in class. Some teachers are trying to solve these problems by making use of their students' work experience in, for example, the development of functional skills, or as the basis for assignment work. What is clear is that where once colleges relied on young people using their 'free' periods to continue their studies in a self-directed manner, they now have to acknowledge that this time is more likely to be spent on the till in the local supermarket.

The nature and scope of young people's life chances are largely dependent on their family background, current level of educational attainment, gender, ethnicity and geographical location. As the work of Furlong and Cartmel (1997) and Hodkinson et al. (1996) has shown, young people's lives do not generally follow the neat linear pattern envisaged by policymakers. Their 'horizons for action', to use Hodkinson et al.'s term, may expand or constrict, sometimes through their choice and sometimes because of circumstances beyond their control. And as Evans (1998: 20) points out, 'Young adults may be caught in disjunctions and contradictions of policies which do not recognise the interplay of the private and public domains and are based on invalid assumptions about common characteristics and needs of age ranges'. For the FE teacher, it is worth remembering that, as Furlong and Cartmel (1997: 41) explain, youth is a 'period of semi-dependency, which forms a bridge between the total dependence of childhood and the independence of adulthood'. It is a time of great experimentation and indulgence, but it can also be a time of great anxiety.

Teenagers can find themselves homeless as a result of family breakdown, they may be coming to terms with having suffered sexual and/or physical abuse, they may be single parents, and they may be responsible for the care of a parent or sibling. As Harkin et al. (2001: 59) point out, 'We know that educational achievement is likely to be as much the product of environmental factors as of any innate tendency to a particular learning style or type of intelligence'. The instabilities of modern life can catapult teenagers into a more adult role than they would wish, or are capable of performing (see also Lumby, 2012; Russell *et al.*, 2011; Thompson, 2011).

As highlighted in Chapter 3, many young people are used to using the Internet and social media as a means to acquire and share information, and are skilled in word processing. Such assumptions can, however, be misleading for teachers, who may find that a significant proportion of their young students have only really used computers to play games. The reliance on the Internet that some young people have developed for gathering information may also have had a restricting influence on their ability to think critically or to study subjects in depth. Although the use of Information and Communication Learning Technologies (ICLT) and social media has to be handled with care, they also offer considerable potential for aiding learner autonomy, for delivering ongoing feedback and, through the use of email and web-based chat rooms, for more creative types of group interaction. Price and Kaid-Hanifi (2011: 185) argue that, at a time of reduced resources for tutorial and pastoral care, e-communication tools, which provide access to online supportive networks, 'could provide individuals with the opportunity to access fellow students for collaboration, assessment advice and transformational motivational support to supplement that which otherwise may have come from more regular face-to-face tutor contact'. Young people (and indeed many older students) will expect ICLT to play a considerable part in their learning experience at college.

In their research into young people's experiences in FE, Bloomer and Hodkinson (2000: 61) developed the concept of the 'learning career', which they define as 'the development of a student's dispositions to learning over time'. These 'dispositions' are affected by experience both within and outside college, but Bloomer and Hodkinson (ibid.) found that the vast majority of the young people they studied were surprised at just how much their dispositions changed during their time in FE. Although, for some young people, the extent and type of transformation they experience as learners will be influenced by their previous life history, in the main, the pattern of one's learning career was not wholly predictable. Some of the many factors that Bloomer and Hodkinson (ibid.) found contributed to changing dispositions to learning were:

- examination results;
- new teachers;
- fellow students in a class;
- course content;
- course assessment;
- learning activities;
- college resources;
- course availability;
- course status;

- financial circumstances;
- job opportunities; and
- access to advice.

Bloomer and Hodkinson (ibid.: 79) conclude that, 'For those entering FE from school, it is a period of maturation, of unfolding and developing personal identity, of transition, transformation and change' (see also Hodkinson and Bloomer, 2000).

Teenagers and young adults can find that being a student does not sit well with their lives outside college. There are a number of difficult issues with which young people may have to grapple:

- personal identity and life goals;
- sexual orientation;
- generation gap with their parents;
- status in society;
- personal finances;
- balancing part-time work with their studies;
- relationship with siblings;
- relationship with peer groups; and
- coping with living apart from their families.

In addition to any personal problems they may have, young people are aware of the fragile nature of the labour market and recognise that they may have to be prepared to change career several times during their working lives. Indeed, the problems faced by young people continue to cause concern throughout the EU and in other countries (for a comparative study, see Brooks, 2009).

We interviewed 16–19-year-old students studying A levels and the BTEC Extended Diploma Level 3 in Business in a large college in the East Midlands to share their views with us on their experiences of college. One group was studying A levels; the other was following a BTEC Extended Diploma Level 3 in Business (for a study of student perspectives on teaching and learning, see also McQueen and Webber, 2009).

In expressing their views on why they had decided to come to college, the overriding reasons for both groups were:

1   dislike of their previous school experience (the majority expressed this view);
2   their schools' unwillingness to accept students into the sixth form who had not achieved specified grades: 'they wouldn't let me take biology because I didn't have C in maths';
3   the absence of an appropriate vocational programme within their school: 'they didn't do music technology at my school'; and

4   the type of learning environment they were seeking as young ad‗
    'I wanted a more adult learning environment'; 'I wanted to meet new
    people'; 'I wanted a new experience'; 'I wanted a fresh start and to get
    rid of my school reputation'; 'schools have kicked people out and they
    end up here'.

In terms of teaching and learning, there was some concern about the variability
of teaching, ranging in the groups' opinions from 'very strict to very relaxed'.
The perceived 'step up' from a Level 2 to a Level 3 programme was a challenge
for some, particularly where large amounts of coursework were required: 'it
is tedious and long-winded'; 'there is so much work to do'; and 'sometimes
we do not know what to study ahead'. Others felt that their tutors, 'really go
that extra mile' to help their students. Clearly, a lot depends upon the
relationship between tutors and students, and where group size is large this is
more difficult to achieve. Above all, the students wanted stronger support
structures to help 'scaffold' their learning: 'they don't always give us the right
information'; 'we need more tests and feedback'. However, they also recognised
that they too had to take more responsibility. Some of the BTEC group
recognised that the move from a Level 2 to a Level 3 programme required
them to be better organised and more self-reliant in terms of taking notes,
accessing resources and preparing coursework assignments: 'it's better than
exams, you need to plan ahead, there's a lot to do, but you can get help if you
need it'; 'it's a more adult environment for independent learning'.

Most students appeared reasonably happy with their course choice,
particularly on the business course, although they suggested that, 'if the tutor
quits, the subject goes'. This reflects a wider concern about the proliferation
of part-time, short-term and sessional teaching contracts. With the A-level
group, several students had been forced to change a subject halfway through
the programme because the tutor had left. There had been significant 'drop
out' from this group. While there is much to be gained from having practising
experts teaching on courses, they too have competing demands on their time.
This is particularly the case within the design sector, where many are self-
employed, and securing a design contract may come before teaching.

The majority of the A-level group, and about a quarter of the BTEC group,
were looking to progress to higher education. The remainder of the business
group had apprenticeship firmly in their sights; one student hoped to find a
job after leaving college. However, it was felt that more help should be provided
for students wishing to apply to university in terms of drafting personal
statements, identifying appropriate courses and preparing them better for
subsequent study.

The students expressed concern about their post-college futures. One
mature student had given up a job to start the course and was keen to ensure
that the sacrifice had been worth it; another said, 'my worst fear is not getting

a job after university'. The interest in apprenticeship reflected these concerns since it was perceived as a route to guaranteed employment. Earning money was very important and over half the students already had part-time jobs, although it was recognised that, in the current economic climate, these were getting harder to find. As one student put it: 'It's really a question of who you know'. Some of the business students hoped that the part-time work might lead to something more permanent.

Students in both groups were overwhelmingly positive about their move to college. Satisfaction appeared to be couched more in terms of the environment: 'meeting different people'; 'treated more as adults'; 'a fresh start'; 'the best place to do business'. There was less enthusiasm, however, for the subjects being studied. They stressed that more could be done to attract more teachers, particularly full-time ones, and to provide a greater range of choice. In other words, satisfaction was expressed in terms of the contexts and processes of learning rather than the content, which appeared to be taken as a given. Nevertheless, a note of sadness was registered by a student who felt that, 'people look down on us because we're at college'. This reflects deeper issues within England related to the academic-vocational divide and a perception that being a sixth-form student in a school has higher status than studying in an FE college.

It would be ridiculous to give the impression that all young people are suffering from stress or experiencing significant hardship. As Lumby (2012: 261) argues:

> As for young people themselves, the YouTube generation does not necessarily see itself as powerless or as a victim of a punitive world (Hull *et al.*, 2009). A counter-narrative presents youth as often agentive, creative and buoyant, moderating and overcoming the hazards perceived by adults (Hull and Katz, 2006).

Mature adults can face many of the problems identified by the younger students above, particularly if those problems are introduced by their teachers and the college in which they are studying, or if they are created by external pressures. In addition, mature students are more likely to face health problems and have the general burden of the responsibility for managing households.

For many mature women, their barriers to learning are wrapped up in the very fact of being female (see the reference to feminist critical pedagogies at the start of this chapter). Their lives tend to be more disrupted than men's as they take time out of education and careers to raise children or to support partners. The following comment from a 30-year-old mother of three captures the battle in which some women have to gain lost ground:

> I'm just getting to the point where everybody else starts. Do you understand what that means? Most people, when they leave home or

graduate from high school, already have an idea of what they are worth. An idea that they go out and conquer the world. I'm just getting to where everybody else is at.

(Belenky *et al.*, 1986: 53)

In order to support women who are returning to learn and who may feel threatened or ill at ease in the company of male students and tutors, some colleges have run women-only courses, though these have declined in recent years due to funding problems. Hillcroft College on the outskirts of London remains the UK's only adult education college providing both day and residential courses just for women. At the time of writing, Newham College in London was providing women-only classes in ESOL, while Bradford College offered women-only courses in construction and engineering. Although many would argue against separating men and women for educational or training purposes, the issues that concern the advocates of women-only courses apply to the central issue of the impact of gender on learning (for more details, see Chapter 5).

Regardless of their age and levels of expertise and experience, all learners shape and are shaped by the context in which learning takes place (see, inter alia, Hager and Hodkinson, 2009; Evans *et al.*, 2006). This argument challenges the deeply rooted assumption that learning is simply a process of the acquisition of knowledge that individuals can transfer from one setting and apply in another. We will return to this issue below.

How do people learn?

A seminal study of adult learning carried out in Canada by Allen Tough and reported in 1971 was particularly influential in seeking to identify the ways in which adults differed in their learning from children. Tough observed the ways in which adults plan and organise their own learning and how they set about acquiring knowledge and understanding. His key finding was that adults are 'self-directed' in their learning for which 'more than half of the person's total motivation is to gain and retain certain fairly clear knowledge and skill or to produce some lasting change in himself' (Tough, 1971: 6). Tough's findings built on earlier work in the US by Johnstone and Rivera, who found that a huge number of adults were engaged in learning outside the formal adult education system, which they termed 'independent self-study' (Johnstone and Rivera, 1965). This and later studies of adult participation in learning showed how the amount of adult learning could be wildly underestimated if the only measure was the numbers attending formal classes in institutions. By recognising the determination of adults to further their learning and that this motivation made them much more self-directed than children, the need for the development of distinctive models of adult learning theory was advanced.

One of the most distinctive theories has been put forward by Malcolm Knowles (1978), who developed the concept of 'andragogy' (from the Greek aner (stem andra) meaning 'man'), which stresses that children and adults approach learning in different ways and that this should be taken into consideration by those who help adults learn. Knowles noted the following differences between adults and children:

1   Children see themselves as dependent – adults see themselves as independent.
2   Adults bring experience to learning and value that experience.
3   Adults are ready to learn for specific reasons as their development is linked to the evolution of their social role – children's development is physiological and mental.
4   Children see much of their learning as being for the future – adults learn as a response to the here and now.

REFLECTION

Given on the facing page (Box 4.1) is a list of instructions based on the Japanese art of Origami for making a salt cellar. (When made up, some of you may recognise the object as one that was, and may still be, popular at school for playing a game of 'choices'.) In order to learn how to make this object, you could do one of the following:

1   Go through the instructions step by step as you would an instructional manual.
2   Ask a partner to assist you – one reading, one folding the paper.
3   Ask a partner to make the object first and then demonstrate to you as in a typical class in which, for example, the teacher demonstrates how to ice a cake or set up a chemistry experiment.

Using one of the above methods, have a go at making the object and record your experiences. When reflecting on your performance, try to consider the following questions:

1   Do you learn best by yourself or do you like/need the support of someone else?
2   Do you follow instructions to the letter or do you improvise?
3   Would you have worked better from a picture?
4   Do you prefer to be shown how to do something?

If you have the time and/or the opportunity, ask a fellow adult and a child (under the age of 13) to attempt the same exercise and compare their learning experience with your own.

Box 4.1 PAPER FOLDING INSTRUCTIONS:

1 Take an A4 sheet of paper.

2 Place paper portrait way up.

3 Fold bottom right-hand corner at 45° until it meets left-hand edge.

4 Take scissors and cut off rectangular unfolded section of paper, and discard.

5 Unfold square paper.

6 Make another diagonal fold, so that there are now two diagonal folds that cross in the centre of the paper.

7 Unfold.

8 Take left edge of paper and fold over to meet right edge.

9 Unfold.

10 Take bottom edge of paper and fold over to meet top edge.

11 Unfold.

12 You should now have a square piece of paper with two diagonal folds and two square folds that cross in the centre of the paper.

13 Fold all four corners, one at a time to meet the centre point.

14 Turn work over.

15 Fold all four corners, one at a time, to meet the centre point.

16 Turn work over.

17 Push diagonal folds together and open out the pockets in each of the corners to produce a 'salt cellar'.

Although much of this work has a common-sense ring to it, there is a danger that the individual learner becomes lost in a sea of generalisations. The vignettes in Chapter 2 show how dangerous it is to generalise. Take, for example, the case of Gary, whose behaviour as a learner seems to have more in common with the characteristics of children as identified by Knowles above, rather than with those of self-directed adult learners. There is a sense, too, with Grace that she may still be at a dependent stage as a learner, owing to a lack of confidence, despite her age and experience.

When you analysed your approach to, and experience of, the paper folding exercise, you may have found yourself engaged in Kolb's learning cycle. You might also recognise some of your experience in the following eight-stage model of learning, which has been advocated by Gagne, an educational psychologist who developed and extended some of the early work on behaviourism. We have summarised and adapted Gagne's model and suggest that the term 'learning' be seen as encompassing knowledge, skills and understanding:

- *Stage 1: Motivation* (student's motives and expectations identified and brought in line with teaching objectives).
- *Stage 2: Apprehending* (teacher gains student's attention by various means).
- *Stage 3: Acquisition* (knowledge, skills and understanding acquired by the student in a form in which they are ready to be lodged in the memory).
- *Stage 4: Retention* (student is helped to memorise and assimilate new learning).
- *Stage 5: Recall* (student encouraged to retrieve learning ready for application).
- *Stage 6: Generalisation* (student transfers learning to range of situations).
- *Stage 7: Performance* (student tries out newly acquired learning).
- *Stage 8: Feedback* (student is helped to judge performance and reflect).

As with all models, this one has a simplicity, which can be misleading – teaching and learning can often be a messy business and individuals do not, necessarily, want to have their learning confined within a chronological framework. Clearly, the stages shown above can be fused and their order might be rearranged or disrupted in order to reflect particular circumstances. It is, however, a useful model for teachers to keep at the back of their minds when they are planning teaching sessions, and it can be used during sessions as an evaluation tool if a teacher feels the right amount of progress is not being made. We return to this model in Chapter 5 when we examine teaching strategies.

You will have seen that Stage 1 in Gagne's model is 'motivation', a word that will figure highly in most teachers' everyday discourses, whether they are thinking about their own levels of motivation or that of their students. Just like the weather, motivation can change from one hour to the next, and it is a difficult concept to unpack. Rogers (2002: 95) explains that motivation can be said to be dependent on either 'intrinsic' or 'extrinsic' factors:

> Extrinsic factors consist of those incentives or pressures, such as attendance requirements, punishments and rewards, or examinations to which many learners in formal settings are subjected or the influence of other persons or organisations. These, if internalized, create an intention to engage in the learning programme. Intrinsic factors consist of those inner pressures and/or rational decisions which create a desire for learning changes.

It is clear that even this differentiation is problematic. Rogers (ibid.: 95) acknowledges that within intrinsic motivation there is a hierarchy of motives. He gives this example: 'a desire to please some other person or loyalty to a

Figure 4.1 Maslow's hierarchy of needs

group, which may keep a person within a learning programme even when bored'.

A key theorist of motivation was Maslow (1968), who devised what he called a 'hierarchy of needs', as shown in Figure 4.1.

In this rising model of motivation, Maslow asserts that adults and children move up the layers as their need in each one is satisfied. Despite its limitations, this model has proved useful to teachers in pointing to the need to remember that their students are individuals with emotional, intellectual and physical needs. Harkin *et al.* (2001: 62) have adapted Maslow's model by filling in some useful detail: they convert 'food' into guidelines for making the learning environment pleasant, including adequate refreshment breaks; 'shelter and safety' refer to non-threatening classrooms, ground rules and induction programmes; 'love and belonging' covers openness of communication, recognition of different learning styles and valuing learners' life histories; 'esteem' relates to setting achievable tasks, giving positive feedback and support for learner autonomy; and 'self-actualisation' is concerned with supporting progression and transfer of learning.

Another theorist whose work offers useful insights for understanding how people learn is Bloom, who distinguished between learning that takes place in the cognitive domain and that in the affective domain (see Bloom, 1965). For Bloom, cognitive learning runs in parallel with affective learning so that at the same time as a learner develops knowledge, his or her behaviour as a learner is also developing. The affective side to learning can be seen as a way to introduce some kind of value system to the learning process so that as one acquires knowledge, one also learns to appreciate the role that knowledge plays, which, in turn, encourages the learner to be committed to the process.

Social, situated and expansive theories of learning

A particularly powerful view of the way in which people learn is that provided by Jean Lave and Etienne Wenger (1991) who introduced the concept of 'communities of practice', which stresses that learning is as much a collective as an individual activity (for a detailed critique, see Hughes *et al.*, 2007). This is a social theory of learning, which sees learning as 'an aspect of participation in socially situated practices' (Lave, 1995: 2). What is important here is that knowledge and skills are seen as not belonging solely to an individual, but things that are to be shared and developed collectively within a context. In addition, it is the historical, social, political, economic and cultural dimensions of any community of practice and the nature of the interactions between members that determine how much learning occurs. Fuller and Unwin (2004, 2010), for example, have argued that the quality of learning on apprenticeship programmes is very dependent on the way in which a company's existing community of practice sees apprentices as primarily learners or productive workers (see also Felstead *et al.*, 2009). They have built on Lave and Wenger's ideas and drawn from the work of the Finnish academic Yrjo Engestrom (2001) to develop the concept of expansive and restrictive learning environments. Fuller and Unwin have examined the way in which different workplaces can be plotted on an 'expansive–restrictive' continuum according to the nature of the learning opportunities created within them. In the workplaces towards the expansive end of the continuum, employees have greater opportunity to share their skills and knowledge, to cross work boundaries and have access to off-the-job training.

The concept of a community of practice, which has tended to be used primarily by researchers exploring workplace learning, can be applied to a college, a classroom or a group of students working together on a project. It can provide a useful device for teachers to examine the social context in which they expect their students to learn. In addition, by examining their own community of practice, whether as members of a department, a course team or at the level of the whole college, teachers can also reflect on how those communities facilitate or impede their professional development and sense of worth (see also Fuller *et al.*, 2005). Central to Lave and Wenger's theory is that learning is partly about 'becoming' – that is, individuals engaged in the social relations that constitute a community of practice learn what is involved (beyond surface knowledge and skills) in moving towards becoming an expert, in whatever type of work, be it plumbing, hairdressing, engineering, bakery, nursing or law:

> The person is defined by as well as defines these relations. Learning thus implies becoming a different person with respect to the possibilities enabled by these systems of relations. To ignore this aspect of learning is to

overlook the fact that learning involves the construction of identities . . .
identity, knowing and social membership entail one another.

(Lave and Wenger, 1991: 53)

A key part of the college element of work-based or work-related programmes
is to provide the codified knowledge and the opportunity to practise skills
within a less pressurised environment than the workplace. This all contributes
to the process of 'becoming', though students will often complain that they
cannot see the immediate connection between what they learn off the job and
what they learn on the job (see Silver and Forrest, 2007). The challenge for
the FE teacher is to create activities that help students make connections, and,
importantly, create space for them to reflect on the aspects of the workplace
learning that they find problematic. This might include issues related to
interpersonal relationships and dealing with superiors.

Practising skills and applying knowledge in simulated or real work situations
enables people to build up a reservoir of tacit expertise. We are all aware that
when we perform tasks we utilise some skills and knowledge that we would
find difficult to describe. Michael Polanyi (1967) developed the concept of
tacit knowledge in the late 1950s and early 1960s as part of an enquiry into
the nature and justification of scientific knowledge and more broadly the
character of human knowledge. He drew a distinction between tacit (practical)
knowledge and explicit (codified) knowledge but acknowledged that the
boundary between the two was not at all clear, arguing that all knowledge was
a combination of the codified and the tacit and that the two worked together
to enable human beings to act. Neisser argued that there is a direct link between
action–centred skills and tacit knowledge:

> The skilled carpenter knows just how a given variety of wood must be
> handled, or what type of joint will best serve his purpose at a particular
> edge. To say that he 'knows' these things is not to claim that he could
> put his knowledge into words. That is never entirely possible . . . The prac-
> titioner's knowledge of the medium is tacit. It is essential to skilled
> practice: the carpenter uses what he knows with every stroke of his
> tool.
>
> (Neisser, 1983: 3)

In terms of teaching and learning, the tacit dimension has always been
understood by vocational teachers and workplace trainers, but some are less
willing than others to create the appropriate opportunities for their students to
develop their tacit expertise through practice. This can, of course, be difficult
due to health and safety regulations, time constraints, and the cost of raw
materials. Awareness of the tacit dimension is also important in terms of
considering students' prior experience. Adult students, in particular, will come

to college with expertise gained through work, but may not have any formal accreditation to prove what they can do, and they may not be able to articulate their skills and knowledge due to lack of confidence or, quite simply, because this expertise is tacit in nature (see Evans *et al.*, 2006). Providing opportunities for students to demonstrate their skills and knowledge can unlock hidden talents and build confidence.

Boreham (2002) has argued that the UK should look to the German concept of 'arbeitsprozesswissen', which roughly translates as 'work-process knowledge', as a way to bring the concepts of tacit and codified knowledge closer together. Work-process knowledge embraces:

> an employee's knowledge of the work process in the enterprise as a whole, including the labour process, the production process and the way in which the various departments and functions are inter-related.
>
> (Boreham, 2002: 232)

This concept is influential in the German 'dual system', whereby apprentices split their week between off-the-job learning in a college or workshop setting and on-the-job training in a workplace. By gaining a much more rounded understanding of how the theory they learn off the job relates to the practical tasks they perform on the job, apprentices are better able to utilise the different types of knowledge and skills they acquire. This process also demands a much closer relationship between vocational teachers and employers to ensure that the former is up to date with regard to changes in workplace procedures.

Lave and Wenger's work has connections to cultural historical activity theory (sometimes abbreviated to CHAT), which builds on the work of the Russian psychologist Lev Vygotsky (see Engestrom, 2001; Cole, 1985). As Guile and Young (1999: 113) explain, Vygotsky was concerned with 'the progress that students make with their studies as they relate their "everyday" concepts – the understanding that emerges spontaneously from interaction with other people and in different situations – to the "scientific" concepts that they experience through textbooks and the formal curriculum' (see also Guile, 2010). Vygotsky developed the concept of the 'zone of proximal development', which he defined as 'the distance between the actual development level as determined by independent problem solving and the level of potential development as determined through problem solving under adult guidance or in collaboration with more able peers' (Vygotsky, 1978: 85).

Where Vygotsky was concerned with child development, researchers such as Lave and Wenger and Engestrom have extended his ideas to adults and to learning outside formal classrooms, including the workplace. Guile and Young (1999) have argued that CHAT could provide a way of linking work-based and school/college-based learning.

Barriers to learning

There are an infinite number of barriers that prevent people from learning, some of which are external in nature, perhaps caused by domestic or financial difficulties, and some of which are internal, arising from psychological or physiological problems. In addition, teachers can, of course, create barriers for their students. These barriers might be created as a result of the following:

- a teacher's personal behaviour towards a student;
- the choice of teaching technique; and
- lack of attention to the teaching environment (for example, too much noise, room too hot or too cold, not enough light, and so on).

REFLECTION

Consider the ways in which you have been prevented from learning during your life and, in contrast, try to identify anything that has been a positive support to your learning. Make your notes in two lists:

List one: Barriers to learning
List two: Support for learning

In the lists you made, you may have identified your family or domestic relationships as a feature in one or perhaps both lists. Clearly, domestic life has a major impact on the way in which children and teenagers learn, but it can be forgotten that young and mature adults can be equally affected by their domestic environment. One of the authors of this book was responsible in the past for running a series of residential training courses for in-company trainers and supervisors. Many of the participants on these courses had not attended a course of study for several years and often not since they had left school. One of the most interesting aspects was to observe the changed behaviour of some of the women who attended the courses. These particular women had not stayed away from their partners and children before and came away worrying about how their families would cope without them. One woman related in detail how she had filled the freezer with meals and separately labelled packs of sandwiches for lunches and had arranged for a neighbour to be on standby to wash and iron items of clothing at a moment's notice. By the end of the third day of a one-week course, the women began to question their attitudes and by the end of the course they were threatening domestic revolution. The last thing the group facilitator wanted was to cause mayhem in families, but the power of the learning situation, and particularly the chance to draw support and ideas from peers, was considerable for those women.

A number of research studies over the past 20 or so years have investigated the reasons why students in post-compulsory education settings leave their courses before completion (see, inter alia, Bariso, 2008; Rees *et al.*, 2000; McGiveney, 1996). Usher *et al.* (2002: 79) have drawn attention to the 'negative imagery' of the concept of barriers to learning. They write, 'The learning process is characterized as one full of blockages and barriers, things that impede or hold back the self-as-learner from attaining various ends, such as efficacy, autonomy, self-realisation or emancipation'. Instead, they argue that the 'postmodern story of the self' means that 'we tell stories about our experience' and that our subjectivity is always 'shifting and uncertain'. This is a complex debate, but the importance of Usher *et al.*'s analysis is that learners' identities are not fixed and, therefore, simplistic notions of what constitutes a barrier to learning might be very misleading when trying to understand learners' needs.

While engaging in the process of learning, individuals also learn 'how to learn' and all teachers play a role in helping their students to develop what is referred to as their 'meta-learning' or 'meta-cognition' capacity (see, inter alia, Hargreaves, 2004; Black *et al.*, 2003). This will clearly be important in also helping students to overcome any barriers they have towards learning. There is a great deal of debate in the research literature about the theory of 'meta-learning' and whether it can be 'taught'. We do not have the scope here to enter into these debates, but we would argue that if teachers can involve their students as much as possible in the planning and organisation of their learning and get them to engage in reflective exercises to review their own progress, then learning how to learn will become embedded in their overall participation in the learning process. This approach will involve teachers and students developing a natural dialogue about the joint enterprise in which they are engaged. There is a danger that if teachers attempt to 'teach' students how to learn, they will invent activities that are too abstracted from the students' interests and will struggle to help students make the connections.

The teacher–student relationship

At the beginning of this chapter, we explored some of the theories that might explain how individuals approach learning. Although most teachers, at some point in their careers, receive thanks and best wishes from their students, most of the time, as in the rest of life, any gratitude that students feel tends to go unspoken and teachers have to plough on in the hope that their work is appreciated. Just as teachers can have a very positive effect on their students, they can sometimes be a negative force, and there are many people who would claim that their insecurities and blocks about learning stem from a certain teacher who made them feel inadequate. The teacher–student relationship is, therefore, a complex and dynamic one and, as such, needs to be treated with care.

Box 4.2 lists a number of labels that can be applied to someone in a 'teaching' role and to someone in a 'learning' role.

Box 4.2 TEACHING AND LEARNING ROLES

Teaching role	Learning role
Teacher	Student/Pupil
Instructor/Demonstrator/Supervisor	Apprentice
Trainer	Trainee
Tutor	Learner
Facilitator	Participant
Assessor	Candidate
Mentor	Colleague
Coach	Trainee

Each of these labels carries with it a great deal of terminological 'baggage', and much has been written about the power of labels in determining behaviour. For example, the term 'facilitator' is used widely in management training, where it is regarded as being much more learner-centred than terms such as 'lecturer' or 'teacher'. On the other hand, teachers in FE colleges are often still referred to as 'lecturers' despite the fact that many of them spend very little time giving 'lectures'. From the point of view of learners, how they are described could denote how they might expect to be treated, the culture and ethos of the institution, and the context in which they are learning. Terms such as 'trainee' and 'apprentice', for example, are generally used in work-based settings, though the term 'trainee' might also be used in colleges for young people on work-based programmes. Labels can also change so that a 'student' might become a 'candidate' at the point when he or she is going to be assessed; or a 'lecturer' becomes a 'tutor' when seeing a student for an individual tutorial meeting.

Teaching in a college will require you to switch between the different roles suggested by each of the labels listed above. Whatever your subject area, you might, in any one session, carry out the following functions:

- spend 10 minutes giving a 'lecture';
- facilitate a group discussion;
- demonstrate how to use a piece of equipment or perform a certain task;
- spend a few minutes with individual students to give them specific tutoring; and
- supervise small groups of students carrying out project work.

To be able to switch from one role to another certainly requires flexibility, but it also demands that the teacher is able to recognise which role is the most appropriate in a given circumstance. (Chapter 6 provides more detail on choosing and applying teaching strategies.) Rory Kidd (1973), building on earlier work by John Dewey, has described learning as a 'transaction' to which both the learner and the teacher have to bring something of value for both parties to feel the transaction has been effective and produced the desired outcomes. In order for this to happen, teachers and learners have to get to know each other and be prepared to change and adapt. This may take time but the process can be accelerated through the willingness of the teacher to create an atmosphere that encourages the following:

- enables students to articulate their learning needs;
- enables students to identify and discuss any barriers that might prevent them from learning;
- enables students to develop the confidence to share their own ideas and actively contribute to the learning situation;
- provides students with constructive criticism and praise so that they feel supported and, in turn, learn how to support each other;
- encourages all students to achieve at their own pace, regardless of ability;
- encourages both teacher and students to work together with a sense of community and shared purpose; and
- promotes respect for individuals within the learning community.

In terms of maintaining order within the teaching situation, whether it be with one or a group of students, teachers will, of course, behave in different ways and choose different methods for ensuring that both teacher and students concentrate on their joint purpose in coming together. As teachers gain in experience, keeping control of the proceedings becomes a subconscious activity, so that neither the teacher nor the students are aware that control is being exerted. Students, too, can be encouraged to develop self-discipline, to control their behaviour in respect of the community in which they are learning, and learn how to maintain order as a group. A useful model for sharing ideas about control and order is transactional analysis (TA), which was developed by the American psychologist Eric Berne.

Berne calls TA a 'theory of social intercourse', and used it to help people understand and improve their behaviour towards others. He wrote:

> Observation of spontaneous social activity, most productively carried out in certain kinds of psychotherapy groups, reveals that from time to time people show noticeable changes in posture, viewpoint, voice, vocabulary, and other aspects of behaviour. These behavioural changes are often accompanied by shifts in feeling. In a given individual, a certain set of behaviour patterns corresponds to one state of mind, while another set is

related to a different psychic attitude, often inconsistent with the first. These changes and differences give rise to the idea of ego states.

(Berne, 1970: 23)

Berne identified three ego states that he believed people move regularly in and out of during their daily lives:

- parental;
- adult; and
- child.

Of the three ego states, the adult (demonstrated when a person is in control and displaying maturity) is thought to be present in everyone but often needs to be uncovered or activated. The child state can be exhibited in two forms: the adapted child, who modifies behaviour under the influence of a parent, and the natural child, who is freed from parental influence to be creative or to rebel. In this latter state, the child can be petulant and difficult to handle. The parental state also has two sides: first, it can be authoritarian ('do as I say'); second, it can be nurturing ('let me help you').

Berne's hypothesis is that problems occur when these ego states are at cross-purposes. For example, if someone who is in the natural child state meets someone in an authoritarian parental state, then they will have trouble communicating. Similarly, if a student in the adult state meets someone in the nurturing parental state, they will feel frustrated or even patronised. The trick, as far as being a teacher is concerned, is to recognise both your own ego state and that of your students. You can also use TA as a model for handling colleagues and running meetings.

The teacher–student relationship will, of course, like any other interpersonal relationship, be constantly tested, and there may be some occasions when it breaks down completely. In the main, however, the relationship will work because most of the people involved will realise that, if it is effective, life for everyone will be happier.

Some of the pressure on the relationship will come from external forces that the teacher or students can do little about, and that can have a positive or negative effect. Figure 4.2 illustrates how those external forces, as well as the internal feelings of teachers and students, can impact on the teacher–learner relationship. The model (adapted from Unwin and Edwards, 1990) is overlaid with three bands – class, gender and race – that exert influence throughout society and from which no relationship can be exempted.

Group learning

Most of the teaching you will do in FE will be with groups of students. As in all sectors of education, pressure on resources demands that group teaching

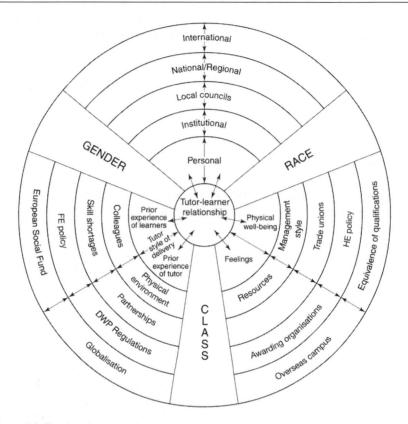

Figure 4.2 Teacher–learner relationship

REFLECTION

You might wish to make your version of the model to reflect the particular circumstances in which you are working. You may, for example, expand some of the bands so that you can include more variables. One way of creating your own version is to use coloured card. The model could also be used with students as a way of encouraging them to identify the variables that affect their relationship with you as a teacher and/or as a group of learners. This works well as a group activity so long as individuals are not forced into isolated positions.

(and often in groups of considerable size) is the dominant mode. Despite the managerial reasons for favouring group-based learning, however, there are distinct benefits that students gain from learning together. We look at specific strategies for achieving effective learning in groups in Chapter 6, but, for the moment, we will briefly explore the general benefits to be gained from group-based learning.

We have paid a great deal of attention in this chapter to the needs of individual students, and you saw in the student vignettes in Chapter 2 how different those needs can be. By bringing students together, they can begin to learn how their own needs compare and contrast with others', and develop shared strategies for advancing their learning and for overcoming problems. Learning in groups can often be much more fun than learning singly, and can facilitate the continuation of learning once the formal session has ended. Students may continue to discuss ideas outside the classroom or workshop and apply themselves creatively to group tasks.

Given the emphasis in current policy on 'personalised' learning, and the increasing use of ICLT, there is a danger that learning in colleges may become too individualised. Although groups of students may be together in the same space, they might all be working completely separately on different tasks or units of competence. For Wildemeersch, such a scenario represents a 'farewell to dialogue and a welcome to individualised technicism' (Wildemeersch, 1989: 68).

The collegiality created by group-based learning can act as an important locus of support for students who lack confidence, have problems outside college, or who gain extra motivation from the discipline of having to keep up with their peers. The teacher can capitalise on that collegiality to encourage the more able students to help others. Jaques (1992) has stated that groups operate at both a task and a socio-emotional level and within both intrinsic and extrinsic dimensions.

He notes that there is a tendency to concentrate on the extrinsic dimension and explains:

> Teaching is often solution-orientated rather than problem-orientated and seems to take external requirements as its starting point rather than the needs and interests of the students. Moreover, a lack of attention to the socio-emotional dimension means that many of the task aims cannot be achieved. Without a climate of trust and co-operation, students will not feel like taking the risk of making mistakes and learning from them. To achieve this, the tutor would have to balance a concern for academic standards with a capacity to understand and deal with the workings of group processes as well as an attitude of generosity and praise for new solutions to old problems.
>
> (Jaques, 1992: 72)

There are groups and groups, of course, and not all will provide the collegiality referred to above. Rory Kidd states that there are three characteristics that have to be present in a group if effective learning is to take place:

1   a realisation by the members of the group that genuine growth stems from the creative power within the individual, and that learning, finally, is an individual matter;

2   the acceptance as a group standard that each member has the right to be different and to disagree; and

3   establishment of a group atmosphere that is free from narrow judgements on the part of the teacher or group members.

(Kidd, 1973: 80)

	Task	Socio-emotional
I N T R I N S I C	Expressing selves in subject	Greater sensitivity to others
	Judging ideas in relation to others	Judging self in relation to others
	Examining assumptions	Encouraging self-confidence
	Listening attentively	Personal development
	Tolerating ambiguity	Tolerating ambiguity
	Learning about groups	Awareness of others' strengths and weaknesses
E X T R I N S I C	Follow-up to lecture	Giving support
	Understanding text	Stimulating to further work
	Improving staff/ student relations	Evaluating student feelings about course
	Gauging student progress	Giving students identifiable groups to belong to
	Giving guidance	

Figure 4.3 Types of aims and purposes in group teaching

Source: Jaques (1992), reproduced with permision from Taylor & Francis Ltd

A college lecturer who researched her own practice of trying to get a class of 'somewhat demoralised' Level 3 biology students in an English FE college to work in groups raises the important issue of physical space and its impact on learning:

> One issue I had not anticipated was that the crowded conditions meant that left and right handed students had insufficient room to write, if sat next to one another: left handed students therefore had to work together, or sit at the end of rows.
>
> (Russell, 2010: 212)

She also came to realise that 'students are far more thoughtful and knowledgeable about work group composition than I had anticipated; however, since they are the ones who work in groups, who manage the personalities and then complete the task, I should have probably foreseen this' (ibid.).

Support services for students

One of the most important ways in which learners can be supported is to give them access to a range of support services. Such support can include advising them as to the most appropriate modules in a course, how to stagger their studies to fit in with professional demands, how to seek financial support for fees, and putting them in touch with professional counsellors if personal problems become too difficult to handle alone. A great deal of support can be provided by organisations and teachers actually listening to students and interpreting their needs correctly.

A major issue here is the extent to which individual teachers accept that they have a role to play in supporting learners above and beyond putting across the actual subject matter of a particular course of study. In particular, the teacher can have a significant impact on a student's sense of well-being, as McGiveney emphasises with this quote from an FE teacher talking about part-time students.

> The reality of formal part-time study is that individual tutors can make or break a learner's experience. The tutor is central to the creation of the essential, supportive social environment of the classroom which reduces drop-out. We can talk till the cows come home about the vital importance of guidance but we are seriously in error if we do not acknowledge the pivotal guidance role of the tutor for the part-timer. For many the teacher is the guidance system.
>
> (McGiveney, 1996: 135)

Colleges arrange their student support services in recognition of the fact that students' support needs stretch from, for example, help with basic skills such as literacy and numeracy, to careers information, but also include the need for

---

As a learner, we aim to provide you with:

- A wide choice of courses
- Information and advice on education, training and career opportunities
- Up-to-date information on sources of financial help available
- An introduction to your course and a clear expectation of what will be expected of you
- A variety of teaching and learning methods to suit differing learning needs
- Tutoring by experienced and qualified staff
- Additional support and equipment if you need this to achieve your learning goals
- Good quality learning materials and equipment
- Your own learning plan
- Regular reviews of your progress

(Extract from Brasshouse Language Centre, Birmingham Learner Handbook)

Figure 4.4a Student support: Example 1: Learner entitlement

Our culture is one where every individual is valued and shown respect.

Students will:
- Abide by and endorse College rules
- Be courteous to others
- Take care of their environment.

Staff will:
- Treat learners as individuals, with individual needs
- Demonstrate good behaviour, being punctual and courteous
- Support and be loyal to colleagues.

Leaders will:
- Spend time with learners and staff
- Share information when appropriate, in a timely and consistent manner
- Encourage transparency, honesty and integrity, leading by example.

(Extract from Burton and South Derbyshire College website)

Figure 4.4b Student support: Example 2: Values and behaviour

The diverse nature of our students creates a rich and stimulating environment and we celebrate this exciting dynamic.

In order for our learners to be successful we will teach them to exploit their diverse talents. We will deliver appropriate and transferable education and training to support them in this.

Our Learner First principles ensure that our offer:
- is customer-focused and makes access to learning easy and personalised
- provides equality of opportunity which removes the traditional barriers to learning
- gives maximum impact on improving employment and skills outcomes by helping students get a job.

(Extract from Ealing, Hammersmith and West London College website)

Figure 4.4c Student support: Example 3: Personalisation and inclusion

access to a confidential service to deal with very private matters. Figure 4.4 illustrates the ways in which colleges support their learners through, for example, student charters, learner handbooks, induction materials and college mission statements. This illustrative 'collage' has been developed from a range of materials reviewed in colleges' student handbooks and on websites.

A key deficiency with many induction programmes is that they tend to be one-off events, whereas the process of induction should carry on throughout a student's lifetime in the college. That is, at various points in his or her career in the college, a student will need to be inducted into a new stage, to meet new tutors and fellow students and so on, or to be re-inducted with parts of the college or course that are long forgotten.

Figure 4.5 shows how a college's guidance and support system should span all aspects of college life from student entry through to student exit.

REFLECTION

Imagine you are about to start a course in a college. What items would you want to see covered in an induction programme? As you make your list, consider the circumstances of the students we introduced you to in Chapter 2.

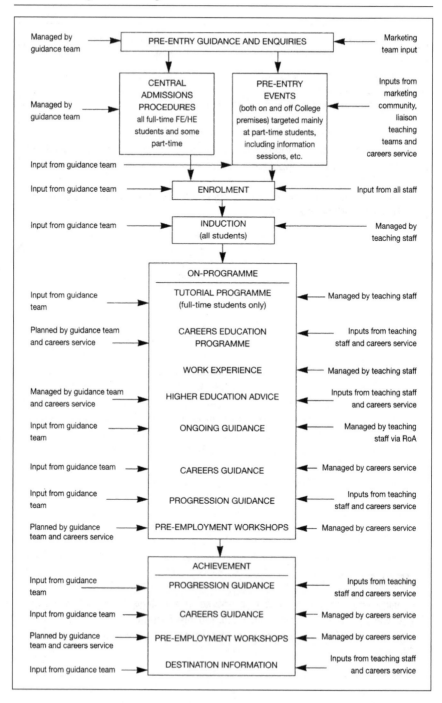

Figure 4.5 Guidance team influence on learner's pathway through college

The teacher's approach to learning

As noted in Chapter 1, just as the student population in FE is extremely diverse in terms of its background and prior experience, so too is the teaching force. This variety provides a reservoir on which the sector can draw to enhance the learning experiences of its students. For example, a majority of those teaching in the sector will have had relevant vocational experience before taking up a career in teaching. Others will still be working within their vocational sectors and perhaps teaching part-time. Some may have taught in secondary education before moving into the post-compulsory phase and others may have been workplace trainers.

Clearly, this will have an impact on the way in which they approach their teaching and their attitudes to learners, and will underpin their own philosophy of teaching.

REFLECTION

Consider to what extent your own gender, ethnicity or social class might influence the way in which you will teach and relate to your students. For example, if you are a young man, how will you relate to mature women or to young teenage girls? If you are a young woman, how will you cope with teaching a class full of 18-year-old male apprentices? If you have an accent that is very different from the predominant one of your students, will that matter? How do your students see/hear you?

We now invite you to reflect further upon the following series of vignettes of typical lecturers to be found in any college. As you did in Chapter 2 with the student vignettes, we suggest you think about the following questions:

1   What perceptions do you have of each of the lecturers and how his or her previous experience might impact on the students?
2   What do you see as the potential staff development needs of the individual lecturers?

Leslie

Leslie is 50; until recently he was head of the hospitality and catering programme area in a medium-sized general FE college situated in an attractive town with a fairly wide rural catchment area. The local economy mostly covers the tourism, hospitality and agricultural sectors.

Leslie began his career in catering, moving through a succession of jobs until he became head chef in a prestigious hotel. When he became tired of the long and unsocial hours associated with hotel work, he decided to move into teaching. He had already had some experience of training younger chefs, which he had enjoyed.

He began by doing some part-time lecturing while running a small catering business. He successfully completed the City and Guilds FE Teachers' Certificate and decided to take on full-time teaching. As his confidence grew in his new profession he was keen to develop his career. He enrolled on a degree programme at the local university and enjoyed part-time study.

When the impact of new funding regimes, targets, qualification reform, and an impending merger began to bite at the college, Leslie became increasingly dissatisfied with his teaching and more interested in developing his own skills as a researcher. He enrolled on a part-time Master's degree and completed a dissertation on 'Changing Employment Patterns in the FE Sector'. The MA successfully completed, he returned to his teaching with renewed critical reflection but little in the way of career progression. The college introduced a redundancy package, but Leslie's application was refused because he was required to lead the hospitality programme area.

Feeling that he would still like to do some personal academic work, but that the pressure of increasing student numbers, changing vocational qualifications and the administrative burden of running a large programme area precluded it, he decided to resign. He is now self-employed, running a training and consultancy business for the hospitality sector, and has registered for an MBA with the Open University.

Andy

Andy is a lecturer in psychology at a city college. He joined the college 10 years ago, having previously worked in a secondary school. Following completion of a degree in psychology and statistics, followed by a PGCE (secondary), he taught A-level psychology and lower school mathematics in a comprehensive school. He was keen to build up the numbers for A-level psychology, but he was irritated by the amount of mathematics that he was asked to teach.

He explored the possibility of teaching part-time (evening) classes at his local college and was offered two evenings a week teaching psychology to students on a 2+2 degree. This was 'the perfect opportunity' for him and he embraced the extra work with enthusiasm. When Andy was told that the numbers for A-level psychology were dwindling at his school and that he would have to make up his timetable with some IT teaching, he decided to change direction. The college was happy to increase his hours and eventually he was offered a 0.75 contract; two years later he became a full-time member of staff.

He is pleased with his decision and enjoys teaching, particularly individual tutorial work with mature students. Andy always volunteers for new initiatives and is keen to be involved with external agencies and curriculum development. He is now HE coordinator for the social sciences programme. His students achieve well and he encourages them to do so. He feels that there is a lot more that he could do if other members of staff were similarly inclined. Although he recognizes that there is insecurity around the college's future and a possible merger with a neighbouring college is under discussion, whatever happens he knows he does not want to return to school teaching.

Clare

Clare is 58 and works in a city college that also serves a dispersed rural area. She has worked in FE for over 20 years and is a highly experienced teacher of English as a foreign language. She worked abroad for a number of years as a teacher of English. Her role has changed significantly over the recent past and her time is spent increasingly on basic skills tuition, in particular IT. Although not an IT specialist, she has had to adapt to the new situation since basic skills teaching is delivered alongside ESOL, a situation that she regards as unsatisfactory.

Her classes include a wide range of learners, with very different prior learning experiences. She describes how, in classes of up to 15 students, there are as many as 12 different nationalities. Many of the students are asylum seekers and present a range of challenges to the organisation of learning. There is 'no whole class teaching'; programmes have to be tailored to the needs of individual learners. This is exacerbated by the fact that learners have inconsistent patterns of attendance and sometimes disappear for lengthy periods, only to reappear again without explanation. This poses problems in recording and reporting achievement against college targets. Programmes are organised on a roll-on, roll-off basis, with the expectation that there will be some achievement in terms of basic skills qualifications. Students are also referred for basic skills provision from other parts of the college, a system that she feels works well.

Clare still enjoys the work, but feels that this is partly because she does not really have to do it. She is considering early retirement and doing similar work on a voluntary basis for a local charity. She feels that for younger staff the situation is unsatisfactory and unsettling. Staff are required to teach in areas where they do not feel comfortable; she has been able to adapt but others find it more difficult.

Jean-Claude

Jean-Claude at 35 is head of department in a specialist language centre based in a large city. He was born and educated in France, came to England many times during his student days, and decided that he definitely wanted to teach here after qualifying.

His first teaching post was at a large general FE college, where he taught French and Spanish on a range of basic language courses, as well as some A-level programmes. He was disappointed by the experience, since languages were not highly valued in the college and enrolments dwindled year on year, to the extent that his post was under threat.

He applied for his current post, little thinking that he would be successful, but recognising that he needed a change of direction. He is happy with his job and sees lots of possibilities for development. He has published several course books. He heads a department of 25 staff, from a range of different countries, most of whom are part time. He finds the atmosphere lively and stimulating and he is encouraged to try new things. Most importantly for him, this college is dedicated to the area he cares most about: language learning. Staff and students share his commitment.

Clifford

Clifford is head of the engineering department at a successful, five-campus college formed by the merger of three former colleges. He has worked here for 12 years and has been promoted several times since his first appointment. He has taught on a wide range of engineering manufacturing programmes from Level 2 to Level 4. Recently, he has been responsible for developing extensive industrial links and designing customised programmes for some leading manufacturing companies. He was also involved in the development of the government-funded apprenticeship programmes in the college. Having spent 14 years of his employed life in the automotive industry, he feels well suited to the job.

He has excellent working relationships with a number of local employers and has enhanced the college's reputation for providing customised training linked to the needs of industry. The partnerships that he has forged with large multi-national companies have enabled him to obtain 'industry standard' equipment for the college. Employers are happy for their staff to attend training at the college, knowing that it will be of good quality, using up-to-date equipment, and will be tailored to their needs. Clifford states: 'That is the way we have always done things here, anyway; that's why we have such strong relationships with our local employers.'

Despite the recent downturn, the local automotive industry has increased its sales overseas and he is optimistic about the future and feels he has 'a great bunch of people to take things forward and a very supportive Principal'. He is also very experienced in identifying opportunities for external funding, whether local, regional, national or European.

Carol

Carol is 32 and a chartered accountant; she is a Newly Qualified Teacher (NQT) and works in the Business and Management Department of a large general FE college. She previously worked as an accountant for a large multi-national company but decided that her real ambition was to become a teacher of business and, if possible, of accountancy. Her employers were very surprised and reluctant to lose her when she enrolled on a full-time PGCE (secondary) programme.

She was disappointed by her first teaching placement in a large comprehensive school; she found some hostility from the teaching staff and did not enjoy her time teaching the younger age groups. She found sixth-form work more rewarding, but it was not what she had expected. Her second placement, in the college where she now works, was exactly what she was hoping for when she decided to change careers. She was warmly welcomed by staff anxious to have a 'real' accountant teaching accounts. She blossomed when teaching adults on vocational courses; she gained an 'outstanding' evaluation for this placement and was offered a job in advance of completing her PGCE.

Carol is now settled in her new role and feels it is exactly what she had hoped for. She has enrolled on a part-time Masters programme and hopes, eventually, to take on a managerial role in FE.

Nadine

Nadine is 41 and teaches part time on a range of beauty courses at her local college. For the majority of the week she is a beauty therapist at a hair and beauty salon. She left school at 16 with five GCSEs and attended a local college, first taking a two-year full-time course in hairdressing followed by a further two-year course in beauty therapy. In addition to the main programme, she completed advanced courses in alternative therapies and theatrical make-up. She took part in national competitions and was always keen to keep up to date with developments in the sector.

Six years ago she began offering beauty students from the local college work placements at her salon. Although initially skeptical, thinking that students might get in the way of actual business, she soon began to enjoy supervising and demonstrating techniques to them. She recognized that she had some competence for training and was enthusiastic about it.

Nadine enquired from the college work placement organiser about the possibility of some part-time teaching. Her offer was enthusiastically taken up and within a few weeks she was in the college salon in front of a class of part-time learners. She found the experience extremely challenging because she had received no training and no proper induction. However, she decided to continue and gradually became more proficient in preparing lectures and practical sessions, though the workload was significant.

Eventually, the college's staff development manager approached her about the requirement to undergo some in-service training if she wished to continue. Once convinced of the benefit of gaining a qualification, Nadine 'threw herself wholeheartedly' into this opportunity for personal and professional development, eventually gaining QTLS. She admits it was 'tough' balancing part-time teaching, a job and family commitments, as well as undertaking the teaching qualification, but feels it has been well worth it. She really enjoys her 'new world' of teaching the subject she loves and being able to continue working in her salon.

Chris

Chris is vice-principal of a medium-sized college of further and higher education located in the southeast. It offers a range of programmes for 14–18 year-olds and adult learners across 15 subject areas. He has been at the college for three years and was previously vice-principal at two other colleges; before that he held a number of positions within both FE and community learning. He has worked in the post-compulsory sector since graduating with a degree in English and qualifying as teacher over 30 years ago.

He had always hoped to become a college principal but recognizes that this will be his last job before retirement. Nevertheless, he still enjoys the work and the challenges faced by the management and administration of a college with aspirations for growth, in particular for outreach work. He has always been interested in the provision of outreach education, basic skills teaching and access issues. For this reason he always chose to work in colleges with a high profile in these areas.

He continues to be active in professional networks and still takes a lively interest in the policy environment, contributing to seminars and conferences. Reflecting on his career in the post-compulsory sector, he has no regrets but recognizes that the challenges imposed by changing funding regimes, institutional targets, and competing with predatory school sixth forms, are deterrents to younger members of staff considering senior management roles within the sector.

Conclusion

There has long been a view that effective teaching comes down to charisma or showmanship – what some might call the 'wow' factor. As this chapter has tried to show, however, charisma might work for part of the time, but, ultimately, teaching is a much more complex business, requiring continual reflection and the trying out of new and different ideas. Getting to grips with the theories and concepts that have been developed over the years to help us understand the ways in which people learn and the relationship between teaching and learning can be a daunting task. Yet, as Harkin's (2005) survey of teachers in 10 colleges in the South East of England found, theory is being used in a variety of ways. Although he found some teachers were hostile to theory and some felt guilty for what they felt was their own lack of understanding, many developed what Schön (1983, 1987) has called 'theories-in-use' (for a further discussion, see Chapter 7). By this, Schön means that professionals integrate a range of theories (gleaned from a variety of sources, including initial training, professional development and their peers) into their continuing practice. As Harkin (2005: 170) reminds us, theory in teacher education in the UK has a contentious history, with some theories labelled in a pejorative sense as 'trendy' or 'plain crackers'. Theories also come in and out of fashion. In Chapter 5, we will see how one theory of learning, 'learning styles', which is used regularly in UK colleges, has been subjected to a highly critical examination.

Chapter 5

Teaching strategies

Flexibility and adaptability

In the opening chapters of this book, we described the complex world of FE and emphasised the need for teachers to be flexible and adaptable in order to meet the demands that their managers, students and external agencies will put on them. It is worth remembering, too, that the pressures on FE colleges to recruit as many students as possible mean that teaching staff will be faced with students who have a wide range of learning needs.

FE teachers are sometimes referred to as 'managers' or 'planners' of learning, involved in a range of activities that stretch beyond the day-to-day business of teaching in a classroom or workshop. Young *et al.*'s (1995) description of the way in which the knowledge that FE teachers need to develop and employ has shifted over recent years remains helpful:

- from subject knowledge to curriculum knowledge;
- from teacher-centred pedagogic knowledge to learner-centred pedagogic knowledge;
- from intra-professional knowledge to inter-professional knowledge;
- from classroom knowledge to organisational knowledge; and
- from insular knowledge to connective knowledge.

Instead of being a teacher who is solely concerned with his or her own subject specialism, FE teachers now have to understand how their specialism 'connects' with the rest of the college's curricular provision and how generic (or core) learning can be facilitated through that specialism (see Fisher and Webb, 2006). This has been particularly problematic in terms of the delivery of key and functional skills, where an integrated approach was axiomatic to successful delivery, and yet where the practice was often found wanting. FE teachers need to 'manage' the process of learning as a whole and not simply be concerned with transmitting knowledge and skills. As 'managers of learning', teachers need to seek the help and support of other professionals, including non-teaching staff, and they will be members of course teams. The shift from 'insular' to 'connective' knowledge recognises the way in which FE teachers have to be aware of and build on their students' prior educational experiences and their future needs.

Elliott *et al.* (2011: 86) pose the question: 'What differentiates a skilled teacher from a less skilled one?' Their answer is: 'One possibility is that, confronted by a potentially challenging situation, the skilled teacher is more likely to select from a range of strategies or tactics the most appropriate way to respond' (ibid.). As such, they argue that teachers need to combine tacit knowledge with opportunities to reflect on practice and connect practice with theory. However, we must always remember that, as Biesta (2008: 67) argues:

> There is no way in which we can assume that what was possible in one situation will automatically be applicable in another situation.

Rather, we must draw on our experience to treat each new situation as an opportunity to assemble strategies in different ways.

An FE college represents a transitional stage for many students as they progress from school education through FE and on to work-based training and/or HE. Adult students may also be experiencing a sense of transition, particularly if they are retraining and building on existing expertise to change direction. Silver and Forrest interviewed college lecturers from a range of work backgrounds who drew on their own professional experience to help their students make connections between their studies in college and the demands of the workplace:

> Learners who are both work-ready and fit for the future need far more than a set of time-limited work skills and have to recognise the impact of new techniques, new materials and new technologies at work. They need to understand the unpredictability and the inevitability of change and shake off the focus on a permanent present that leaves younger learners, especially, unprepared. Excellent practical teachers open their eyes by demonstrating the radical ways that work has transformed over time, and signposting the future. They build in an expectation that skills will need constantly updating, and show that technical skills alone are not enough. Drawing on their own extensive experience, these teachers were able to tackle the behaviours commonly associated with employability but often claimed to be unteachable. Developing those generic behaviours that would secure the learners a future as well as a place at work was all part of 'becoming one of us'.
>
> (Silver and Forrest, 2007: 73)

This sense of going beyond the transmission of prescribed knowledge and skills is also reflected in Robson *et al.*'s (2004: 190) research with vocational teachers in FE. They argue that such teachers are concerned with the 'whole person' as opposed to seeing their students as one-dimensional individuals in a classroom or workshop:

The fostering of criticality, creativity and pride in one's work positions the vocational teacher as concerned with the student as a 'whole person', as a potentially valuable member of a professional group and not just an employee. These teachers are not concerned simply with producing 'work fodder' nor with the narrow and commercial demands of one particular workplace. They have a broader perspective and in their expression of it, their narratives support a wider discourse of professionalism, concerned with expertise, commitment and care for others.

When they visit colleges, inspectors concentrate, in particular, on the organisation and management of the learning situation and note the strengths and weaknesses of the following:

- level of coherence of schemes of work;
- level of teachers' subject expertise;
- level of rapport between staff and students;
- clarity of aims and objectives;
- appropriateness of the pace of learning;
- range of teaching techniques in use;
- opportunities for students to participate actively;
- quality of resources (for example, technology, equipment, handouts, visual aids, etc.);
- clarity of assessment criteria;
- classroom/workshop management (for example, punctuality of staff and students, behaviour of students);
- quality of feedback on students' work;
- quality and usefulness of tasks set and appropriateness of coursework; and
- quality of record-keeping to inform students of their progress.

Choosing a strategy

Students attend colleges to acquire skills, knowledge and understanding related to their area of study, whether it be English literature, welding, social care or applied statistics. Separating out the skills, knowledge and understanding components within any one learning encounter is not, of course, a straightforward process, as in most encounters the three are bound together. As shown in Chapter 4, teachers also need to consider how best to ensure their students get the opportunity to develop their tacit expertise.

Given the underpinning complexity of the learning encounter in terms of content, there is also the diversity of your potential students to consider. You are clearly going to need to develop a range of strategies for helping your students to learn effectively. Once you gain some experience as a teacher, you will find that you can create your own strategies that reflect your personality and are designed to respond to your students' particular needs. Always remember that different strategies work differently for different teachers. You may be the sort of person who will never be comfortable giving a lecture or facilitating a role-play exercise, but able to get excellent results from designing group-based problem-solving exercises. Then again, you may shine as a lecturer, providing your students with stimulating talks that capture their imaginations. Gaining confidence as a teacher is important, and all teachers tend to stick with the strategies with which they feel most comfortable. Your students, too, as we saw in Chapter 4, have their own preferences when it comes to teaching strategies.

There is a danger, therefore, that both teachers and students can settle into a cosy learning relationship in which neither is challenged or pushed into expanding their learning horizons. On the other hand, if the teacher disregards the preferences of the students and sticks to the teaching strategy they feel least happy about, then the learning environment is put under stress and the outcomes may be unsatisfactory for both parties. Essentially, the key message is to provide a variety of learning experiences to cater, as far as possible, for the needs of all learners.

Depending on the nature of your subject area and the level at which you teach, you will need to be very aware of the literacy and/or numeracy capability of your students (Swan and Swain, 2010). Handing out written instructions and information sheets and using PowerPoint slides may seem to contribute to good practice, but you will need to pay careful attention to the level of literacy required to use them. In their research on the different types of literacies within FE, Ivanic et al. (2007) discovered that teachers can both underestimate and overestimate their students' abilities, and could make more of what Fowler (2008: 426) has called 'the text-rich environment of the FE college' (see also Edwards and Miller, 2008).

Learning styles

There has been a great deal of interest over about 20 years in the much contested theory that individuals' preferred learning styles can be identified and measured, and it is now widely practised in FE colleges. Honey and Mumford's 'Learning Styles Questionnaire' is one of the best known commercial products to have emerged from the development of a theory that has been heavily promoted by government agencies. One of the attractions of the theory is that it offers a way for teachers to gain a better understanding of the different ways their students approach learning and so provides clues as to how they might best be supported. Such a theory has also proved to be very attractive to college managers who see it as a way to improve retention and attainment. Coffield et al. (2004) undertook a major review of the learning styles field and found 71 models, of which they categorised 13 as being worthy of attention. They found widespread disagreement among learning styles theorists and a 'dearth of rigorously controlled experiments and of longitudinal studies to test the claims of the main advocates' (ibid.: 64). They concluded that:

The main charge here is that the socio-economic and the cultural context of students' lives and of the institutions where they seek to learn tend to be omitted from the learning styles literature. Learners are not all alike . . . they live in particular socio-economic settings where age, gender, race and class all interact to influence their attitudes to learning.

(ibid.: 65)

We would argue that using a learning styles inventory can be a fun exercise to stimulate students to consider the ways in which they approach learning. Using Honey and Mumford's (1982) *The Manual of Learning Styles* will provide an 'instant' diagnosis of where your students sit in the following categories:

1   Activist (rolls up sleeves and rushes into action).
2   Reflector (contemplates the problem and considers how to approach).
3   Theorist (consults 'experts', researches the issues before acting).
4   Pragmatist (selects the most appropriate form of action given the circumstances).

This might well trigger a discussion about the extent to which students recognise themselves and, more importantly, how they would evaluate the inventory. To base your pedagogical approaches on such a contested theory would, however, be highly inadvisable.

In choosing an appropriate teaching strategy, you have to consider four equally important issues:

1   Given a specific curriculum objective to be achieved, which teaching strategy will be most effective for transmitting the necessary skills, knowledge and understanding to your students?
2   How can you ensure that your students will fully participate in the learning process so that they learn for themselves rather than just listening to or watching you demonstrate your learning?
3   Given your knowledge of the group of students, how can you incorporate their prior learning and overcome any barriers to learning they may have?
4   How much time can you allow for this particular curriculum objective?

There are a number of strategies at your disposal, and they can be arranged on a continuum (Figure 5.1) that stretches from teacher-centred methods at one end to those methods that encourage students to take more responsibility for their own learning at the other end.

The chart in Figure 5.1 is not judgemental. It is not saying that giving a lecture is wrong or that the best way to teach is to engage students in role plays and problem-solving exercises. It is, however, a means of illustrating how different teaching strategies will affect different learning outcomes.

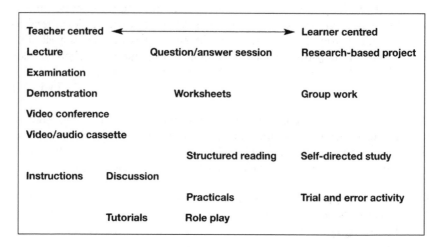

Figure 5.1 Teaching strategies continuum

Aims, objectives, goals and learning outcomes: 'what are we supposed to be learning here?'

All students come to their course with preconceived assumptions about its content and will react differently to its separate components. In addition, each student will have certain expectations about how much he or she will gain from the course. The course team has to be aware of such complexities in the student profile when constructing the learning materials and will attempt to cover as many of what it judges to be potential areas of interest. In terms of choosing the inputs or content of a learning programme, it is the teacher or course team, in most cases, who has the main responsibility. Once a learner begins to study, the teacher's control begins to diminish. What goes into a learning programme and what comes out at the other end may not, necessarily, be all that closely related, as Rogers (1986: 12) explains:

> The planning agent (teacher-provider) initially determines the goals of the learning process. The agent has in mind certain expected outcomes, the results that will flow from the learning undertaken in changed attitudes and behaviour. However, most of the student participants come with their own intentions, which may or may not be the same as those set out by the agent; they will use the learning opportunity for their own purposes, to achieve their own outcomes. Each of these sets of purposes influences the other. The teacher's intended outcomes to help shape the learners' expectations and the learners' intentions and hopes should affect the formulation of the teacher's intentions. Both sets of proposed outcomes may well be different yet again from the effective outcomes of the educational process. Since those

being taught consist of a mixed group of learners, each of whom responds to the learning in a different way, there will always be a series of unexpected outcomes. The teacher-agent needs to keep these differences in mind when planning the learning encounter.

In the case of competence-based programmes, it could be argued that teaching inputs must be determined by the prescribed competences in the various elements and units, but we would argue that the teaching and learning relationship is more sophisticated than even the purest competence-based approach would assume it to be. And, in most other sorts of programmes, teachers and learners still have some freedom to strive for undetermined outcomes. It is important, therefore, for teachers to be able to identify the aims and objectives of a particular teaching session, albeit with the flexibility to amend their original ideas. Furthermore, there are valuable opportunities here for teachers and students to work together to determine what each wants in the way of learning outcomes, and so negotiate a micro-curriculum.

The language of learning can be so complex as to suppress understanding. Indeed, many professional educators and trainers, and particularly academics, are guilty of constructing a highly technical and often impenetrable set of terminology that shuts out teachers and students alike. It is common practice for teachers to set aims and objectives when designing learning programmes, so what is the difference between aims and objectives and learning outcomes? Furthermore, what might be the value of specifying or identifying the outcomes of learning? Box 5.1 shows an example of some learning outcomes set by a teacher educator for a group of trainee teachers on a PGCE programme.

Box 5.1 LEARNING OUTCOMES

By the end of this session you will be able to:

■   understand the role of assignments within the assessment process;
■   discuss the implications for the planning of assessment;
■   practise developing and writing assignments; and
■   test out your assignments in classroom situations.

As you will see, these outcomes are both cognitive and applied in nature – from 'understanding' through to 'testing'. Similarly, the following learning outcomes for the 'fixing floor joists and laying flooring' unit of a Level 2 course in carpentry require the student to combine theory and practice (see Box 5.2).

Try the exercise shown in Figure 5.2 (page 129). The teaching and learning involved in the exercise will have reflected the personalities, capabilities and learning styles of the two people involved. As the teacher, you will have had to:

- think carefully about the nature of the instructions you supplied;
- communicate those instructions effectively; and
- listen carefully to your partner's questions and reactions.

In judging the success of the exercise in terms of how closely your partner managed to reproduce the diagram, you will have considered to what extent each of you contributed to the exercise. Over and above the physical reproduction of the diagram, you may have discussed other outcomes: for

---

Box 5.2 LEARNING OUTCOMES

The candidate will be able to:

1   Interpret drawings and specifications for floor construction and floor coverings.
2   Install floor joists and coverings according to instructions.
3   Use and maintain a range of tools and equipment and store them safely.
4   Protect the work and surrounding areas from damage and maintain a clean and safe workspace.
5   Dispose of waste.
6   Measure, mark out, fit, position, secure and finish the work.

REFLECTION

In this reflection, we hope you will engage in some lateral thinking about learning outcomes from the point of view both of the teacher and the learner. Similar exercises to this are often used in relation to developing communication skills.

Study Figure 5.2 and follow the instructions – you will need a partner to help you. The basic outcome should be for your partner to achieve as close a representation of the original drawing as possible. When you have finished the exercise, you might find it useful to discuss with your partner the following questions:

1   To what extent was the basic outcome achieved?
2   Can you identify any other outcomes of this exercise in terms of (a) your learning and (b) your partner's learning?
3   In terms of the overall outcomes of this exercise, how important was the achievement of the basic outcome?

You could extend this exercise by reversing your roles, though you would, of course, need to use another diagram!

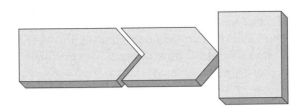

Instructions

1 Study the picture and consider how you would describe it to someone.
2 Sit back-to-back with a friend/colleague who has not seen the picture and give him or her a sheet of paper.
3 Give verbal instructions to enable your partner to draw the picture.
4 When the new picture is complete, examine it to see how closely it matches the original.

Figure 5.2 Reflection exercise

example, your partner may have learned that he or she needs to practise following verbal instructions. By simply concentrating on the physical outcome, we can miss a great deal of associated learning, which could include generic or transferable skills, as well as the tacit dimension (see Chapter 4).

The process of learning is often seen in terms of what goes in rather than what comes out. Trainee teachers spend a great deal of time constructing lesson plans detailing how they will cover a particular subject in a given period of time. Most curriculum planning takes the form of a stockpot into which ingredients are thrown until the chef decides there are enough to make a decent soup. Some thought will be given to the balance of subjects, the depth to which each should be discussed and, importantly, the presumed expectations of the potential learners. At some point, the curriculum planners, often a course team in a college, will have identified certain broad aims by which their deliberations and choices are guided. These aims tend to relate to the whole curriculum or large parts of it:

> Not infrequently, such statements reflect philosophical or educational beliefs and values. Statements of aims are generally vague and tend to have little operational value (descriptively or prescriptively) in relation to the planning, development and implementation of curricula. They can, however, act as a 'reference' against which the tenability of more specific statements of intent (e.g. curricula goals and objectives) can be appraised.
>
> (Heathcote *et al.*, 1982)

Heathcote *et al.* found that when curriculum aims were translated into more specific goals, it was to serve two closely connected but alternate functions: the first function involves the teacher acting as an agent for the curriculum planner by teaching directly to tightly defined goals; the second function sees the teacher as a much freer agent who interprets the curriculum planner's goals in the context of each specific group of learners. In some cases, of course, the teacher may have complete control over both the design and implementation of the curriculum.

The pre-eminence of either function depends, according to Heathcote *et al.*, on the following variables:

1   the amount of direction that the curriculum planner wishes to impose on the implementing teacher;
2   the extent to which the curriculum emphasises student autonomy in relation to learning outcomes;
3   the ability and previous experience of the students for whom the curriculum is intended; and
4   the curriculum planner's perception of the constraints imposed and opportunities offered by the subject matter.

We would add a further and, in the light of the competence-based approach, increasingly dominant variable that concerns the teaching or learning system within which the teacher has to function. Heathcote *et al.* distinguish between the use of curriculum aims as a base from which the curriculum planner exerts control over the teacher who delivers the curriculum, as opposed to a 'staging post' where control passes to the teacher who then translates the aims into more specific objectives. They see the first approach as being objectives-based and the second as being process-based. The distinction here is that the process-based model focuses on the role of the teacher who adopts appropriate pedagogical methods in order to achieve the broad aims of the curriculum. Under the objectives-based model, the activities of the teacher are seen as merely the means to an end (that is, the attainment by the students of the specified learning outcomes). In the case of distance learning materials, the materials themselves become the main 'agent' of the course team, but can involve a tutor or 'secondary agent' who interprets the materials for students.

What is looked for is a change in behaviour on the part of the learner, change that Bloom's Taxonomy (Bloom, 1965), still widely adopted by both teachers and trainers, classifies into three domains:

1   *Affective* – attitudes and emotions.
2   *Cognitive* – knowledge and information.
3   *Psychomotor* – practical or physical skills.

Each domain is subdivided into a hierarchy of categories that demonstrate the different levels at which a learner may operate or be asked to operate. Bloom has been criticised, particularly for separating the cognitive from the affective, and other people have developed alternative taxonomies (see, for example, Gagne, 1988). Despite the criticisms, however, Bloom's domains and categories, when taken together, do provide a useful and fairly straightforward structure of learning. As such, they can be used as a basic template for the teacher when planning learning sessions and can also be used for the purposes of evaluating the effectiveness of a particular session.

The *affective domain* has five categories:

- receiving (taking in messages and responding to a stimulus);
- responding (taking responsibility by responding and seeking to find out);
- valuing (recognising that something is worth doing);
- organising and conceptualising (the individual develops his or her own way of arranging responses to stimuli and develops particular attitudes based on a set of values); and
- characterising by value or value concept (bringing together ideas, beliefs and attitudes in a coherent whole).

The *cognitive domain* has six categories:

- knowledge (facts, categorisation of facts and knowledge in general, theories and abstractions);
- comprehension (making sense of what things mean and how they relate to each other);
- application (applying knowledge to different situations);
- analysis (breaking down knowledge into its constituent parts to gain a clearer understanding of the whole);
- synthesis (bringing together the separate constituents to create a new whole, which involves making choices); and
- evaluation (reflecting on knowledge and making judgements).

The *psychomotor domain*, as developed by Harrow (1972) from Bloom's work, has six categories:

- reflex movements (in response to stimuli);
- basic fundamental movements (build upon reflex movements);
- perceptual abilities (used to interpret stimuli and behave accordingly);
- physical abilities;
- skilled movements (involve practice); and
- non-discursive communication (involves creative and artistic behaviour).

As we saw in Chapter 3, behavioural objectives have been heavily criticised for a number of reasons and, as discussed earlier, too much emphasis on a predetermined outcome can result in a dangerously narrow approach to learning. All teachers, however, do need to have a sense of what it is they want their students to achieve by the end of a particular session and over a certain period of time. Those 'objectives' might be largely predetermined and written in the form of 'outcomes' or they may be framed more loosely but in such a way as to help the teacher give a structure to the learning. On some programmes, it is possible, and often desirable, for the teacher and students to negotiate a set of objectives and for the negotiation itself to be regarded as a central part of the learning process.

So far, we have been discussing 'objectives' for teaching and learning and there has been some reference to 'outcomes'. Teachers also talk about 'aims' and 'goals'. Although there is little point in getting too pedantic about terminology, it might be helpful to separate these terms and use them to differentiate between the distinct elements of a teaching/learning situation.

The following example is taken from the 'Recruitment in the Workplace' unit of the GCE in Applied Business. This is a mandatory AS level unit and is assessed internally through portfolio work. This unit is broken down into a series of topics ('What you need to learn' in specification-speak), all of which have to be covered, and for which students need to provide assessment evidence. One of the topics is titled 'The Recruitment Process'. The specification states what students need to understand and be able to demonstrate in their evidence, for example:

- preparing person specifications and job descriptions;
- carefully planning how and when to advertise;
- identifying the strengths and weaknesses of job applications, curriculum vitae and letters of application;
- shortlisting candidates;
- how recruitment interviews are planned, carried out and evaluated; and
- the legal and ethical responsibilities relating to equal opportunities.

(OCR, 2009: 23)

The teacher knows in advance, therefore, what is expected in terms of learning outcomes, but in order to ensure that students achieve those outcomes, the teacher has to construct a teaching plan. This is where aims and objectives come in. We asked a trainee FE teacher to devise a plan for teaching this section of the unit. She began by setting down an overall aim, followed by a set of objectives:

Aim:

To understand the process involved and the skills required when applying for a job.

Objectives:

- to understand the recruitment procedures when applying for a job;
- to respond to a job advertisement;
- to complete an application form in a clear, accurate and professional manner;
- to produce a covering letter to accompany the application form;
- to complete an employer aptitude test; and
- to attend an interview with a personnel officer.

We can see from this that the aim encompasses the topic as a whole, whereas the objectives indicate the separate components that the student needs to master in order to fulfil the aim. In addition to demonstrating his or her ability in the subject area – that is, business – the student may also be able to demonstrate his or her ability in a number of generic skills (functional skills and PLTS, see Chapter 3). For example, this particular assignment offers many opportunities for developing communication skills as well as IT skills. The teacher may want to extend the prescribed learning outcomes in order to reflect the needs of the students, or to develop PLTS (for example, 'problem solving'; 'team working'; 'creative thinking'; 'independent enquiry'). Additional outcomes might include, for example:

- developing the students' confidence outside the classroom;
- developing the students' independent research skills; and
- improving the level of written work among the students in general.

In defining these additional outcomes, the teacher would place them within the context of the course as a whole. An outcome related to the students' research skills would, therefore, be associated with more than one aspect of the assignment. Other outcomes might appear as a result of the teacher (or students) identifying a particular weakness in a previous session, which requires attention.

In designing her teaching plan, the teacher is required to make judgements not just about the subject matter, but about a variety of other factors likely to have an impact upon learning. Examples here could include gender, ethnicity, students with 'special educational needs', prior learning experiences, the resources available; the list is not exhaustive. What this suggests is that teaching strategies have to be differentiated in order to take account of different learning needs and circumstances. Planning for differentiation usually presents a challenge for the majority of beginning teachers, and, it has to be said, for more experienced teachers as well.

A common method for approaching this is by identifying what essential knowledge, skills and concepts all students must learn; what additional material the majority of students should be expected to cope with; and what some more advanced learners could achieve. At an individual class level, differentiation might also be accommodated by providing differentiated materials/resources (for example, large font handouts). Tasks may also be differentiated according to the level of challenge presented. Some students may be allowed extra time in which to complete tasks; others may be given additional support from the lecturer or from a learning support assistant. Expected outcomes might also be differentiated. For example, some students might produce a written report; others might choose to present their findings as a poster display.

If we return to our trainee teacher's plan, we can see that she has set 'goals' for different sections of the plan. For example, objectives 1 to 3 will be covered in three weeks; or one of the objectives will involve a group discussion or activity. It is in the planning where the teacher can be creative, despite the prescriptive nature of the specification. Our trainee teacher decided to divide the content into seven sections and to employ a range of teaching strategies (TS) as follows:

Section 1: General overview

In this section, students are asked to discuss their attitudes to unemployment and the different ways in which people can apply for jobs.

TS: 'Thought shower' as a group to get initial views; ideas can be captured on the whiteboard or on a flipchart; ask students to consider a set of case studies of people seeking work; ask students to choose two job vacancies from the local newspaper and obtain the necessary application forms (use telephone, send letters and visit the job centre).

Section 2: The recruitment process

Students learn about how a typical company sets out to recruit staff.

TS: Teacher uses information from an actual company (in this case, Royal Mail) to explain the recruitment process. Teaching aids include PowerPoint and company materials. Alternatively, a company representative might agree to talk to the group. Students are also encouraged to talk about their own part-time jobs and how they were obtained.

Section 3: Letters and job specifications

Students learn how to construct a letter of application and interpret job advertisements.

TS: Students have been asked to bring in copies of job advertisements from local newspapers and to select three jobs they could realistically apply for; the students work in pairs to assess the quality of a sample of specimen letters of application; the teacher goes through the key requirements in writing a letter of application; the students work on their own to produce a letter of application for one of the jobs they selected earlier.

Section 4: Application forms and curriculum vitae

Students learn how to complete an application form and construct a CV.

TS: Students work in groups to assess the quality of specimen completed application forms; group discussion about what the applicant needs to do when completing a form; teacher reinforces the requirements by presenting a list on PowerPoint. The process is repeated for CVs. Students use computers to generate CVs, thereby covering some IT skills.

Section 5: Equal opportunities and contracts of employment

Students learn about the legal obligations employers have to adhere to when recruiting staff.

TS: Role play between teacher and student to demonstrate how certain questions could contravene equal opportunities legislation; group discussion of why equal opportunity matters in recruitment; students work in small groups to analyse a sample of contracts of employment; teacher reinforces legal knowledge with handouts.

Section 6: Preparing for interviews

Students learn how to prepare for an interview and how to conduct themselves in an interview.

TS: Teacher shows a DVD illustrating good and bad interviews and students take notes; group discussion of DVD; teacher reinforces points related to how to prepare for an interview and how to behave as an interviewee.

Section 7: Being interviewed

Students take part in mock interviews, acting as both interviewees and interviewers.

TS: Mock interviews held using video cameras and external interviewers brought in; students watch the videos and analyse their strengths and weaknesses; teacher draws together all aspects of the element.

In devising her teaching plan, the trainee teacher was determined to provide her students with a lively and varied learning opportunity; hence, she has deliberately chosen a range of teaching and learning strategies.

Assignments

The use of assignments as vehicles for encouraging participative, student-centred learning has been a central feature of college life for many years.

Assignments can enable students to see their programme of study as a coherent whole in which all the parts are related to each other and through which they are encouraged to apply their knowledge, understanding and skills. In this way, assignments are an important means for enabling students to engage in learning by doing and for emphasising the integrated nature of their courses. The student-centred nature of assignments and their facility for including both individual and group tasks means that they highlight the process of learning as well as being agents for delivering outcomes of learning. When assignment work is assessed (either by teachers, or through student–peer assessments, or both), valuable lessons can be learned by reviewing the process through which the learning took place (see Chapter 6). Common features of assignments are:

- they include an element of independent student activity to be carried out individually or in groups (usually referred to in the assignment guidance as 'tasks');
- they are based on realistic scenarios drawn from vocational practice;
- they can be of varying length;
- they encourage students to apply knowledge, understanding and skills to meaningful (authentic) tasks in a realistic contexts; and
- they allow functional skills and PLTS to be integrated into the learning process and assessed as part of the overall learning outcomes.

Assignments can be created by individual teachers, or by course teams, who wish to create greater coherence between the modules or units that comprise the distinctive parts of a programme of study. Designing assignments can be divided into three areas:

1   *Task* – what a student does, often resulting in a product or other outcome.
2   *Activities* – the process used in order to achieve the task.
3   *Assessment* – the benchmarks or criteria for the product and the process.

For example, if an assignment was built around the design and use of questionnaires, the three areas listed above would translate as follows:

1   *Task* – devise and use a questionnaire.
2   *Activities* – select sources and obtain information about questionnaire design; plan the questionnaire; pilot it; amend as necessary; use the amended questionnaire; collect data; evaluate and present data.
3   *Assessment criteria* – range of methods used in obtaining information; fitness of resulting questionnaire for purpose – language, tone, degree of complexity, depth of analysis; clarity of presentation; adequacy of evaluation.

There is enormous scope when identifying appropriate scenarios for assignments for teachers to be creative and to utilise the expertise and ideas of a range of people. When designing an assignment, the following stages should be followed:

1   Choose the unit/topic you wish to cover.
2   Formulate a scenario, exercise or brief for the students to work within (be realistic about the amount of time available for students to cover the work involved).
3   Correlate possible tasks with evidence criteria that will have to be fulfilled for the purposes of assessment.
4   If applicable, identify the generic skills that will be assessed through the assignment.
5   Decide if this will be a graded assignment, and, if so, how marks/grades will be allocated.
6   Write the assignment as a series of tasks with guidance for students.
7   Write assessment guidance (including grading criteria if applicable), indicating the nature of the evidence to be obtained.
8   Design any necessary documentation for assessment purposes (for example, grids, question sheets, logs, etc.). (Awarding organisations provide examples of these on their websites and you should always ensure that you are using the most recent examples offered by the awarding organisation with whom your students are registered.)

By evaluating the implementation of an assignment, the teacher (and/or course team) can refine the different elements in order to improve it and ensure its continued applicability and viability. Once a set of effective assignments has been created, the pressure on the teacher to produce teaching materials is reduced and more time can be spent supervising the actual learning process. One serious note of caution is imperative when talking about assignment work. There is a misguided belief by some that assignments are a way of keeping students occupied and of letting the teacher off the hook. Assignments should never be used as an excuse for simply sending students away 'to get on with assignments/coursework'. In order for students to submit satisfactory coursework and to complete assignments, they must receive adequate and appropriate teaching input, they must be supported through their independent research, they must be given timely and focused formative feedback, their progress should be logged and action plans drawn up for next steps. Assignments and coursework should never be regarded as an easy option; in order to support students appropriately and to ensure that learning takes place, they require just as much planning as any other learning experience.

Being creative

As discussed in Chapter 4, teachers have to be aware of the different ways in which their students approach learning and try to create a learning environment in which those different approaches can be accommodated. But creativity in teaching involves risk.

The following question and answer section helps you to think about some of the implications for teachers when designing outcomes-based, student-centred programmes.

What teaching will I need to devise and deliver?

The teaching will have to be designed to contribute to the assignments; in other words, to provide the underpinning knowledge that students require in order to complete the assignments. This will not always be provided by the teacher, but the teacher may act as a facilitator in pointing the students in the direction of suitable learning resources. You need to check the specifications carefully to see how much teacher support is permitted. This is currently a highly contentious issue and we have already seen in Chapter 3 that the amount of coursework now permitted within some qualifications has been reduced, and that there may be further reduction. However, it should be borne in mind by practitioners and policymakers that, within the context of vocational learning, technical knowledge and practical competence must go hand in hand. In order to achieve higher grades, students are expected to demonstrate independence in their learning. They need to be able to show evidence of synthesis and evaluation. Teachers need to ask themselves: what do students need to know in order to fulfil the assessment criteria for this unit? Supplementary questions then follow.

Where or from whom can this knowledge be accessed?

The important point here is that there is a wide range of resources and sources from which knowledge can be accessed and the teacher should exploit the interdisciplinary nature of the college environment, as well as drawing on resources available through the college's external networks. There is also a wealth of information available on the Internet, although its sheer volume can make the job of selecting appropriate material daunting. A word of caution is required – students should not simply be directed to websites before their content has been assessed for suitability in terms of its appropriateness and relevance to the topic being studied. Surfing websites can be a huge timewaster, and students do not always have the necessary research skills to select effectively. These are skills that need to be developed through appropriate induction processes.

How and where will the learning take place?

The answer to this question could be as wide as individual teaching staff wish to make it. If it is accepted that the opportunities for learning are constrained neither by the time nor the place at which it occurs, nor by the age of the learner, then the opportunities presented by a wide range of diverse contexts and experiences are limitless. However, if teachers subscribe to the view that learning can only take place in classrooms where the teacher stands at the front and talks, then it will be extremely difficult to deliver vocational programmes effectively.

Examples of work-related learning activities include:

- work experience placements on employers' premises;
- work shadowing;
- projects undertaken in companies specifically for those companies (for example, product testing);
- simulations;
- organising and running events in the college (for example, open days, careers fairs, catering and general reception duties); and
- practical experience in the college's restaurant, beauty salon, crèche, workshop.

The importance of vocationally relevant and realistic learning environments, as described within the model for the 14–19 Diploma in England (see Chapter 3), and as already well established within many existing vocational programmes, requires close cooperation with, and support from, employers and the local community. Some variation in provision across different colleges and different programme areas exists, and there are clearly capacity issues if employers are expected to take an even more active involvement in the sector in the future as recommended in current government policy documents. The best interests of individual employers are not necessarily the same as the best interests of learners, the wider economy or local communities. There is insufficient space here to explore in detail the relationship between education and the wider economy (for a fuller discussion, see Huddleston, 2012), but, in the best-developed examples, assignments have been designed in conjunction with employers. Well-planned work placements allow students to collect assessment evidence from their experience. In some cases, assessments can be undertaken by workplace supervisors and later verified by college staff. There are obvious implications for quality control when parts of the programme are, in effect, being devolved to employers but in the best examples drawn from apprenticeship training this is exactly what is happening. Some colleges have been able to develop effective partnerships with companies by arranging for staff teaching on vocational programmes to have work placements in business and industry.

What sort of students will be involved?

While many students following full-time vocational programmes in colleges will be 16–19 years old, by no means all of them will fit this age profile. Part-time students cover a much wider age range, and since, as the former Qualifications and Curriculum Authority (QCA) in England used to talk about the curriculum 16–90, it is worth remembering that we cannot neatly put our students into clearly defined age groups. It should also be remembered that many of these students also have part-time, and full-time, jobs and these can provide rich sources of vocational experience and information on which they can draw. Too often, we fail to recognise this wealth of experience. In addition to age differences, there will be differences in terms of gender, ethnicity, prior learning experiences, cultural and social norms. Think, for example, of the issues Clare is facing in developing teaching strategies for her groups of students (see Chapter 4).

How will assessment be organised and carried out?

Assessment is continuous throughout the programme and may be based on a series of assignments, or other forms of coursework, including practical workshops or studio activities that are completed during the programme. This can be in addition to, in some cases, a series of externally set and marked tests, even formal examinations. There has been a great deal of discussion recently about the balance of coursework and external assessment within qualifications, and there have been demands for a reduction in the amount of coursework permitted within GCSEs, A levels and even in vocational programmes for pre-16 students, which we discussed in Chapter 3. However, as asserted in Chapter 6, 'fitness for purpose' should be the guiding principle in assessment design and practical activities, coursework, learning logs, investigations all play important roles within the teaching and learning process.

Evidence for assessment is often collected in a student's portfolio. The student has to satisfy the assessment criteria for each unit of the course and has to provide sufficient evidence that this has been achieved. We discuss portfolio building more fully in Chapter 6.

Choosing a strategy

It is clear that teaching strategies are chosen for reasons that go beyond being a mechanism for ensuring that the students achieve the subject-specific outcomes. Certainly, achievement of those outcomes is vitally important but the teacher also has to ensure that students develop their abilities as learners and build relationships with each other that contribute to an effective learning environment. We can portray this as a model for effective learning (see Figure 5.3).

Once you are clear about the outcomes to be achieved in a session, and have taken account of any constraining factors, you can select one or more teaching strategies. As noted earlier, those strategies will obviously reflect your preferences as a teacher but you may want to try out different approaches, albeit on a small scale at first until you begin to gain confidence in using them.

The following checklist can be used to evaluate the extent to which your proposed plan for a particular session (or 'lesson') has taken into account the different needs that have to be met. You might like to use this checklist when devising your lesson plans (Figure 5.4).

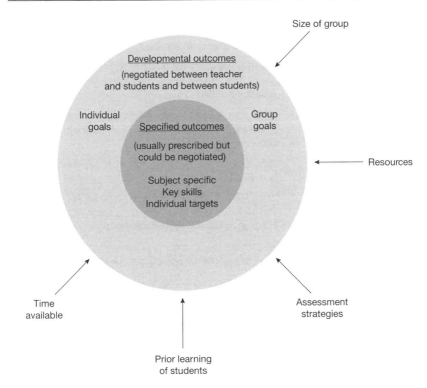

Figure 5.3 Model for effective learning

In the following section, we identify the characteristics of a range of teaching strategies and suggest tasks that students can be asked to perform in order to ensure that they participate as fully as possible in the learning situation.

Managing learning: handling 'difficult' students

In the opening chapters of this book, we stressed the diversity of college life and, in particular, the need for FE teachers to appreciate that their students will reflect a range of abilities, needs and levels of motivation. Unlike schools, where all the students are legally required to attend, colleges expect their students to attend as a result of acting as responsible adults, rather than from the threat of legal sanction. Some learners, it is true, may be attending courses selected by their employers and, in the case of government-sponsored trainees or apprentices, some students may have their wages reduced for missing classes, but, even in these cases, a college would hope that the students concerned could develop enough maturity to understand the need to fulfil their obligations as course members.

Ask yourself	Quick check (some ideas)
What am I going to teach?	Topic, e.g. customer service.
Who are the learners?	Group (e.g. Level 2 catering and hospitality), size of group, age, gender, ability range, prior learning, equality and diversity issues.
Where will the teaching take place?	Classroom, laboratory, workshop, sports centre (are there any constraints in terms of location: health and safety issues?)
When will the class be timetabled?	Length of session (too long, too short, will this present a challenge? How should I structure the time?)
What are the intended learning outcomes?	What is it that I expect learners to be able to know and understand by the end of the session? Think about all, most and some (differentiation).
How?	What strategies am I going to use – whole group, small group, one-to-one support, peer support?
What range of activities will I provide?	Demonstration, speaking and listening, making notes, role play, practical work, performance, completing worksheets.
What is the balance of activities?	Teacher-led, student-led, mutually configured, supported by others (learner support staff, technicians).
How will the learning be assessed?	What strategies will I deploy, during the session, at the end of the session, in the coming weeks to confirm learning – Q and A, written test, observation of practice?
What resources will be required?	What do I need to make it happen – equipment, artefacts, PowerPoint presentation, handouts, DVDs?
What are my personal targets?	Build my confidence in working with this group; improve my classroom management skills; make a potentially 'dull' topic more interesting.
How will I evaluate this session?	In terms of students: learning, behaviour, interest, involvement, attainment.
	In terms of my teaching: giving information, questioning, providing feedback, time management, assessment, working with support staff.
What targets/action points do I want to set for next time?	Improve time management; provide more realistic and relevant examples drawn from the vocational context for students to consider; design better differentiated material.

Figure 5.4 Checklist for lesson plans

The replacement of the EMA with a student bursary (as discussed in Chapter 1) raises issues for relationships that colleges enjoy with their students and vice versa. For example, college staff are cast in the role of financial arbiters and enforcement agencies; they will decide who is eligible, how, when and for what purposes bursaries will be paid. Tutors may be required to sign weekly attendance and performance reports in order for the students' bursaries to be paid; the student/teacher relationship has, in some cases, been realigned, although this was already evident in the former EMA. One of the authors was recently observing a class where a young man, whose behaviour was particularly problematic, was heard saying to the lecturer, 'You can't throw me out because I'm on the allowance'.

All colleges, of course, have to comply with the funding criteria laid down by the relevant funding body, part of which puts particular emphasis on maintaining acceptable levels of student retention. This can lead to disputes between teachers and managers in cases where the former wish to remove particularly disruptive students from courses and the latter decide that the need for student retention overrides any difficulties in the classroom. All teachers need to feel that they have the support of their managers when faced with difficult students and should be apprised of their college's disciplinary procedures and policy on exclusions. Indeed, induction programmes for new staff should include a session on this important area and should ensure that teachers have a clear picture of the support structures that exist to help them, should the need arise.

The presence of increasing numbers of 14–16 year olds in FE colleges, as discussed in Chapter 3, has brought a different cohort of young people into colleges with very different learning needs. The following is an example of a college's experiences with such groups.

Northside and Southside College

Northside and Southside College is a large general FE college operating across two campuses, brought together through the merger of two separate colleges. The main campus is situated in a medium-sized town (formerly a mining community) serving a dispersed rural area. The town is a focus for the logistics, distribution and transport sector, being adjacent to the motorway network and several major distribution centres. The second campus is located in a smaller town, 10 miles away; employment opportunities have dwindled there since the demise of the mining and textile industries.

The provision for pre-16 learners at the college began in 1999, with the intention of providing an alternative curriculum for school students focusing upon its vocational excellence. Originally designed for Level 1 learners who wanted access to more practical learning, it now offers nine programmes, from entry Level 1 to

Level 2, across 10 subject areas, including horticulture, child care, floristry, catering and construction. A dedicated team of staff work with partner schools in selecting students who would benefit most from access to these vocational programmes. A college manager is responsible for coordinating the programme in college and liaising with schools, parents and other colleagues, who have now been brought into the team. The manager also gives talks to other providers about the provision, which was graded as 'outstanding' by Ofsted.

Pupils attend college one day a week and are working towards nationally recognised qualifications, which also allow for progression beyond 16; this is seen as a strength of the provision. Pupils work to industry standards and there are high expectations in terms of dress, attendance, punctuality, working practice, time management and professionalism. The success of the 14-16 partnerships derives from the fact that pupils' needs are identified and carefully matched to course provision; there is a strong system of pastoral care and support; staff teaching on the programmes do so because they enjoy teaching this age group; students have access to high-quality workshops and industry standard equipment that motivates and engages them; and there are clearly marked progression routes into apprenticeships, or other programmes post-16.

It is important for all teachers to realise that some of their students may have problems that require the intervention of specialists and that, as teachers, they are not equipped to deal with such problems beyond the initial stage of encouraging and supporting an individual student to seek help. Deciding where the line falls between those students who need specialist help and those who can be supported within the everyday teaching and learning situation is, however, not a straightforward process. Avis *et al.* (2011: 54) have researched the ways in which trainee teachers sometimes construct their students as being in need of care and therapy:

> There is a paradox in that the discourse of the 'bad' student mirrors that of care, with both constituting particular students as inadequate and in need of some sort of intervention. This process needs to be placed alongside 'the other', the 'good student' who is set against these learners in state policy discourse. That is to say the potentially high achieving, often white middle-class learner who needs to be pushed to meet their potential. This is the student who has to be stretched and challenged and who should encounter a demanding educational experience, not least so that selecting universities are able to differentiate between applicants . . . Whereas the 'bad' student is in need of care so that they avoid becoming disengaged and disaffected.

They conclude that investing so much in the 'care' of students has significant implications for the health and well-being of teachers as so much 'emotional labour' is involved (see also Robson *et al.*, 2008). This research echoes the concerns of

Ecclestone and Hayes (2008), who have lambasted what they see as a shift to a therapeutic approach in FE, one that focuses more on supporting students rather than on their educational needs. Hyland (2011), however, challenges this view, arguing that Ecclestone and Hayes overlook the importance of support in teaching and learning. Similarly, Jephcote et al. (2008: 168), in a study of FE teachers in Wales, stressed the value of what they term 'highly supportive pedagogical strategies', which students regarded as a 'crucial determinant of their learning'.

The more experience one gains as a teacher, the more adept one becomes at managing the learning process and spotting potential flashpoints. As discussed in Chapter 4, if teachers demonstrate that they have empathy with their students, they are much more likely to create conditions that are conducive to cooperation with, and between, their students and in which all parties trust and respect each other. We also noted, however, that the pressures on students in terms of the lives they lead outside college can cause them to display behavioural patterns that appear disruptive in the classroom or workshop. But that pressure may also come from within the college if, for example, a student is struggling to keep up with his or her written work or if he or she is being bullied. And, of course, disruptive behaviour may be the student's way of telling a teacher that the sessions are boring, poorly organised or pitched at an inappropriate level. Changes in behaviour can usually be seen as signals of stress or anxiety, and the teacher must be able to recognise those signals and act appropriately before the situation gets out of hand.

A key factor in the effective management of any learning situation is for the teacher to involve the students in the whole process. This involves the teacher in an exercise in sharing with students as follows:

1   Discuss with students your expectations (as a teacher) of them and identify their expectations (as students) of you. For example, try to establish a code of practice regarding lateness, the handing in of work, eating/drinking in class, dress codes, health and safety in workshops, etc.
2   Explain to students the nature of what is to be covered in a particular session and how this relates to the rest of their course.
3   Explain clearly (and review at intervals) the assessment procedure you will operate – this includes both the informal (criteria you use to monitor student progress) and the formal (externally imposed criteria for summative assessment) criteria you will employ.
4   Discuss with students the constraints under which you and they must work (for example, presentation of work to satisfy external examiners, coverage of certain elements of a curriculum, the lack of sufficient computers or textbooks, etc.).
5   Review your working arrangements as a group, giving students the chance to discuss whether they should be given more time to hand in work or to receive more support with a particular part of the course – this may require you to recognise any inadequacies in your initial preparation for a course or to accept that you have made mistakes.

By sharing the necessary ingredients of the learning process with students, they are given the opportunity to act responsibly and with the same degree of professionalism as the teacher. At the same time, the teacher has to be prepared to show the same degree of respect to the students and to try not to retreat into a position of isolated superiority when challenged. Working with students does not necessitate a blurring of roles to the point where teacher and student become indistinguishable. Both teacher and students have to recognise the demands of each other's roles and that the teacher, like any manager, has to take responsibility for ensuring that the collective goals of the group are achieved.

Rogers (2002) makes some very helpful suggestions for dealing with behaviour management issues, which are widely applicable across a range of teaching/ group situations. He emphasises the importance of routines, clarity, reinforcing desired behaviour and dealing unobtrusively with problems when they occur. He suggests the following principles as general good practice:

- treating all with respect in the class (peers as well as teachers/support staff);
- establishing appropriate protocols of communication in class (listening to others, speaking in an appropriate manner);
- establishing learning behaviour (how to seek support from a teacher/others, how to support others in their learning);
- movement about the class (respecting other's space); and
- dealing with problems (settling misunderstandings/arguments/potential flashpoints).

Team teaching and learning

One of the most stimulating and natural ways to teach and to learn is to work with a colleague or team of colleagues. As we saw in Chapter 4, social theories of learning highlight the relational nature of learning, with human beings coming together to share and 'teach' each other in domestic as well as work contexts. Mentoring is widely used across the professions, both formally and informally, and with differing degrees of success, to facilitate the sharing of expertise and experience, and it can also play a part in encouraging students to support each other (for a critical discussion, see Cunningham, 2012; Colley, 2003).

Forms of team teaching range from two people taking it in turns to address the class, to larger groups of teachers adopting a variety of roles, including facilitating small-group discussion, working on a one-to-one basis with students and coordinating project-based activities. Such teaching can be used to counter prejudice along gender and racial lines, and to overcome the difficulties in mixed-ability classes. It can also help to stimulate greater responsibility on the part of students who have to learn to cooperate with teachers who display different pedagogical approaches and styles.

A particularly useful role for team teaching is during induction periods when 'ice-breaking' activities can help cement a sense of group identity and

community among students and teachers. In their classic text, *Gamesters'*
Handbook, Brandes and Phillips (1985) describe a number of activities, games
and strategies that can be used to promote personal development and social
cohesion.

Box 5.3 shows a few ideas that we have used as 'ice-breaker' activities.

Box 5.3 'ICE-BREAKER' ACTIVITIES

Find a mate

On entering the room, each student is given half of a definition on a strip
of paper (for example, 'balance of . . .'). Another student will have the other
half of the definition on a similar strip of paper (for example, 'payments').
Students move around the room until they find their match. When they have
done so, they will take their partner to sit down and decide exactly what
the definition means.

What's my line?

Tutors prepare large cards with a job title on each one (these should be
taken from job roles within the vocational area the student is studying). Each
student has one pinned on to his or her back so that it can only be seen by
others in the group. Students move around the room and attempt to
discover what their 'line' is by asking questions of other students. Responses
must be restricted to 'yes' or 'no'. Once the 'line' has been discovered,
students sit down. When all have finished, each student describes what the
role entails.

Tell me a story

Students are asked to form groups of fours; tutors hand out paper bags
containing five everyday items (one bag per group); groups are asked to
construct a short story involving the five items. After 10 minutes, group
stories are recounted to the whole class.

True or false?

Tutors prepare a set of laminated cards displaying 'true' or 'false' (these can
be used many times). Each student is given a set of cards and is asked to
respond to statements that the tutors make (for example, 'Photosynthesis
is the process by which plants use energy from sunlight to build up complex
substances from carbon dioxide and water').

From distance to e-learning and using ICLT

Distance learning has been available in the UK and throughout the world for much of the twentieth century, beginning with correspondence courses in which there was no contact between tutor and student other than by post. The establishment of the British Open University in 1969 led to a number of similar institutions being set up around the world. The OU was notable for allowing people to study for undergraduate degrees without any entrance requirements and for combining distance learning via multimedia materials with attendance at residential summer schools. Many FE colleges are designated as study centres for OU students who attend a limited number of face-to-face tutorial sessions in their local areas, and some colleges provide courses on study skills (sometimes called 'return to learn') for adults who are considering enrolling with the OU. The term 'distance learning' has joined a lengthy list of other terms, some of which are used interchangeably. These terms include 'flexible learning'; 'flexi-study'; 'resource-based learning'; and 'independent study'. Although the expansion of distance learning has been largely aimed at adult learners, some of the techniques involved in the preparation of study materials have been used in schools, and the learner-centred approach that drives many (though not all) distance learning programmes has influenced classroom-based and work-based teaching and learning. Now, through the rapid development of ICLT and the availability of faster access to the Internet, e-learning is making its mark.

e-Learning can cover a spectrum of activities from the use of technology to support learning as part of a 'blended' approach, to learning that is delivered entirely online. These flexible learning approaches are promoted in terms of their ability to provide access to learning to large numbers of people who need the flexibility of being able to study when and where they choose. The European Commission (EC), in particular, and some national governments, have extolled the virtues of flexible learning for some time. Some critics argue, however, that these newer forms of learning have grown in stature and availability as a result of the reduction in spending on staff development, training and adult education in general.

Edwards (1993) takes these arguments a stage further and suggests that the growth of open learning (which he uses as a generic term) reflects a wider societal change that is witnessing organisations shifting from Fordist (mass production lines, labour intensive) to post-Fordist (part-time working, flexible work patterns) structures. He is particularly concerned with the way in which open learning, as used in some industries, can separate employees from each other, thus reducing the opportunity for critical discussion of shared concerns. Many teachers, in common with managers and other professionals, now gain their professional development through flexible learning courses, which include master's degrees and doctorates. Although Edwards's fears deserve constant attention, flexible approaches to course provision and learning are very popular, particularly with people whose professional and domestic lives allow them little time to study in conventional ways. Well-structured flexible learning programmes include opportunities, often through residential weekends, for students to come together to share ideas and enjoy the experience of being 'real' students.

Hargreaves (2004: 48) stresses the motivational power of the new technologies:

> They do this in a variety of ways. They make the work easier. Redrafting an essay is much easier to do with computer-based text than with written text, where the whole piece has to be rewritten, slowly and painfully. The Internet or the use of some commercial software can make the task of finding relevant material to support or illustrate an argument much more efficient than searching through books. They also often make the work more interesting. They give speedy access to material that is often of inherent interest: in the exploration of new sources one stumbles across the unusual and fascinating.

He describes how technology can be used to design online formative assessment tools that deliver feedback much more quickly than through more traditional means, and the important role technology can play in getting learners to take more responsibility for their own learning. In Chapter 6, we examine the dark side to ICLT – the rise of plagiarism.

If you are involved in teaching on courses that have an open, distance or electronic format, you may have the opportunity to prepare learning materials in the form of written, self-study texts, audio cassettes, instructional videos, video-conferencing and interactive computer programmes. You might also be involved in placing teaching materials within what are called 'virtual learning environments' using interactive platforms such as 'Blackboard' and 'Moodle'. The use of VLEs has grown dramatically in colleges, partly as result of the 'personalisation' agenda. The extent to which you can become proficient in these media will be determined by the amount of training available and the level of resources devoted to this mode of teaching. The development of e-learning is bound to have a profound effect on the types of media available in colleges and, although one should not get too carried away by the hype surrounding such developments, it is clear that both teachers and students will need to keep abreast of the electronic revolution.

Mayes (2002) argues that ICLT, and e-learning more generally, cannot just be absorbed by teachers and students; rather, these developments require us to ask some fundamental questions about the pedagogical skills needed to utilise them properly (see also Kenway, 2001). He says that we need to think about 'how technology can support the learning cycle, the goal-action-feedback loop that provides a basic model for all learning' (Mayes, 2002: 164–5). In their research in colleges in the Netherlands and Scotland, Rommes *et al.* (2005) found that women-only classes were particularly effective in encouraging female students to develop their use of ICLT for three particular reasons: positive role model effects; mutual encouragement and support among trainees; and the safety to speak openly.

Students, of course, need support in mastering the skills required to use the new learning technologies effectively. Thus, most colleges now have learning resources centres. These are usually 'drop-in' centres where students can use the technology available in order to complete assignments or where they can access additional units to support other learning. They may also be able to access such material remotely. As we have seen in earlier chapters, with this more personalised approach, there are implications for student guidance and counselling. Students need help in accessing the parts of the curriculum that meet their needs. They also need guidance in constructing a coherent and integrated programme of learning from the wide range of offerings available.

The promotion of e-learning, and the use of new technologies in general, has its critics. Some are concerned about the emphasis on the individualised nature of this type of learning. For example, Field (2000: 55) points out that, 'From the perspective of an older type of adult education – dedicated to enlightenment, social improvement and the support of social movements – this individualism represents an abandonment of social purpose' (see also Field, 2006). Guile and Hayton's (1999: 123) concerns raised some years ago are also still very pertinent. They cautioned against the prevalent and very misguided belief that 'the individualised, technological approach to delivery is a cheap option'. They also noted that research in the UK and the US showed that ICLT is not, by itself, a vehicle for assisting people to become acquainted with new ideas or for enabling them to think in theoretically informed ways, but rather 'that the effective use of ICLT involved teachers rethinking the relationship between the process of learning and their role in supporting such learning' (ibid.).

Some technologies, such as video and DVD, have been used in colleges for many years. Mitra *et al.* (2010) point out, however, that the development of websites such as YouTube, Google Video and TeacherTube mean that a much greater amount of material is now available and easily accessible by students themselves. They stress that, as with all aids to teaching, teachers need to think through how they want video-based technologies to support learning: 'How lecturers themselves use video will determine whether or not the video is an effective learning tool or simply a passive time filler for students' (ibid.: 413).

Conclusion

This chapter has explored a range of teaching strategies that can be employed in college and college-related settings. Individual teachers have to try on these strategies, rather like new clothes, to see how they feel and fit, as not all the strategies listed here will suit everyone.

The culture and context of the setting in which you are teaching will also affect the extent to which you can be innovative and can take risks. Your managers may not welcome seeing you trying out something untested the week the inspectors call! Finally, your students play a key role in helping you decide which strategies to use, and your relationship with them will often determine how 'safe' you are in your teaching style.

Chapter 6

Assessment and recording achievement

The role of assessment

An important and integral aspect of your work in teaching is the assessment of your students. In England and Wales in particular, assessment has been the focus of increased interest, and indeed reform, during the past 15 years or more. At the time of writing, the DfE in England has placed emphasis on the need to streamline the assessment process not only to reduce the burden of assessment, but also to improve its transparency, rigour and consistency. More controversially, the DfE has also made clear that it wants to see more external tests and examinations, thus reducing the amount of assessment undertaken through coursework. In this context, within general education programmes, coursework has already been replaced by controlled assessment, which requires stricter controls over the way in which these types of extended assessments are conducted in terms of task-setting, task-taking and task-marking.

At the time of writing, a consultation on A levels is ongoing, again with an emphasis upon 'stretch and rigour', the desirability of external examinations, reduced opportunities for re-sits, and linear rather than modular design. But, of course, A levels are not the only 'game in town'; most of us working within the post-compulsory sector will be teaching and assessing on vocational programmes that may involve external tests, or examinations, but that will also include a large proportion of coursework, the demonstration of practical skills, the production of artefacts, and the compilation of portfolios of evidence to confirm that outcomes have been achieved. In short, a wider range of assessment techniques than those associated with academic programmes are at our disposal. This creates challenges as well as opportunities.

The debate around the purposes and design of assessment, its reliability and validity, is set to run for some time and you will note through your reading of the educational press, and through discussions with colleagues, that practitioners' views on assessment can give rise to heated debate. Assessment can also engender severe anxiety among our students. Remember from your reading of the student profiles in Chapter 2 that some of them had been scarred by previous negative experiences of assessment; for some, it resulted in their being excluded from a course of choice. Whatever your views on the broader landscape, it is clear that a range of assessment strategies are necessary in order to provide sufficient evidence to confirm that learning has taken place not just by issuing an end of unit test, but through questioning and feedback, which should be built into all your lessons and workshops. Within vocational programmes, for example, assessment through coursework, or other forms of practical activity, may provide more reliable evidence than a written test.

Evidence of assessment, and its outcomes, is not only a mandatory requirement of awarding and validating organisations for whose qualifications you are preparing students, but you will need to assess in order to maintain a record of students' progress and to assist them in planning their own learning. It is also a necessary check on the effectiveness of your teaching, since we cannot assume automatically that what we teach is the same as what students actually learn. In a target-driven education and training climate, evidence that outcomes have been met, standards reached and qualifications achieved is often required to trigger funding.

At the heart of this dilemma is the need to provide accountability across a wide range of learning experiences and programmes of study, to confirm learning and to measure standards and effectiveness, as well as to contribute to the personal development of students. It is clear from this that assessment performs a range of functions:

- providing a framework in which learning goals, aims and objectives can be set;
- providing the benchmarks for monitoring students' progress and for planning future learning;
- providing a framework for identifying learner needs; and
- providing a framework for designing feedback.

Assessment, then, is not simply seen as something that is used for grading work, or for processes of selection; it is increasingly recognised as an important part of the learning process.

Ecclestone (2000: 144), in a wide-ranging analysis of assessment and critical autonomy in post-compulsory education, reminds us that 'ill-formed, and often contradictory, theories of learning and motivation underpin all assessment regimes in different ways'. She gives the example of the behaviourists' 'belief in the power of extrinsic motivation through externally set targets, rewards and punishments', which contrasts with the 'humanist belief in people's innate need to learn, the need to cultivate intrinsic motivation'. While recognising the many debates about 'good' and 'bad' assessment approaches, Ecclestone calls for formative and diagnostic assessment to be placed 'at the centre of teaching and learning instead of being a separate afterthought, or merely an instrumental process to generate summative targets' (ibid.: 156). In this way, teachers and learners can engage in a community of assessment, a concept that has its roots in the community of practice model described in Chapter 4. Brown (1994: 271) suggests that, in terms of young people:

> Assessment, therefore, now has several functions including the diagnosis of causes of young people's success or failure, the motivation of them to learn, the provision of valid and meaningful accounts of what has been achieved and the evaluation of courses and teaching.

When asked 'Why do we assess students?' a group of trainee teachers gave the following responses:

- It's a measure of feedback for students.
- It helps us to plan our teaching more effectively.
- We do it to grade students.
- Assessment is formative.
- It's to help them prepare for exams; give them an idea of what to expect.
- It's for selection.
- It helps us to know if the students have understood.
- To empower the student and teacher to move forward.

The variety of responses indicates the multi-faceted nature of the assessment process. Assessment is not so much something that is 'done unto' students, but often involves negotiations with students and sometimes with employers as well. Both its purposes and practices have changed during recent years. Some of these changes are associated with changes to the structure of qualifications and programmes. The introduction of mandatory assessment within the national curriculum in England in the compulsory phase of schooling is mirrored by similar changes in the post-compulsory sector.

Throughout life, we are both being assessed by and assessing other people, whether it is formally, as in the case of a teacher, magistrate, employer or parent, or informally, as when we meet someone for the first time or attend a concert. Sometimes those initial assessments are hard to shift as well. In education and training, assessment is a powerful process that can both empower people as well as damage them. There are many adults who carry the scars of their encounters with assessment throughout their lives. Some, for example, remember failing the 11+ examination for entry to grammar school, whereas others may never forget the agonies of oral spelling tests or being made to write their answer to an arithmetic question on the blackboard in front of the whole class. Smith (1989: 119) asserts that both the assessor and the person being assessed need to understand the nature of the assessment process and that:

> The more aware both assessors and assessed become of the relationship between the outcomes of the judgement process and the sources of evidence from which they derive, and the more honest assessors become

about the sources of evidence from which their judgements derive, the more equitable and generally acceptable they are likely to be.

Fitness for purpose should be the guiding principle in considering assessment design. There is a wide variety of assessment techniques. Whichever method is selected, it is important to recognise the purpose of the assessment and what it is designed to measure. Different methods of assessment will be necessary to assess practical skills from those designed to assess students' abilities to engage with a theoretical concept. In designing an effective assessment strategy, a useful checklist should include:

- Is this assessment valid (does it assess what it sets out to assess)?
- Is it reliable (likely to produce consistent, repeatable results)?
- Is it practical (not too difficult or expensive to undertake)?
- Is it fair (does not make unreasonable demands on learners, bearing in mind equality of opportunity and access)?
- Is it useful (does it contribute to the learning process)?

REFLECTION

Box 6.1 shows some examples of different assessment methods, which you may have used yourself or seen used by others. Consider where, within your own particular subject area, you might use them. The first one is already completed; consider also 'fitness for purpose' issues.

As we saw in Chapter 3, the introduction of an outcomes-based model of vocational qualifications, and particularly occupationally focused qualifications, has resulted in the measurement of achievement in terms of learning outcomes (that is, through the demonstration of competence, usually within the work place). However, the term learning outcome connotes different meanings for different people. A major employer within the travel and tourism sector recently interviewed by one of the authors described them thus: 'We prefer to talk about particular competences, attributes and attitudes that we are looking for (in trainees), rather than learning outcomes', while a representative of an awarding organisation suggested that for her it is: 'What the learner will be able to do . . . things that the learner can take away and use elsewhere'. However, there can be a danger of the assessment dominating the learning process if achievement is measured solely in terms of outcome and bears scant regard to the process by which those skills are acquired. Assessment for assessment's sake is unhelpful and does little to enhance the learning process. Assessment should be an integral part of learning and should help to identify

---

Box 6.1 EXAMPLES OF DIFFERENT ASSESSMENT METHODS

	Activity	Subject area
Role play	Mock interviews	Business studies (Human Resources); Key skills (Communications)
Assignment		
Case study		
Short answer test		
Multi-choice questions		
Essay		
Data response		
Practical test		
Presentation		
Other examples?		

---

evidence of achievement, as well as inform the design or redesign of learning programmes:

> Assessment means much more than only measuring and judging; it should play a crucial role in the whole learning process. More emphasis is placed on congruence between instruction and assessment, which should both focus on stimulating the development of competences needed to perform various professional roles and on stimulating reflection and lifelong learning skills by involving students as active participants in the learning process.
>
> (Gulikers *et al.*, 2009: 174)

Much more emphasis is now placed on formative assessment. Research undertaken by Black and Wiliam (1998: 9–11) outlines some guiding principles for effective formative assessment. These stress that: feedback should emphasise the qualities of the work and areas for improvement and not make comparisons with other students' work; students should be trained in self-assessment so that they can see what they need to achieve; students should be provided with opportunities to reflect on their performance; and written work and tests should be relevant to learning aims. You may wish to reflect on these features as you begin to design your own assessment strategies.

Work on theories of learning has also influenced the debate on how we carry out assessment. We have discussed some of these in Chapter 4. Views on the ways in which individuals learn are contested. Broadly speaking, the current debate flows from two theoretical traditions: 'symbolic cognition' and 'situated cognition'. Symbolic processing, it is suggested, separates the learner from the environment, whereas theories of situated cognition place emphasis upon the contexts in which learning takes place. Learning is achieved by 'doing' as well as 'knowing' and by interacting with others through that learning process. Murphy (1999: ix) presents the difference as follows: 'The focus in understanding learning in this approach (symbolic cognition) is therefore the individual's internal mental processing and the symbolic representations of the mind. In the situated approach human knowledge and interaction are seen as inseparable from the world.'

In the context of apprenticeship learning, 'becoming' could be added to 'doing' and 'knowing' since apprentices are being introduced to communities of practice to which they hope to gain access (for further discussion, see Fuller and Unwin, 2004, 2010). The competences required to demonstrate 'becomingness' are, of course, more difficult to assess and run the danger of assessor subjectivity. The demonstration and assessment of personal, learning and thinking skills (PLTS) have posed similar challenges in this regard.

Gulikers (2006) has proposed a helpful Five Dimensional Framework for consideration when planning assessment. This includes:

1 the need for authentic assessment tasks;
2 consideration of the physical context in which assessment takes place (for example, workshop, laboratory);
3 the social context of assessment (for example, the relationship with workplace supervisors, other workers);
4 the output/form of assessment (for example, artefact, report); and
5 assessment criteria that clearly state what is being assessed.

It is important to remember that in designing assessment strategies we need, as teachers, to be aware of the different ways in which our students learn and also their preferences for assessment. Some students dislike having to make presentations in class; others become extremely anxious in examination halls. A catering student's ability to make a soufflé will ultimately have to be assessed by the production of the finished product, not by writing about it. Nevertheless, a written test may be used to assess the student's knowledge of the underlying food science theory, or this could be assessed by means of oral questioning. Similarly, trainee teachers are assessed on their ability to convert lesson plans into practical teaching activities. Subject knowledge and classroom practice have to be assessed equally but using different techniques. Bringing the two together can create significant challenges for beginning teachers/trainers, especially when faced with students who are not as enthused by the subject/topic as the teacher/trainer.

The focus of assessment should be on the student and the measurement of his or her achievement. Testing as a means of 'catching people out' does little to develop confidence or to identify real learning. Similarly, 'teaching to the test' may simply identify those with good memories or reflect a teacher's ability to spot questions, or to 'drill' students into producing model answers. Most of us will probably remember our attempts to revise only 7 out of the 10 available topics for an examination, in the hope that some of them would 'come up'. A quick glance at the education section in any bookshop will reveal that producing 'how to' guides and revision aids is a profitable business, but does little to encourage deep learning.

In our research for this book, one FE teacher remarked, 'Our business is to help students achieve'. At another college, a poster displayed in large print on the wall of the Learning Resources Centre read: 'Tell us what you want to learn and we'll do our very best to help you.' This should be a guiding principle in the design of assessment strategies. Such strategies should be formative and motivational and appropriate in their design for the purpose for which they are intended. Whereas assessment will be used for the purposes of selection, it should always have a strong emphasis on the recognition of achievement. It may now be useful to consider the different types of assessment:

> The term assessment refers to all those activities undertaken by teachers, and by their students in assessing themselves, which provide information to be used as feedback to modify the teaching and learning activities in which they are engaged. Such evidence becomes 'formative assessment' when the evidence is actually used to adapt the teaching work to meet the needs.
>
> (Black and Wiliam, 1998: 2)

Formative assessment

It is now generally recognised that assessment is most helpful when it forms an ongoing and integral part of teaching and learning so that feedback can be used at each stage in the planning/teaching/evaluation cycle. To be formative, assessment must have a feedback and a feed forward function (Brooks, 2004: 110; see also Black et al., 2003). Ecclestone et al. (2010: 33) note that:

> There is currently no watertight definition of formative assessment. It is often described as 'assessment for learning' as distinct from 'assessment of learning'.

The purpose of formative assessment is to provide a continuous process that charts achievement, identifies areas for development and indicates next steps for both teachers and learners. This latter point is crucial, as teachers need to draw on what they learn from the assessment process to refine their own practices and possibly even the curriculum. Formative assessment can be either formal or informal, or a combination of both. Ecclestone *et al.* (ibid.: 35) argue that:

> From a pedagogic perspective, assessment activities cannot be understood as formative unless evidence from feedback is actually used to adapt teaching and learning activities, either there and then or in future planning.

Action planning may be a part of the formative assessment process in that students should be encouraged to reflect on what they need to do in order to move on with their learning. All colleges now have continuous assessment procedures in place. Many vocational programmes require students to complete portfolios of evidence that testify to their achievement of each individual unit, and all the associated learning outcomes, of the qualification. You can find examples of such 'tracker' sheets and achievement logs on the websites of awarding organisations. These also provide a record for external verifiers. They provide a summary of achievement, but they provide no real feedback on how the student is progressing. They simply record the steps along the way to achieving the full award; the emphasis is on the 'can do' rather than the 'will do'.

A formative assessment should consider the 'will do' in that it should help to inform the next steps of the student's development. As teachers, we are constantly involved in formative assessment through informal means. For example, we find ourselves making the chance remark: 'That's very good, but next time why don't you think about including some conclusions at the end of your report?' or 'It would be really great if the next time you shampoo a client you ask if the water is at the right temperature' or 'Please ensure you clear your bench before using the saw'.

We should also encourage our students to reflect upon their performance. We may ask them to consider such questions as:

- In which parts of this assignment did I do well?
- In which parts of this assignment did I not do so well?
- Did I manage my time effectively?
- Are there areas that I would wish to improve?
- Do I need to access the Learning Resources Centre?
- Did I work effectively with other members of my team in completing this assignment?

Ideally, any formative assessment should involve a dialogue between student and teacher. Sometimes, this may take the form of a record that may be signed by both parties (see Figure 6.1 for an extract from a student's profile that is designed to provide formative assessment). The emphasis in the student's profile is on what has been learned and on what needs to be learned in the

STUDENT PROFILE

Name _____

Programme of study/course _____

Group _____

Date _____

Date of last tutorial _____

What assessed work has been completed since the last tutorial? (List)

_____

_____

What grades/marks/comments were received? (List)

_____

_____

Do these marks reflect a fair assessment of my performance?

_____

_____

In which assignments/tests did I do particularly well? (You should not just consider the overall grade, but did you make a significant improvement on previous work, or did you succeed in spite of some practical or personal difficulty?)

_____

_____

In which assignments/tests did I not do so well? (Why was this?)

_____

_____

Are there any areas in which I require help? _____

What are they? _____

_____

What do I intend to do about this? _____

_____

What do I want to achieve by the time of the next tutorial? _____

_____

How shall I achieve this? _____

_____

Signed   .... Student

          .... Tutor

Figure 6.1 Student profile

future. The purpose of the assessment should be to improve learning. Placing a tick or simply writing 'well done' at the end of a piece of work gives little indication of how the piece might be improved further. Tests may be useful in identifying what students know, or do not know, but unless accompanied by some feedback, they may provide no diagnosis as to the reasons why students do not know. It may simply give rise to students comparing marks. It may reflect some unsatisfactory teaching. There is always a danger too that some of the correct answers may have been arrived at through guesswork.

One of the most important uses of formative assessment is to establish a student's level of ability at the outset, or before they join a programme. This is important for all students, but particularly so when teaching those for whom English may not be their first language. A part-time lecturer in beauty therapy interviewed by one of the authors expressed concerns that some of her students had insufficient command of English to cope with the theoretical aspects of the course, although their practical skills were strong. She had not discovered this until some time into her teaching on the programme because she only works at the college in the evenings and has very little face-to-face contact with the course manager. Communication is often through notes left in the register, or brief emails. She became aware of the problem when she set a written test. She is concerned that the students' lack of written communication skills will hinder their progress. She feels that an ESOL screening test should have been given at induction so that professional help could be appropriately targeted; although she says she 'is happy to help', she recognises that she does not have the expertise required for supporting ESOL.

It is interesting to note that within the current specification guidance, emphasis is placed on the importance of initial assessment in order to determine the appropriate level at which a student should prepare for functional skills. Good practice dictates that this should be the starting point for any programme of study, and that appropriate guidance and induction should be provided for all students embarking upon a course of further education. Inappropriate course choice can be an important factor in student retention (Huddleston, 2004). The recommendations for increasingly personalised learning make the initial induction assessment process central to appropriate course choice and eventual successful outcome.

Brooks (2007) offers some very helpful guidance in terms of providing positive feedback to students. She suggests, for example, the importance of giving clear indication within an assignment brief of the criteria for assessment. In this way, it is easy to demonstrate the extent to which these have been met and for students to plan, and later to evaluate, their work against the criteria. If you look at the qualification specifications for, say, applied A levels, you will see that the assessment criteria are clearly indicated, including guidance on what would constitute achievement across the grade bands. Brooks also stresses the importance of timely and balanced feedback – highlighting positives and drawing attention to areas for development.

It is helpful to look carefully at the specifications for the qualifications for which you will be preparing and assessing students. As in this example taken from the Level 1 Introductory Certificate in Basic Construction Skills (6217-01), it clearly states what learning outcomes are required in order to pass the unit (for example, Unit 1 'Fixing skirting to a timber background', states 9 specific learning outcomes that need to be demonstrated from practical activity and a further 11 learning outcomes that are required in terms of underpinning knowledge). Of course, the underpinning knowledge should also be clearly demonstrated within the practical activity.

Let us put the two together to see how this also helps to contextualise the learning. Using the same unit specification example, Unit 1 'Fixing skirting to timber background', learning outcome 4 states: 'candidate will be able to safely use and store tools and equipment' during the practical activity. If we look at the learning outcomes listed within the 'Underpinning knowledge' section of the specification, learning outcome 10 states: 'candidate will be able to state how maintenance of tools and equipment is carried out' (source: www.cityand guilds.com). Clearly, the two are interrelated; if the student does not understand the importance of maintaining tools in good and safe working condition, he or she cannot fulfil the practical activity adequately. Remember that earlier in this chapter we referred to a tutor's comment: 'Please ensure you clear your bench before using the saw'. This is exactly the type of formative feedback that could feed into the successful achievement of the learning outcomes just described. When the tutor is cast in the role of assessor, he or she will be looking to see if this informal feedback has been incorporated into the student's practice.

Summative assessment

Summative assessment is used to ascertain whether the aims of a course or programme have been achieved (for example, through the setting of a final examination). Examinations, or written tests, often have an important role in selecting or deselecting those for the next phase of education (for example, from FE into HE or from a BTEC Level 2 programme to a Level 3 programme). For this reason, summative assessment is often referred to as 'high stakes' assessment because, frequently, much depends upon it. Harlen and Deakin Crick (2002) suggest that summative assessment:

- narrows the curriculum and encourages rote learning;
- widens the gap between high and low achievers;
- promotes high anxiety levels among students; and
- erodes the self-esteem of low attainers.

Summative assessment has increasingly assumed an important accountability function for colleges, since they are required to provide detailed information on assessment outcomes. There are funding implications too (for example, in government-supported programmes for apprenticeships, or programmes for job seekers, where colleges receive a final payment when qualification outcomes have been achieved). Within competence-based qualifications, summative assessment is made to ensure that all units of the qualification have been achieved. In many vocational programmes, the student's portfolio is the collection of work that provides the evidence that the requirements for each unit have been met. This evidence can be derived from a variety of sources: written tests, witness statements, artefacts, photographs, musical or theatrical performances, longer written coursework assignments.

REFLECTION

In the example below, a lecturer has prepared an assignment for students following Edexcel AS GCE (Single Award: 8761) in Leisure Studies. The assignment focuses on Unit 3 of the specification, in particular 3.2 'Operational aspects related to the leisure customer'. Read through the assignment and consider the extent to which the lecturer has provided clear guidance on what has to be achieved and by what criteria the piece will be assessed. How has he used the formative feedback provided by the examiner's report to inform the design of the assignment and the guidance provided for students?

UNIT 3 THE LEISURE CUSTOMER

3.2 Operational aspects related to the leisure customer

Background

At the end of last term, Jane Bailey, the manager of Sunny Park Leisure Centre in Boomtown, presented to the group. She outlined details of the centre's vision for customer service, along with procedures in place to ensure continued high levels of customer service. Jane also shared with us examples of customer feedback from the 'comments box' in the foyer.

Jane would like to improve the levels of customer service further and is looking for your advice!

You are required to investigate a different leisure organisation and evaluate its levels of customer service.

Using the information you obtain, you are required to prepare a report for Jane outlining your findings and making recommendations on what Sunny Park Leisure Centre can learn from the organisation you have studied.

It would help if the leisure organisation you study is involved in similar activities to Sunny Park (i.e. swimming, gymnasium, etc.) although this is not essential. Please ensure you get my agreement on your choice of organisation before you start.

Please read through the next section in detail as it outlines exactly what you have to do.

Spring term assignment

The leisure customer – operational aspects

1   Choose a leisure organisation (preferably a fitness organisation) near to you. It may help if it is one that you or your family are familiar with.

2   Make a 'mystery visit' to the organisation. Gather in-depth information about the organisation's provision of customer service that you experienced. This should include, but is not limited to:

- quality of the service you experienced;
- helpfulness of staff;
- cleanliness of facilities;
- access for customers, signs, etc.;
- price;
- opening times;
- range of services on offer; and
- reception procedures.

3   Interview the manager about how they approach customer service. Review any relevant documents like mission statements (often on display), or customer service training manuals or procedures. Evaluate whether these are effective and suitable in providing customer service.

4   Reflect on your findings and produce some key learning outcomes about good customer service that you can use to make recommendations for Sunny Park.

Required outputs

Your full report is required by the *end of this term*. You have 10 weeks left, so please plan your time carefully.

You will need to produce two documents:

1   a word-processed report (at least six pages), containing each of the four sections of the assignment; and

2   a PowerPoint presentation summarising some key recommendations for Sunny Park (you should plan for a presentation of about 8–10 minutes).

Report

Section 1: Write a section that describes the leisure organisation you have chosen, including its location, range of services and other background details. Include what sort of leisure customers the organisation is aimed at.

Section 2: After your 'mystery visit', write up this section of the report based on the detailed notes you took during your visit. (Write a list of the areas you are going to look at *in advance*.) You are required to *evaluate* each aspect of customer service you experienced, so under each heading, make sure you write the service you experienced and how effective you felt it was. Separate the positive and negative points. This should be the longest section of the report.

Section 3: After you have interviewed the manager and collected documents relating to customer service, write up a review of how *effective* and *suitable* they are. If you cannot get an interview, often documents such as mission statements are up on display.

Section 4: This is the conclusion. Reflect on the previous three sections and summarise the *positive and negative* aspects of customer service that you experienced. Where you highlight any negative aspects, try to make *recommendations* on how these could have been improved.

Presentation

Using your assignment report, prepare a presentation for Jane Bailey of Sunny Park Leisure Centre. Outline your key learning outcomes from the different areas of customer service you experienced and apply these to Sunny Park in the form of some recommendations.

The presentation should last for 8–10 minutes.

Assessment criteria

To gain access to the highest mark bands:

*   Your report should give examples of a range of aspects of customer service you received on your mystery visit.
*   You need to evaluate how successful the organisation is in serving customers.
*   This should be possible through your conclusion as you assess its strengths and weaknesses.
*   You also need to get hold of a range of documents such as mission statements, training manuals and customer comments forms, and comment on their effectiveness and suitability. To do this, you will need to have secured an

interview with the manager or other member of staff. You will also need their permission to include these.

Special notes for your assignment

*   Please ensure you have agreed with me the leisure organisation you choose before you make your mystery visit.
*   Before you make the mystery visit, please tell your parents/carers where you are going.
*   When conducting your mystery visit, do so as part of a general 'look around' the organisation. Do not pretend to be a potential member and have a sales manager show you around, as they are busy people.
*   If you are unable to find a suitable leisure organisation, Jane has given the group permission to use her other local facilities, which are:
    –   Marsh Field Swimming Pool
    –   Brook Farm Recreation Centre
    –   Cherry Common Leisure Centre.
*   Please do not take photographs inside any organisation unless you have prior permission. Do not take photographs inside any changing area.
*   As part of this assignment, you may want to interview some customers. Please make sure you ask permission from the manager first. Also, you will need to show the manager and me your questionnaire in advance.
*   Remember that many organisations have their own websites. You can use these as part of your work. Please make sure you remember to include any websites visited in your references.
*   Please enclose any extra resources as appendices to your work. These could include photographs, leaflets, photocopies of mission statements or customer service policies, questionnaires, interview notes.

And, finally

*   Please check your work before you hand it in for errors or for poor English.
*   Please make sure all pages are numbered and that you have completed each of the four sections of the report, as well as the presentation.
*   Please confirm this coursework is all your own work before you submit it.
*   This work is due in its *final form* on *2 April*.

In the following section, the lecturer provides a rationale for the assignment design. Consider how effectively he has taken into account the needs of assessment in its design.

RATIONALE FOR THIS ASSIGNMENT

This assignment was designed for the Edexcel AS GCE in Leisure Studies (Single Award: 8761) and specifically for Unit 3.2 'Operational aspects related to the leisure customer'.

The starting point for designing any piece of coursework is the 'what you need to learn' section of the qualification specification. However, it is wise to look much further than this, as has been done in this case.

The 'Introduction' to the unit clearly states that 'theoretical and practical' activities are required, and that these should lead to 'analysis' and 'interpretation' of leisure organisations. The assumption has been made that the class time has been quite theoretical, so this assignment has been designed to be wholly practical in nature, centred on a mystery visit.

The assignment has also been designed so that some points of 'analysis' are made during the visit, and that a presentation of recommendations will require 'interpretation' and 'evaluation', therefore allowing higher ability candidates to reach the highest mark bands.

As well as the specification itself, the teacher's guide, mark scheme and examiner's report were also studied from the Edexcel website. These also helped to guide the development of coursework and contributed to the rationale for this particular assignment.

The teacher's guide contains 'mock' coursework. This was a useful basis for constructing this particular assignment. It also contains examples of students' work with both teachers' comments and the examiners' comments. Again, these all help to shape an assignment that directly meets the requirements of the examiners, ensuring that the students get every opportunity to gain the highest marks possible. A good example is that only in the teacher's guide does it become clear that for section 3.2 there is only requirement for one organisation to be analysed in depth. Without viewing this, one may have created an assignment where students analysed several organisations, which would have sacrificed depth of analysis and, therefore, marks.

The examiner's report is a very useful resource as it is the one document written after the setting of the specification and mark scheme and, therefore, gives a very practical viewpoint on common errors made by students. In the case of this assignment, the examiner's report was relied upon to create an assignment to help students avoid common pitfalls that result in lower marks.

In terms of the specifics of this assignment, it has been designed around a fitness/swimming establishment, to which it is hoped most students would have access. The assignment has also been designed to include a talk from a leisure centre manager so the area is familiar to them.

The context of the assignment is that a real leisure manager wants 'recommendations' from each of the students. This is designed not only to motivate them, as the coursework has a real purpose outside the qualification itself, but also to make it feel more like a vocational piece of work that is not just theoretical in nature.

The assignment is also designed so that, while students are encouraged to use leisure centres, there is flexibility (with the lecturer's approval). It is also acknowledged that not all students are members of, or would have access to, their own centres. For this reason, agreement with the Boomtown manager has been arranged so 'sister' organisations can be visited by students if necessary without further specific permission.

The 'What you need to know' section of the specification makes it clear that a mystery visit needs to be undertaken to gain information about customer service. This is, therefore, the central theme of the assignment and the largest section of the report. In addition, the section of the specification requires understanding of 'mission statements', 'customer service policies and procedures' and 'training programmes'. Again, all these are central to the assignment to ensure that students are clear about what they need to do to access the highest mark bands.

Wherever possible, the language of the examiners is used to ensure students are encouraged to undertake the correct level of work (for example, 'evaluate', 'apply'). The assignment goes further than this, however, in being a practical piece of work requiring a final presentation to a 'real' customer with recommendations. This encourages the students to think about converting the data they have collected into information, and then evaluating this information to be able to make useful recommendations.

It is acknowledged that not every student will be able, or motivated, to obtain the highest mark bands. For this reason, the assignment allows for differentiation. For example, in order to obtain mark band 3, a review of several documents needs to be undertaken. The assignment encourages students to interview a member of staff and gain access to these documents, but also encourages students who are unable, or unwilling, to do this to collect evidence such as mission statements from the public areas. This could get them to mark band 2.

The assignment spells out the key assessment criteria in the students' own language, so the whole process of access to different mark bands is transparent.

Towards the end of the assignment, several practical issues are covered, such as parental/carer knowledge, photography in changing rooms, permission for interviewing customers, etc. It is important for assignments to contain this sort of information as it is wholly inappropriate for lecturers to set pieces of work that could encourage students to act in inappropriate ways or put themselves at risk.

The assignment provides students with an opportunity to understand customer service around the leisure customer and to experience it for themselves. It also covers all the areas detailed in the specification, and with the reality of the 'feedback presentation', it directs students towards the higher skills and, therefore, higher mark bands.

The assignment is also designed to address some areas of key skills development. The data collection is qualitative, so while there is little opportunity for application of number, the assignment is designed around several other key skills. Communication is addressed through interviewing leisure managers and, of course, through the final group presentation. IT is developed through research and through the report and presentation. Improving own learning and performance is developed through allowing the students to plan their own work schedules to complete the assignment in the allotted 10-week period.

In the case of NVQs/SVQs, or in those qualifications that have now been incorporated into the QCF and have replaced NVQs (see Chapter 3), candidates will present themselves for summative assessment whenever they consider they can demonstrate that they have met the learning outcomes for the unit (that is, through the production of evidence that can be judged in terms of its meeting the assessment criteria for the unit). Evidence may take a variety of forms, for example:

- copies of documents appropriately word-processed;
- artefacts produced in practical classes;
- log books signed by supervisors testifying that certain procedures have been undertaken (for example, in retailing, stock rotation);
- witness testimonies;
- observation;
- simulation; and
- APEL.

Essentially, the purpose of the assessment is to verify that the candidate 'can do' what is described in the learning outcomes for each unit and has demonstrated the underpinning knowledge and understanding required to operate in the work environment at the required level for the qualification. Much of the assessment evidence will be derived from observing the candidate in the workplace, for example: 'Prepare to receive goods in the retail environment' (learning outcome 3, Unit BO3 'Receive goods and material into storage in the retail environment' from the Level 2 Retail Skills qualification). However, underpinning knowledge and understanding may have to be confirmed by questioning, for example: 'Show that they know legal and company requirements for maintaining security and safety while receiving deliveries' (assessment criterion 7, learning outcome 2, Unit BO3).

Although summative assessment plays an important part in assessing students and, it could be argued, is the only means of assessment in competence-based qualifications, ideally, this type of assessment should always be underpinned by a diagnostic process that will help students identify how they can improve their performance next time. Competence-based qualifications attest to candidates' abilities through a series of 'can do' statements; however, there is little scope for indicating how well a candidate 'can do' something over a period of time. As individuals, we all know that we can perform a whole range of activities, but that we will perform some of them much better on some days than on other days, and under different sets of conditions and circumstances.

As teachers, we need to be aware of the range of assessment techniques available to us and to select those most appropriate for the piece of work we are trying to assess. In practice, we are likely to adopt a range of approaches within our teaching programmes. We now consider some of these different approaches.

Extended writing, examinations and written tests

There has been a considerable shift away from terminal examinations involving essay-type assessment under controlled conditions during recent years, particularly within vocational programmes. However, criticisms concerning 'lack of rigour' in coursework assessment procedures, coupled with the increasing opportunities for plagiarism via the Internet, have led to the inclusion of externally set and marked tests in both GCSE and GCE programmes. In GCSE programmes, assessment, which initially included a fair proportion of coursework, has reverted to examination-based terminal assessment, with a corresponding reduction in coursework. This trend is likely to continue and reforms to assessment within A level, for example, are likely to include emphasis upon terminal examinations, a move away from modular design, restrictions on the opportunity for resitting examinations, or modules thereof. In many programmes, coursework has already been replaced by controlled assessment (that is, assessment where the tasks set are regulated by the awarding body, even if internally set) and the conditions under which the work is undertaken are restricted, in terms of time, location, materials, degree of teacher and other external support. At the time of writing, these issues are being hotly debated and you will need to keep abreast of current developments within your subject area. Make sure you check the websites of the awarding bodies for whose qualifications you are preparing students. You must ensure that you enter students for the current specification.

With essay-type tests, care has to be taken over the extent to which the assessor's subjectivity gets in the way of making reliable and consistent judgements. With only one assessor, a considerable degree of subjectivity can 'creep in'. In an examination constructed around essays, within a tightly regulated timeframe, there is only a limited capacity to cover the entire syllabus. This may result in some candidates being unable to show their real ability if they have 'spotted' the wrong question. In contrast, those who favour the competence-based approach would argue that this method of assessment ensures complete coverage in that the achievement of every learning outcome for every unit must be demonstrated. Nevertheless, the essay does test students' abilities to organise material, present arguments and interpret the question in their own way. It allows for a degree of creativity and individuality, though this individuality can create problems in the marking. Since no two essays will be alike, it is important to establish clear criteria, in advance, by which the resulting essays can be reliably assessed. An enormous number of candidates may sit public examinations. It is, therefore, essential that marking is standardised and that it is subject to checks and double-checks. Currently, there is significant development in the area of e-marking.

As a beginning teacher in FE, you should take every opportunity to learn from others: more experienced colleagues, perhaps some who already act as verifiers and external examiners; attend the training events offered by awarding bodies; try to visit some of the workplaces where your part-time students work and observe how workplace supervisors assess work-based qualifications. Look at examples of assignments, past examination papers, mark schemes and examiners' reports displayed on the awarding body websites.

In all externally set and marked examinations, there is always some process of verification and moderation, often several layers of checking in large 'high stakes' public examinations. That is, an external examiner or moderator will check a sample of scripts to ensure that marking is consistent across the range of candidates and markers. One useful way of doing this for new teachers is to sample a range of scripts and to mark them according to the stated assessment criteria, and then cross-check the results against those of an experienced teacher, preferably one who has also acted as an external examiner or verifier. Try to identify if, and why, differences have occurred.

You should always keep in mind that many of your students will be alarmed at the thought of having to undertake extended pieces of writing, to sit in examination halls, to produce results under timed conditions. For those who do not have to sit examinations, but who have to produce coursework assignments, which often include extended writing, there are often other problems. A group of students to whom we spoke during researching this book told us that: 'there are just too many assignments'; 'they all come together'; 'as soon as you've done one, there's another'; 'the staff don't seem to know what they are doing'; 'it's just doing my head in'. For their staff, it also means a huge marking workload.

There are, of course, other ways of assessing students than through essay writing. These can range from simple questions requiring tick-box answers to those questions that are more unstructured or open-ended and require a student to think more deeply about a topic, to analyse, reflect and present arguments. Obviously, this form of extended written assessment is far more suitable for some courses and topics than for others. For example, in childcare programmes, students may be required to develop an in-depth case study of a child in an early years setting. This type of extended writing also requires very strict ethical controls to be in place, including parental consent, guaranteed anonymity to respondents, security of data, and access to drafts in order to check matters of fact.

Highly structured questions are, obviously, much easier to mark than unstructured questions. Multiple-choice questions are used by some awarding bodies and the answers can be pre-coded for ease of marking, nowadays often electronically. In designing such tests, care has to be taken in eliminating ambiguity from the possible answers offered, since there must only be one 'right' answer. This method of testing purports to offer wide coverage of a syllabus but it offers nothing in the way of analysis or interpretation, dealing primarily with recall. Minton (1991: 194) suggests that, 'Multi-choice objective tests of the kind used by examining boards are best left to experts to compile. Few people have the skills to write them.' They can, however, provide a useful means of checking from time to time on students' learning. They can identify any misunderstandings that might have occurred. However, a balance has to be struck between the time given to testing and that given to real learning. If too much time is spent preparing for tests, including teaching to the test, then this will impede the overall learning process. It can also be demotivating for students. Testing should be seen as part of an overall learning strategy in which there are a variety of assessment methods.

In writing short-answer questions, it is important that the teacher makes absolutely clear what is required; questions should be unambiguous. It is useful to include guidance on marks awarded for each question so that a student can see the relative importance of the questions and plan the timing accordingly.

Box 6.2 shows a short-answer question suitable for Level 2 Business Administration. It covers the topic of reception duties.

Objective tests require very little judgement on the part of the marker, because there is only one predetermined correct answer and they can be easily marked online (computer-assisted assessment). In some cases, the students will receive the results online immediately on completion of the test. Examples of objective tests include: multiple-choice questions; matching questions; true/false statements; assertion–reason questions.

Box 6.3 shows an example of a matching question that might be used with some Level 1 catering students.

Assessing 'generic skills'

> Generic skills have been an element of education policy and practice in the UK for over thirty years, although variously labelled, for example transferable skills, common skills, core skills, key skills, essential skills, employability skills, enterprise skills, functional skills and personal learning and thinking skills (PLTS).
>
> (Fettes, 2012: 116)

Box 6.2 LEVEL 2 BUSINESS ADMINISTRATION

'Receive and direct visitors'

1 List 3 skills/qualities required by a good receptionist

i) _____

ii) _____

iii) _____

(3 marks)

2 What procedures should be followed when a visitor with an appointment arrives at your company?

_____

_____

_____

(5 marks)

3 What information should be included when leaving messages for members of your company that have been left on the reception answerphone?

_____

_____

_____

(5 marks)

4 Where would you find the following information?

• a copy of the company's Annual Report _____

• the telephone extension of the Personnel Director _____

• the nearest first aid box _____

• the telephone number of a local taxi company _____

• a brochure of the company's product range _____

(5 marks)

Box 6.3 MATCHING PAIRS

Draw lines to link the type of pastry with the correct dish

Hot water crust   Apple dumplings

Choux pastry   Sausage rolls

Short crust pastry   Pork pie

Suet pastry   Eclairs

Puff pastry   Plum tart

                                   Peach crumble

                                   Yorkshire pudding

                                   Fruit cobbler

Generic skills are different from subject-specific or sector-specific skills because they cover a range of abilities that are useful across a range of contexts, occupations and in life more generally. Examples include: 'the ability to work in teams'; 'communicating effectively'; 'being able to solve problems'; and 'planning effectively'. As we discussed in Chapter 3, functional skills (English, mathematics and ICLT) are replacing the broader key skills, but many courses will retain the aim of supporting students to recognise that they can apply similar strategies across a range of learning contexts.

Functional skills are included in the specifications for vocational qualifications. If you look at these, you will see that the notion of 'embededness' is seen as being central to their successful development (in other words, context is the key). For example, the NPTC Level 2 Diploma for Veterinary Care Assistants (0448-02) Unit 203, learning outcome 1 includes assessment criteria that require learners to 'communicate with clients, colleagues, other industry professionals and members of the public using appropriate methods of communication to meet the needs of others' and also 'to produce client invoices and receive payments'. Both of these activities could contribute towards the achievement of functional skills in, for example, English – 'speaking listening and communicating'; and mathematics – 'identify and obtain necessary information to tackle the problem'. Although functional skills will be separately assessed, both externally and internally, in order to achieve the qualification, students can gain valuable experience of developing and practising functional skills during other parts of their programme. The qualification regulators in the UK all stress the need to connect the assessment of functional skills to meaningful contexts:

Assessment must focus on functionality and the effective application of speaking, listening and communication, reading and writing skills in purposeful contexts and scenarios that reflect real-life situations.

(Ofqual, WGA, CEA, 2009: 14)

Some of your students may be less than enthusiastic about 'doing' maths and English, which they thought they had left behind at school, but when it is situated within the context of their vocational programme and it is seen to have a purpose, then it can be potentially motivating. After all, it is quite important for a trainee chef to know: how to 'scale up' a recipe for a larger number of diners; what the appropriate profit margin should be on a pot of coffee; and how many portions can be obtained from roast duck and how many will be needed for the banquet.

Box 6.4 shows a short-answer test that could provide some experience for practising functional skills (mathematics, Level 1) 'add, subtract, multiply and divide whole numbers using a range of strategies'.

Box 6.4 EXAMPLE OF TEST FOR PRACTISING FUNCTIONAL SKILLS

Here are the figures for 'Krazy Kuts' hair salon during the last week.

	Mon	Tues	Wed	Thurs	Fri	Sat
Cut and blow dry	6	10	8	16	25	20
Perm	2	3	2	5	7	10
Shampoo and set	5	8	7	13	21	20
Tints	4	2	0	4	5	16

1   How many more perms were sold on Saturday than on Tuesday?

2   How many 'cut and blow dry' appointments were made during the week?

3   If a perm costs £53, how much revenue have I received from perms this week?

4   Which is the least popular treatment?

5   A tint is priced at £35 and a cut and blow dry at £28. If I offer a 15% discount to customers booking both treatments, how much will the customer pay?

6   If the salon decided to close on one day of the week, which day should it be? Why?

REFLECTION

Try to think of the opportunities presented for functional skills development within your own professional subject area. This is often referred to as mapping. In order to do this, you might use the planning matrix in Box 6.5.

Box 6.5 PLANNING MATRIX

Functional skill	Opportunities
English	Select, read and understand and compare texts and use them to gather information, ideas, arguments and opinions. (Skill standard Level 2) **Examples:**
Mathematics	Apply mathematics in an organised way to find solutions to straightforward practical problems for different purposes. (Skill standard Level 1 Analysing) **Examples:**
Information technology	Use simple searches to find information; select relevant information that matches requirements of given task. (Skill standard Entry 3) **Examples:**

Source: Ofqual, WGA, CEA (2009) Functional Skills Criteria for English, mathematics and ICT.

Oral test

Oral tests are now an integral part of student assessment. Many programmes often include some form of presentation to a variety of audiences. At Level 4, they often form a substantial component of assessment; for example, when presenting design solutions (art and design programmes); and presenting marketing plans (business programmes). Presentation skills are included within the specification for functional skills English; for example, at Level 2, a candidate would be expected to 'make effective presentations' (skill standard) including 'adapt contributions to suit audience, purpose and situation', 'present information and ideas clearly and persuasively to others' (coverage and range statement) (Ofqual, WGA, CEA, 2009: 12). Most students would benefit from being able to contribute to a discussion or give a short talk regardless of the level or nature of their programme.

The assessment of such skills is challenging and can, of course, be highly subjective. The assessor has to be very clear about what is being tested and has to make this known to the candidates well in advance. There should be a mark sheet available, and it is helpful to have another marker or moderator present in the audience. This can help to eliminate tutor bias. A sample mark sheet is shown in Box 6.6. The relative weighting of the marks can be adjusted according to the purpose of the assignment. If you were assessing students' abilities in public speaking, for example, one might want to include marks for diction or, in the case of a poem, a mark for interpretation.

Box 6.6 SAMPLE MARK SHEET

	Marks awarded	Maximum marks allowed
Content:	____	20
Structure:	____	15
Suitability of language for purpose:	____	10
Clarity of exposition:	____	15
Accuracy of information:	____	20
Use of visual aids:	____	5
Ability to handle questions:	____	10
Appearance:	____	5
	____	100

As with all assessment, feedback is extremely important in this type of activity, and it has to be handled with great sensitivity. It is often less threatening to students if they begin by making short group presentations in which each can play a small part before asking them to embark on individual presentations. This requires detailed knowledge of the group and a supportive environment in which to work.

Assignments

As we saw earlier in this chapter (Sunny Park Leisure Centre), these are much longer pieces of assessed work and form a very important element in the assessment strategy of vocational qualifications. The assignment is central to the learning process and should bring together and integrate different components of the programme (for example, covering and making clear the connections between learning outcomes across a unit; why learning in one area of the programme is relevant for application in other parts of the course). The young carpenter needs to be able to measure accurately the length of timber required to complete the skirting board. Assignments should enable students to learn and develop their knowledge and to practise applying their skills in a vocational context. The assessment is based on the evidence submitted within the assignment. Designing and writing assignments is a complex task and is very different from writing essay questions or short-answer tests. In Chapter 5, and earlier in this chapter, we looked at the design of assignments. Every assignment should carry with it a set of assessment criteria and students should be absolutely clear about what is required and how marks are allocated.

Within qualification specifications, clear assessment and grading criteria are expressed within the unit guidance in such a way that teachers and candidates know exactly what is required to achieve a pass, merit or distinction grade, or, in other cases, a numeric or literal grade.

Full details on assessment procedures for all qualifications are available from the awarding organisations and, because they are subject to revision from time to time, readers are advised to ensure that they have the latest available guidance.

The marking of assignments requires cooperation among different staff members teaching the programme. If the assignment is to be truly integrative, then it should be jointly designed and written by the course team as well as assessed by them. Coverage of the learning outcomes will be cross-checked against the evidence provided in the assignment. This evidence may take a variety of forms. Within the same assignment a student may be required to:

- produce some written work (for example, write a report);
- undertake some practical activity (for example, change an oil filter);
- give a short oral presentation (for example, on work experience);
- produce a set of drawings (for example, for a draft design/prototype);
- record audio video tapes (performing arts); and
- complete artwork.

Assessment within vocational programmes may involve using a variety of evidence and need not be done on the basis of paper-based evidence alone. Teachers have sometimes been reluctant to design assignments that will allow students to present evidence in different forms (for example, using digital recordings, photographs or log books). This may, in part, reflect the culture of academic teaching where the only acceptable evidence is the production of written work, often under examination conditions. Group work may be seen as tantamount to 'cheating'. The issue of plagiarism raises serious concerns for the integrity of the examinations and awarding system. There is a further concern that relates to the difficulty of providing valid and reliable methods of assessing work that is not written.

In designing practical assignments, it is necessary to strike a balance between the assessment of the finished product/design/result and the skills and knowledge used in achieving that result. For example, what percentage of the marks should be given to manual skills, to the selection of appropriate tools or materials, and what percentage to the final product? If a student worked with little regard to health and safety procedures, should this invalidate the finished result? All these considerations need to be taken into account when drawing up the assessment criteria for an assignment.

It can be a useful strategy to show students examples of work that have been completed by former students, subject, of course, to their agreement. With a teacher's help, students can be encouraged to identify the strengths and weaknesses of different approaches. This is particularly helpful in the case of adult students who may be returning to learning after a considerable break and who may be anxious about the production of assignments. You have already met some of these students in Chapter 2.

You will gather from all of this that the process of assessment and recording achievement is an extremely complex one. The teacher is required to act in a number of different roles, ranging from being purely a marker to being a guide, counsellor and mentor. Some of these roles are potentially conflicting. As a tutor, you may know that a student is undergoing a series of personal difficulties, which you feel may have impinged upon the production of a good piece of work. How, then, are you to assess the work? In terms of a strict 'standards' methodology, the work does not meet the criteria. As tutor, you are aware of the reasons why this work may not meet the standards. This brings us back to the fundamental purposes of assessment and the balance between the formative and summative elements. The tutor has to strike a balance between directing the students and 'letting the students go'. Writing from the context of adult education, Jenny Rogers (1992: 63) writes:

> Some teachers, who rightly pride themselves on the standard of their own work, sometimes find their students' mistakes too painful to contemplate, and will often seize the work and do the difficult bits themselves, sometimes under the impression that students are grateful for such professional

additions. There may be occasional students too placid to object, but most people feel cheated if someone else does all the hard work for them. They want the satisfaction and sense of achievement of learning to cope for themselves.

Students may be encouraged to involve themselves in both peer and self-assessment. Peer assessment needs to be handled very sensitively and should not be embarked upon until the teacher has a good knowledge of the group. Guidance should also be provided on the criteria to be applied in making peer assessments. Comments such as 'that was great' or 'that was rubbish' are to be avoided. On the other hand, self-evaluation is an important part of the learning process because only the individual knows his or her objectives in undertaking the programme and should, therefore, be best able to judge whether or not such objectives are being achieved. This may be a new idea to some of your students and they will require guidance in developing techniques of reflection and self-evaluation. You may wish to provide some standard form on which students can record their own evaluation or you may prefer simply to provide some prompts. As students become more practised, they will probably be able to write a short evaluation for each assignment undertaken.

Marshall and Rowland (1993) have drawn attention to the importance of self-evaluation in the learning process and of its role in helping to provide student independence. Students should also be encouraged to discuss their assessments with tutors and there may well be a case for involving students in joint marking with tutors. This can be highly motivational.

In summarising its research findings on assessment and classroom practice, the Assessment Reform Group (1999) emphasises the following key points in ensuring that learning is central to the assessment process. Although its research focused upon learning within the compulsory education phase (hence the use of the term 'pupils'), the points are valid for learners of all ages:

- the provision of effective feedback to pupils;
- the active involvement of pupils in their own learning;
- adjusting teaching to take account of the results of assessment;
- a recognition of the profound influence assessment has on the motivation and self-esteem of pupils; and
- the need for pupils to be able to assess themselves and understand how to improve.

(Assessment Reform Group, 1999: 4–5)

Competence-based assessment

As shown in Chapter 3, and referred to earlier in this chapter, in competence-based assessment the assessor must make judgements concerning the sufficiency of evidence supplied by the candidate to ensure that all learning outcomes have been achieved. Evidence can take a variety of forms but the assessor needs to be assured of its validity. The assessor will want to make sure that he or she has satisfactory answers to a number of questions, including:

- Is this the candidate's own work?
- On how many occasions was this task performed?
- If a 'real-life' situation is unavailable, how reliable are those results achieved through a simulation?

The following all provide legitimate forms of evidence. You may wish to consider how you would reliably assess them:

- displays and presentations;
- practical demonstration of skills;
- planning and organising events;
- creative use of photographs;
- making and producing models/drawings/paintings;
- group work;
- designing products and services;
- projects undertaken by individuals or groups; and
- role-play work.

Evidence can be derived from observing the performance of a student within a 'real' working environment (for example, a candidate could be observed welding metal within a workshop situation). The candidate could also be assessed on a finished product. If processes cannot be directly observed by the assessor, then evidence from videotape or audiotape may also be used, providing it can be authenticated. Evidence could also be collected by questioning the candidate. There must be sufficient evidence to meet all of the assessment criteria for the unit.

Often, evidence collected to fulfil the criteria for one learning outcome may be relevant to, and provide evidence for, the achievement of other learning outcomes. It is not necessary to generate a separate piece of evidence for every criterion – the role of the teacher is to help students identify what evidence may count towards the achievement of those criteria.

Let us consider an example. 'Maintaining a safe and healthy working environment' is central to workplace practice and appears as a unit in the majority of occupational qualifications. The achievement of this unit cannot be assessed in isolation because sound and safe working is an essential element of good practice. Evidence of this should permeate the candidate's work across all units of a qualification. Those responsible for making assessment judgements must have regard to this across the whole qualification.

Assessment involves making judgements about the evidence that the candidate provides. This assessment may involve observing a candidate's performance in the workplace, where performance evidence cannot be assessed; supplementary evidence may be used to infer performance. For example, you may want to question a candidate about certain activities or set some form of written test. However, it should be remembered, when considering performance and supplementary evidence, that the two sorts of evidence complement each other. Activities that provide supplementary evidence do not exist in a vacuum. They are designed to support the performance evidence you have collected by confirming the knowledge and understanding of the candidate; for example: 'Why did you decide to use that particular product on this client's skin?' or 'Why did you select that story for your group of 2 year olds after lunch?'

Competence-based assessment may be carried out by college staff within the college, even for candidates who are in employment, though sometimes college staff may go to the employers' premises to carry out assessment. Where assessment is carried out within the college, it is very important that the conditions under which it is performed are as realistic as possible (that is, as far as possible under the normal conditions and pressures of the workplace and with the use of appropriate equipment and facilities). Within colleges, assessment may be undertaken in training restaurants, hairdressing salons, motor vehicle workshops, or training offices where services are offered to the public.

For full-time students working towards competence-based qualifications, work placements have to be found so that they can demonstrate competence to workplace standards, as in the case of college-based apprenticeships. Here, assessment may provide challenges since it will depend upon the goodwill and cooperation of those employers willing to provide work placements. In some sectors, it is extremely difficult to access sufficient placements and there is often competition for them. Consistency across work placements may be variable; while some may provide excellent opportunities for candidates to demonstrate competence, others may be of a poor standard. Some colleges often have productive links with industry and provide specialist courses for employers, often tailored to the specific training requirements of the company. In return, the college may benefit from the donation of industry standard equipment (we saw some of these in Chapter 2).

There are some key questions upon which you may wish to reflect concerning issues of assessment within such qualifications:

- Who is assessing?
- What is being assessed?
- How valid and reliable is the evidence?
- Is there consistency of standards across different units of the qualification?
- Where is the assessment being carried out?
- What is the balance between performance evidence and supplementary evidence?
- Do the candidates understand the assessment process?
- How is evidence being recorded?

Assessing portfolios

Throughout this chapter, we have been talking about the centrality of the student's portfolio in assessment within many vocational programmes. Portfolios can be confusing documents for the beginning student; navigating the apparently endless paper trail is a daunting task, particularly if its purpose is not made clear. The portfolio provides the evidence that the student can meet all the assessment criteria set out in the specification for that programme. Let us take a specific example. Within a unit on Business Finance, a student may be required to investigate a range of financial products or services suitable for different customer groups, to compare costs and evaluate the benefits. The evidence in the portfolio must demonstrate that the student has collected information from a range of financial services providers, has calculated the costs of certain products for specific customer groups and drawn conclusions from actual data. The evidence should always be suitable for the purpose for which it is provided, and authentic; in other words, it must be the student's own work. It must also be sufficient (that is, it must include all that is required to meet the criteria). If, in the example above, the student omitted to include calculations of costings, then all the criteria would not have been fulfilled.

This may seem relatively straightforward. However, the organisation of the material into a coherent portfolio is often challenging. Some organising strategies can help students to overcome the difficulties. The guiding principles are:

- appropriate induction, so that students understand clearly the purpose of the portfolio and its role in assessment;
- a clear map through the course indicating exactly where, in which units, and at what time in the programme the pieces of evidence will be produced that will go into the portfolio;
- copies of the assignment brief attached to the front of the student's assignment together with a copy of the assessor's comments and grade awarded;
- good systems that help students to organise their work, including, for example: files with dividers; and tracking sheets on which students record where in the file the evidence is located, identifying the unit for which they provide evidence – signed off by assessors and dated;
- an index that also contains relevant information about the candidate and the centre; and
- keeping portfolios up to date – trying to complete them retrospectively is a recipe for disaster.

In the first instance, students' work is assessed by the appropriate tutor for the unit. All colleges offering vocational qualifications that include a portfolio assessment must appoint internal verifiers in order to ensure consistency across different markers and across programmes. This is part of the quality assurance system that is required by the awarding bodies, and ultimately by the regulators (for example, Ofqual). In addition, the awarding organisations appoint independent standards moderators to ensure that internal assessment and verification is consistent across different centres, thus ensuring national standards.

If you are involved in the delivery of vocational programmes, you should ensure that you keep up to date with developments through your awarding organisation, or organisations, since you are likely to be teaching on qualifications offered by more than one body. All matters relating to assessment should be referred to the awarding organisation.

e-Assessment

The use of technology is now widespread across a range of contexts to support a number of assessment purposes including: question setting; online testing; e-marking; standardisation; examiners' discussion forums; providing feedback; peer review; and student satisfaction surveys. The increased use of technology by students for learning purposes and for the production of assignments suggests that assessment should also take account of the changing digital landscape. In this context, all the major awarding organisations have increased their use of technology for testing and assessing. Online, on-demand testing has also increased in volume, particularly in relation to the testing of basic skills. e-Marking is now used for some extended written answers, as well as for marking multiple-choice questions.

It is suggested (JISC, 2010: 6) that technology can be harnessed to improve the quality of formative assessment and feedback for students by 'integrating a wide range of technologies into their practice, enabling learners to experience more varied and appropriate assessment and feedback strategies at all stages of their learning programmes'. These advances also permit the development of self-assessment through the use of learning logs, blogs and online discussion groups, in any location and at a time to suit learners. However, the same guiding principles for effective assessment (as outlined earlier in this chapter) should apply whatever the form or context of the assessment. Technology should be used to enhance the learning experience and to improve teaching quality, not just to save time or cost. It should also help learners to become more confident about reviewing and evaluating their own work.

The JISC (2010: 9) report sets out the benefits of technology-enhanced assessment thus:

- Greater variety and authenticity in assessment design.
- Improved learner engagement, for example, through interactive formative assessments with adaptive feedback.
- Choice in the timing and location of assessments.
- Capture of wider skills and attributes not easily assessed by other means, for example, through simulations, e-portfolios and interactive games.

- Efficient submission, marking, moderation and data storage processes.
- Consistent, accurate results with opportunities to combine human and computer marking.
- Immediate feedback.
- Increased opportunities for learners to act on feedback, for example, by reflection in e-portfolios.
- Innovative approaches based around use of creative media and on-line peer assessment.
- Accurate, timely and accessible evidence on the effectiveness of curriculum design and delivery.

REFLECTION

Given the advantages listed above, consider how you are incorporating some of these principles into your own use of technology for assessment purposes (for example, using interactive games as 'starter' activities; and the use of discussion groups for sharing ideas/feedback/resources across distance learners).

Conclusion

You will have realised that assessment is a complex and time-consuming business. The nature and forms of assessment in FE have changed considerably during the past 15 years. The contexts in which assessment is undertaken have also changed. It is not just a matter for the examination hall but for the workplace, and in many other settings as well (for example, within community settings and voluntary organisations). The incidence of e-assessment is now widespread.

The process of assessment has become more transparent, and greater emphasis is placed upon the dialogue between the assessor and the assessed. There are also more opportunities now to challenge assessment decisions through a range of appeals procedures. Increasingly, assessment serves a variety of purposes. It helps to identify starting points and, in this sense, it is diagnostic. It may help to identify previous learning for which a student may wish to claim credit, as in APEL procedures. This type of assessment can help to inform the learning plan and avoid unnecessary duplication.

Assessment, in its formative aspects, maintains a record of ongoing progress. This type of assessment aims to improve the quality of what is being achieved and helps to structure learning. On the other hand, summative assessment may be a summary of the formative assessments already carried out of what a student can do at a given time. Of course, summative assessment may be used to select, or de-select, students from the next stage of their learning journey.

In designing assessment plans for our students, we need to ensure a balance of different types of assessment. We can collect evidence in a variety of ways and over different time periods. We can also collect evidence provided in different contexts; we all know that our students may perform differently on employers' premises from the way that they perform in our practical classes. We should also consider the motivational and personal development opportunities implicit in a negotiated record of achievement or profile.

We should not neglect the opportunities provided by assessment to review our teaching and the way in which we organise learning, and to judge its suitability for the students for whom it is intended. The concept of 'assessment for learning' requires both teachers and students to be engaged in a cooperative venture that should help not only in improving the learning experiences of students, but the teaching and support that we offer them. The success of such an endeavour will depend, in large part, upon our ability as teachers to make critical assessment decisions when students enter programmes, throughout the course of their study, and at completion.

Part III

Professional development

Chapter 7

Evaluation, reflection and research

Introduction

> The activity of reflection is so familiar, that as teachers or trainers, we often overlook it in formal learning settings . . . reflection is a vital element in any form of learning and teachers and trainers need to consider how they can incorporate some forms of reflection in their courses.
>
> (Boud *et al.*, 1985: 8)

> Stimulated by surprise, they turn thought back on action and on the knowing which is implicit in action . . . it is this entire process of reflection-in-action which is central to the 'art' by which practitioners sometimes deal well with situations of uncertainty, instability, uniqueness and value conflict.
>
> (Schön, 1983: 50)

> (We) need to challenge vigorously the incorporation of the concepts of reflection and reflective practice into processes of scrutiny and regulation, appraisal and control. Instead, we propose that a critical understanding of reflection and reflective practice – one in which reflection is no longer seen as an isolated, individual activity but one which has the potential to bring about social and organisational change – will move us beyond the caricature that reflective practice has become.
>
> (Zukas *et al.*, 2010: 194)

In this chapter, we examine the benefits that teachers can gain from applying the concept of the 'reflective practitioner' as a means of evaluating and considering their own practice, and by helping their students use the same concept to reflect on their development as learners. In that respect, as Canning (2011: 614) has argued, there is a 'mutual dependency between trainee teachers and students'. He adds: 'This is a hard lesson for novice teachers to learn as it requires suspending judgement and staying with the needs of students at a time when they are naturally overwhelmed by their own concerns and anxieties' (ibid.: 615).

As you will gather from the opening quotations to this chapter, there has been a concern that the process of reflection and the concept of the 'reflective practitioner' has been highjacked over the past 20 or so years by policymakers and organisations in order to put further pressure on professionals. Writing in the same volume as Zukas *et al.* (2010), David Boud, one of the major contributors to the development of reflective practice and the author of the first quotation, argues that while the concept of reflection is robust enough to withstand further interrogation, 'we need to find ways of rehabilitating some key aspects of reflection that have been eroded through unthinking use' (Boud, 2010: 36).

Throughout this book, we have been asking you to reflect on your own learning, on some of our ideas, and on your approach to teaching. Reflection is a natural part of human life, but for professionals and students, structured reflection can provide a framework within which they can examine their strengths and weaknesses and identify strategies for improvement. In addition, professionals can use reflection as a bridge to help span what is often regarded as a chasm between the reality of their practice as teachers and the theoretical models and concepts put forward by academics who research education.

Reflection can sometimes turn into 'navel gazing', a pleasant enough pastime for some, but not one that will necessarily take the reflector any further forward or cause any changes to his or her practices! This is why we are advocating the need for reflection, whether by teachers or students, to be structured and fully incorporated within the formal framework of a course or teaching career.

Later in this chapter, we discuss ways in which teachers in colleges can build on the reflective process and begin actively to research their practice. By turning one's reflections into ideas for research projects, those reflections can be sharpened and scrutinised, and lead to real and worthwhile policies for improved practices (and policies) for both individuals and institutions.

Reflection for students

In his book *The Enquiring Tutor*, Stephen Rowland explains his commitment to student-centred learning:

> At the heart of this approach is the view that, both morally and practically, it is worth taking our students seriously. What they have to say about themselves provides us with the most significant information about their own learning, and thus our teaching. If we can give voice to our students' experience, we have come a long way towards understanding our own practice.
>
> (Rowland, 1993: 6)

There are many ways in which teachers can and will encourage their students to reflect on their learning but, all too often, reflection becomes confused with assessment. As we saw in Chapter 6, constructive feedback that arises out of assessment can, of course, facilitate reflection, but students need to learn how to reflect and come to regard it as a natural process in its own right.

In order to reflect, you have to ask yourself questions, some of which might be difficult or awkward. The identification of those questions may be straightforward if, for example, you have been struggling to write an essay and cannot decide how the story ends, or you may have been cooking and discover that you have left out a key ingredient from the recipe. If, however, you are reflecting on why you find it so difficult to learn how to conjugate verbs in French or how to turn what you have read in a book into a summary using your own words, then the questions you need to ask become more complex. Students, therefore, will have to practise reflection, and to do that they need some guidance.

One way of helping students to reflect would be to ask them to analyse themselves as learners. They could, for example, do the exercise at the beginning of Chapter 5 in which you were asked to consider whether you were a 'good' learner. Whichever method is chosen, however, the student has to learn to reflect in a way that suits his or her own style and needs, and the teacher has to create a supportive atmosphere in which this can take place. We asked a number of students in different colleges to reflect on their learning experiences. In the first set of examples, three 16-year-old students (two full-time and one part-time) give their reactions to their tutors' assessments of a piece of work.

BTEC group assignment: a student reflects on how the group worked together

I think the grade is fair because we all really put a lot of work into this. I mean, just writing the letters and arranging the company interviews took ages. As usual, Angela did practically nothing, but I think Mrs Bennett [the tutor] knows this because she gave her a lower grade, which is only fair anyway. I wasn't too happy about the marks for the oral presentation because I think we did as well as we could have done. I mean, we're not all bloomin' TV presenters! I don't see why we should have so many marks for oral presentation when it's all in the file anyway.

I think Kamal did a brilliant job with the accounts; it really helped our assignment. I am pleased he was given a higher mark for that because he really deserved it. What I especially liked about this assignment was that it really gave us a chance to get together out of college. I mean, in the evenings, we used to meet up at someone's house and do all the planning – it was really great. Sharm's Dad gave us lots of help as well, like where we could find out things, and he even brought us some company brochures and reports.

I used to think people in our group were, well, sad until I got to know them through this assignment. Now I know they're OK.

An A-level student reflects on the comments she received for an essay on *Hamlet*

I must say I am very disappointed with this mark. I put a lot of effort into this, practically regurgitating all the notes that we had been given. That always seemed to work at GCSE. English was my best subject. If the lecturer can't tell us the answer and give us a decent set of notes, what can he expect? He talks about critical reflection; I don't even know what he means. I don't see how he can expect me to go off and find the stuff when he hasn't told me what to look for. After all, he's paid to teach us and get us through the exam. I don't see why I should have to 'look things up'. Perhaps I should buy a set of those revision notes.

Perming hair: a hairdressing student reflects on an activity in the college's training salon

Well, I think that the perm was all right. I mean, not brilliant but all right. Mrs Smith [the tutor] thought it was a pass but she said it wouldn't be fast enough in a real salon. Well it ain't a real salon anyway and the people who come here know that – that's why it's cheap. Anyway, I think Mrs Smith has got it in for me since she caught me using the mousse in the practice salon. I don't care because the gaffer [manager of the salon in which the student works when not at college] thinks I'm OK and that's what matters. He says the college don't know what they're talking about because they don't have to run a business. Anyway, college is a laugh. We have a great time and as long as I just get by that's OK. There was nothing wrong with the perm, anyway.

These reflections capture the emotional tensions that formal assessment can engender. In the first example, the experience of learning within a group structure has enabled the student to recognise the strengths and weaknesses of individual group members and to celebrate the social enjoyment to be found in working closely with colleagues. In the second and third examples, we see the students struggling to accept criticism of their work and behaviour. These students instinctively blame the tutor rather than examining their own weaknesses. They may have legitimate reasons for criticising their tutors but unless they are given opportunities to discuss the thinking behind the assessments, they may have difficulty in demonstrating their true abilities. When tutors and learners reflect together about the learning process, both parties can confront each other's level of contribution, thus identifying ways in which that process can be improved.

In the second set of examples, three mature students (one full-time and two part-time) reflect on their individual progress after six months on a course.

Adult basic skills student: 45-year-old Jack has been unemployed for three years

I finally started to understand where I'd been going wrong with maths when I stopped blaming myself for having failed at school. It was this week the penny dropped and I've been here nearly six months. I just sat in class on Tuesday and I heard Brenda [a fellow student] shout at our tutor. She said, 'I'm really good at some things, you know. I might not be any good at these sums you give us but I used to get good marks at school for my writing'. I thought, she's right; just because we're not much cop at maths doesn't mean we're stupid, and then I seemed to lose my fear about what Brenda calls 'sums'.

Information technology student: Frances is a 33-year-old secretary

I still don't really like coming here. I'd rather be at work but my boss wants me to learn about this stuff and I know I need to really. It's not the tutors; they're smashing. Well, I suppose it's the effort of having to concentrate on learning new things when at work I seem to get by so easily and I feel in control. When there's a test, I just go to pieces and my husband says he can tell I'm worried about college because I take it out on everyone at home. I'll be glad when it's finished . . . awful isn't it? I should be grateful for the chance, really.

Catering student: Edward is a 27-year-old former policeman who is now training to be a chef

If only I'd done this years ago, I would have been much happier. The course is going well but then I know I've got a good attitude, better than some of the others who are a bit up and down about the whole thing. I can't wait to get into the kitchen and the pressure doesn't bother me at all. I'm much more motivated about this than anything else I've been on and it really makes a difference to your standard of work. I never knew I could learn so fast.

In these examples, maturity helps the students to reflect more deeply on their learning experience and they can relate back to earlier experiences to gain insights into their problems and successes.

Constructing a reflective journal

A 'reflective journal' can take many forms and should be a very personal record, so you can be as creative as you wish. You might decide to use a typical diary format, making entries for each day or week in a notebook. You might keep a box file or shoebox in which you can store any jottings, cuttings from newspapers, cartoons, photographs and so on. Or, you might keep a very visual record using diagrams or pictures to illustrate your journey through the teaching year. If you feel happier with a more formal structure for the journal, here are some suggestions for dividing the diary into sections to include:

- a record of newly acquired knowledge, understanding and skills that are important to you;
- a commentary on your personal/professional development as you progress through the year;
- a commentary on the interesting (and perhaps contentious) issues and concepts that arise out of your professional experience; and
- responses to critical incidents.

Here are two extracts from reflective journals that show how experienced college teachers record their concerns and queries about their students. The first extract records a teacher's thoughts after an induction meeting with a group of adult students on a 'two plus two' degree course:

> This seems a pleasant enough group. It's a real 'mixed-bag' though. One or two obviously have the impression that they know it all and tend to dominate the rest, mainly through their attempts to monopolise the discussion and to 'name drop' one or two key texts. Mrs Baker is a bit of a worry because she obviously knows quite a lot but is anxious about expressing her opinions. I must remember to let her take a more active role next time. Perhaps I should let her act as a rapporteur for feedback on group work.
>
> Greg seems particularly anxious. I notice he was hovering at the back afterwards waiting to catch me on my way out. Did he really need to check the time of the next class or was there something more important that he wanted to discuss? I noticed that he moved away very quickly when Tony came up.
>
> I must remember that Winifred is repeating this year; I need to keep her interest. I must draw on her knowledge and expertise to help me and the group. It's going to be tough for her because her son is in hospital again. I think I might suggest we plan a group get-together at the local pub or bowling alley to help establish a real group identity.

The second extract is from a catering tutor's journal, written after she assessed a group of students working in the college restaurant:

> On the whole, the group performed well with one or two notable exceptions. Ros was late and Chris didn't have his white jacket. Nevertheless, Ranjit, who was maitre d'hotel for the evening, handled the

situation very well. I must remember to enter his performance under functional skills in his portfolio. His communication skills were particularly appropriate.

The main courses were well presented and service was competently handled. Must remember to tell Gill about her mistake with the cutlery although I don't think she was the only one. Lee should have noticed that the water jugs were empty before the customer had to ask. The dessert trolley was the least well handled. This group is very poor at describing the individual dishes to customers. It's not that they don't know, I think they are too scared to say. I must speak to their communications lecturer. We need to develop some role play situations so that students can practise before they meet real customers.

It may seem daunting to try to find the time to record observations and ideas in this way, but the two extracts above show how a number of important details can be logged by teachers in a relatively short diary-style account. In the next extract, from a trainee teacher's record of a session with a full-time vocational intermediate class that was being observed by the teacher's tutor, we see an example of how a teacher can reflect on a critical incident:

It was a disaster, I just totally lost it. I thought I had it all planned and organised and it all went dreadfully wrong. There are some real trouble-makers in this group. I should have realised that, I just wasn't prepared for it. I should have realised that the trouble was starting once the two at the front began banging the cupboard doors. I should have separated them. I can't think why I let them sit together, the whole thing just became worse and there was nothing I could do about it.

I realise that while my attention was being taken by the troublemakers others were starting to become restless. Then those who were working well were not being given any attention. I really need to think about everyone in the group and not just concentrate on those who are causing trouble. I couldn't believe it when they started throwing the paper darts. Obviously I was an easy target. I knew then I had lost it. My real worry is how I am going to face them next week.

The trainee teacher's tutor also recorded her own reflections on the session she had observed and provided her student with these comments:

A) Opening

Try to be on time and establish control before taking the register. What about the young lady loitering at the door; was she supposed to be in or out of the class? Close the door to show that the class has begun.

B) Introduction

You need to recap on previous class. Make sure everyone is attending before you start. What was that boy doing wandering around? You must ensure that:

- everyone understands the task and is fully prepared; and
- everyone is working through the task.

Try to deal with one question at a time. You broke off in the middle of answering one boy's question to answer another. It gives the impression to the group that you are not fully in control. You must deal with the boy at the back who kept shouting. There was a lot of constructive work going on in some parts of the class; try to capitalise on this. Class eventually settled down well to the task.

C) During lesson

Make sure that the troublesome elements are also on the task. Don't leave people too long before checking up on them . . . the boy next to me was drawing cartoons.

D) Feedback from activity

Make sure all the class is ready to engage in the activity: people were still writing, others talking among themselves. You must draw the whole group together before attempting a debrief from the exercise. How should you deal with the paper darts incident? The disruption with the cupboard was very unfortunate – one strategy would have been to move the boy away from the cupboard rather than have the confrontation. The class was aware that you were losing control. It is a great pity that those who were working on the task and who had some good ideas were not used more; the disruptive students were really dominating the class. In fact, if you notice, there are only five, at the most, disruptive students; the rest of the class is fine so capitalise on them.

E) Rounding off

Keep your eye on the time so that you allow sufficient time to draw everything together and reinforce any key points. The lesson didn't have a proper ending but just stumbled to a close.

F) Reflection

- What do you feel the students learned from this class?
- How would you sum up your classroom management?
- What went well?
- What did not go well?

Put together, the two sets of reflective notes create a much more meaningful critique of the lesson than if one simply had access to just one person's account. Clearly, the trainee teacher has written his notes from a fairly acute sense of failure and, to some extent, foreboding, given that he will have to meet this same group again. His account gives the impression that the majority of students in the group were behaving badly, that the noise level was high and that he lurched from one crisis to the next. His tutor's notes provide a more coherent account (having been written from the relative calm of the back of the room) by breaking the lesson down into a chronology of pedagogical principles. We learn from this that the trainee teacher apparently arrived a little late for the lesson and so may have created the wrong impression with some students. In addition, we learn that a very small number of students caused the disruptions whereas, for the trainee teacher, it was as if they had completely taken over the proceedings. Finally, the general lack of organisation in the classroom is obviously something that the trainee teacher cannot blame entirely on five 'troublemakers'.

We are, of course, surrounded by examples of people learning, whether at home, at work, in the street, in the pub, or at the football ground. The list is endless. Try to observe your friends, relatives, colleagues and even strangers if you see them in a learning situation and record your observations in your 'reflective journal'. In fact, treat the everyday world as your research laboratory and don't forget to include yourself too!

In Chapters 4 and 5, we discussed some of the theoretical literature related to teaching and learning, and tried to show how theory can inform and illuminate the teacher's role. The individual teacher should have the opportunity to contribute to and engage with the theory, and this is where the process of reflection can have real meaning and purpose. For Quicke (1996), theory needs to be balanced with reflective practice, otherwise it is in danger of putting a 'straight-jacket on teacher thought'. He gives three reasons for this:

> First, they [theories] may no longer be relevant. Although conceived originally as a way of clarifying and helping to resolve problems with which common-sense knowledge was no longer adequate to deal, they now address problems which are no longer salient. There may be new agendas in place in relation to which old theories may be obsolete. Second, theories may become reified. This problem is not so much to do with the content of a theory as with the manner in which the theory is held . . . Thirdly, theories are not so much irrelevant in terms of the issues they address but are irrelevant as theories. There may be other theories which address the same problems 'better' by constituting them differently or it's possible that common sense has already been informed by such theories. What is required is reflection on existing common sense using ideas from other aspects of common-sense knowledge.
>
> (ibid.: 21)

Teacher as researcher

The concept of the 'teacher as researcher' has been promoted for some considerable time, certainly since the 1970s when the work of Lawrence Stenhouse advocated the need for practitioners to become researchers in their own right (see Stenhouse, 1975). In the current climate of change that has swept through FE colleges, the concept should be re-examined, for it has the potential to act as a vehicle for enabling college staff to investigate collaboratively the key questions and problems that concern them. FE teachers are familiar with researchers, evaluators and representatives of management consultants who visit their colleges to interview students and staff, collect statistical data and observe teaching and learning. Ironically, however, the concerns of the FE teachers themselves may – though this will be rare – form the focus of this externally generated and externally led research activity. In the main, the teachers are left with their concerns and the external researchers move on to another set of problems.

Academics in HE have, of course, their own legitimate reasons for carrying out research, and play a crucial role in helping practitioners tackle the theoretical underpinning they need in furthering their understanding of and ability to examine critically the educational context in which they practise. But this relationship can be limited and much of the important work that it generates is hidden from view. There is a need, therefore, for the two communities to work much more collaboratively to ensure the following:

- that research outcomes are disseminated widely and acted upon;
- that teachers and other professionals play a more proactive part in determining the research questions to be addressed;
- that teachers contribute their professional experience and expertise to the whole of the research process rather than just a small part of it;
- that researchers are made to challenge their research practices and findings through collaborative enquiry and ongoing dialogue; and
- that researchers pass on their skills to others and demystify the process of research.

This new relationship cannot, of course, be simply formed in order to meet the needs of one of the partners. It has to be recognised that university education departments are struggling to maintain adequate student numbers at postgraduate level. Gone are the days when the local education authorities and institutions would pay teachers to attend courses and give them time to study. Teachers and other professionals are having to pay their own fees and may, in some cases, be actively discouraged from attending certain courses by their managers. The pressures on college staff to meet retention and attainment targets and meet the demands of external quality assurance means that professional development becomes less of a priority.

From the colleges' point of view, a collaborative relationship with HE should not be driven solely by management priorities or imposed on staff as yet another workload clause in their contracts. Staff who are told on a Monday morning by the college principal that they are all to become 'researchers' are unlikely to react positively when a group of academics arrives to begin work. The considerable amount of pedagogical, curricular and policy change that has affected colleges in recent years, and the increased emphasis on the role of FE in terms of rising post-compulsory participation rates, have presented college staff with a plethora of problems and concerns to be investigated. Given the pressures of workload affecting all staff and the demands of external bodies for information about individual college performance, it will be necessary to ensure that institutions separate routine data gathering and monitoring from a more searching research programme that combines quantitative and qualitative methods and draws on a range of different research traditions and method-ologies. At the same time, college staff will need to be supported over a realistic time span in their research activity by both their managers and the academics with whom they are to collaborate.

Andrew Culham sounds a realistic note in relation to teacher researchers when he writes, 'The realities of practitioner research are, in my experience, very different from the optimistic view reported by educational institutions and research journals. With all this "enthusiasm" why is it still difficult or impossible for FE practitioners to conduct research?' (Culham, 2001: 27). Culham goes on to suggest that four key factors affect practitioner research in many colleges:

- lack of time and funding;
- no 'active' research culture within FE;
- no 'value' of research within colleges; and
- few opportunities for dissemination.

He calls for 'a greater understanding of the relevance and value of practitioner-based research . . . embedded within further education philosophy and policy development as part of an active promotion of a college's research effort' (ibid.: 28). The difficulties facing FE teacher-researchers are, however, not to be underestimated. Anderson *et al.* (2003: 507) argue that, in the light of the 'outcome-driven culture' of many colleges, there is limited internal capacity to 'overturn the dominant paradigm of "performativity"'. Further-more, they note that 'many colleges cannot distinguish between "criticism" and "critical voice", and can be defensive' (ibid.). Their experience has, however, enabled them to think through the different ways in which a more robust research culture might be developed across FE. For this to happen, research needs to be seen as part of a 'wider cultural change process that will make colleges fit to thrive in a changing environment . . . Teachers will share the fruits of that success through improved security and greater recognition of their professional role' (ibid.: 513).

Conclusion

Working as an FE teacher is highly demanding and it is often difficult to find time to stand back from the daily pressures to reflect and take stock. This chapter has explored some ideas to help you build on your experience, to learn from both your successes and your mistakes, and to create ways to make reflection an integral part of your working life. As discussed in Chapter 1, FE teachers come from a wide range of backgrounds and many already have had careers in other fields before coming into teaching. The process of learning to become an FE teacher will often involve the need to switch from one identity to another and, in the process, new identities will emerge. For example, the following comments come from an FE tutor in Performing Arts:

> I am an actor and also work as an actor–in–residence at a secondary school, teach Performing Arts BTEC at a college, teach a summer school on 'Shakespeare's Drama' and also teach on the PGCE/Cert Ed Performing Arts in a university. I think the duality of performers who teach is quite complex. Firstly, there is an unspoken, inherent sense of 'failure' for a lot of performer/teachers in the self-questioning caused by the old saying 'those who can, do, those who can't, teach'. I suspect a lot of performers actually teach out of economic reality rather than any sense of 'vocation'. However, any 'negative' motivation might possibly be counteracted by the fact that performers come to the classroom with an inherent under-standing of audience needs, storytelling skills, the use of dramatic effects and a tendency towards charismatic modelling that positively affect their teaching. However, it might also be true to say that performer/teachers are foremost performers and are always highly conscious of their teach-ing as a form of performance and are interested in monitoring its effects for their own benefit. The classroom can become a substitute stage where the teacher is the unquestioned solo actor/director and critic and if this happens, the students' learning can take second place to the gratification needs of the teacher. Teacher-led activity can take precedence over student creativity and autonomy. At best, however, teacher/performers are innate motivators who understand student's need for affirmation and praise due to their own development as 'fragile' performers. They also tend to be curious about people, open-hearted, empathetic, creative thinkers and ensemble players – all of which make them useful teachers.

From their research with teachers and nurses, Stronach et al. (2002) have argued for a new perspective on the concept of 'professionalism' in order to capture the plurality of the professional role. Stronach et al. (ibid.) found teachers and nurses constantly juggling the different aspects of their daily lives as they tried to conform to the different, and often conflicting, expectations of their work held by policymakers, managers, clients and students. In her research with schoolteachers, Watson (2006) has found that teachers find it helpful to recount their daily practice in the form of stories or narratives as these expose the way in which they have to shift their perspective to suit the changing contexts in which they work and, hence, be more aware of the different possibilities available to them.

As an FE teacher, you might find you work in a range of 'spaces' and 'places' (including, for example, teaching in classrooms and workshops or assessing students in workplaces) and this diversity of environment will also have an impact on the formation of your professional identity/identities. James and Diment's (2003) research has shown that FE staff who work away from the traditional classroom setting may need to develop different forms of practice in order to adapt to the nature of the learning environment and the needs of their students. They refer to this as 'underground' practice. Trainee FE teachers, who are on placement in a college as part of a full-time course leading to a teaching qualification, sometimes find that the realities of college life are somewhat different from the picture painted by their tutors. Bathmaker and Avis (2005) found, for example, that trainee teachers in their study in England often felt isolated from the community of practice they were seeking to join and were not, necessarily, impressed with the practices of the experienced teachers they were working alongside (see also Bathmaker and Avis, 2007). Recording these different experiences in some form can help teachers make sense of the different ways in which they have to 'perform' and can also reveal how strategies that have been effective in one setting, might be transferable to another one.

Chapter 8

Professional development

Introduction

In previous chapters, we have emphasised the multi-skilled nature of the FE teacher. Given the diversity of FE life and the volatility of curricula within colleges, every FE teacher has to make plans to ensure they have access to relevant and appropriate professional development opportunities. Given also that teachers in FE stretch from those who concentrate on basic skills, through to those teaching at undergraduate and postgraduate level, the scope of professional development must, necessarily, be broad enough to encompass the wide range of professional needs.

In Chapter 4, we discussed the role that theory plays in developing our understanding of teaching and learning. In their study of initial teacher training (ITT) for FE, Lucas *et al.* (2011: 15) found that:

> there is no consensus about what is meant by the term 'learning theory' nor about what theories should be included in ITT courses. Teacher trainers interpret the meaning of theory in different ways. Indeed from our research, even what constituted theory was unclear. In some course handbooks the university criteria of assessment wanted to see 'theory research based evidence used', while other handbooks referred to 'being critical', 'reflective practice' and 'teacher knowledge'.

Your own ITT course may have included a study of theoretical concepts and the research underpinning them, but it is important to try and maintain some connection with the developing research field throughout your career. In addition, you will also need to ensure your specific professional area of expertise is kept up to date. Michael Eraut, who has made a key contribution to our understanding of professional knowledge and competence, sees the 'disposition to theorise' as the 'most important quality of the professional teacher' as once they gain this, teachers will:

> go on developing their theorising capacities throughout their teaching careers, they will be genuinely self-evaluative and they will continue to

search for, invent and implement new ideas. Without it they will become prisoners of their early . . . experience, perhaps the competent teachers of today, almost certainly the ossified teachers of tomorrow.

(Eraut, 1994: 71)

For Michael Tedder, writing from his experience of teaching in colleges, the concept of professionalism has many meanings in FE:

Many of us use the term 'professional' regularly to convey a range of meanings among which might be identified the possession of a body of knowledge and expertise, normally accredited with academic or vocational qualifications, and the awareness of a set of values or a code of conduct that governs our relationship with 'clients', the ethics of our profession. Professionalism also implies a relationship with colleagues that includes responsibility for monitoring the standards in our practice and an acceptance of responsibility or a sense of accountability to the community we serve.

(Tedder, 1994: 74)

Professional development is itself a concept in need of some clarification. A more familiar term might be staff development, but often, this will tend to refer to largely in-house, short and management-led initiatives rather than activity that is determined by the individual teacher to fulfil personal development goals. Staff development in colleges has had a mixed history. As Castling (1996) has shown, the 1970s was a period in which staff development probably meant being sent on an external course for updating related to one's teaching area, whereas in the 1980s, more emphasis was placed on colleges creating internal staff development programmes, often using ideas generated by the then FEU. LEAs also played a key role in the 1980s as they managed government funding targeted at staff development, while HMI ran national conferences for staff development officers. The levels of nationally available funding gradually decreased, however, and now staff development is very much seen as a cost to be borne by colleges themselves.

Robson (1996: 3) has pointed out the danger in assuming that terms such as professional development or staff development privilege the needs of staff, whereas in reality, the inspectors have a more college-centric outlook: 'Staffing needs will be derived from analyses of the college's objectives and staff development activities will be determined less by perceived individual need than by the college's academic and strategic plan'. Thus, the majority of activity that falls under the umbrella of professional development tends to be related to servicing an immediate need (for example, health and safety training, new assessment procedures, ITT requirements, etc.) or, where it is seen as servicing a long-term goal; as Robson states above, it will be closely tied to the college's strategic plan. There is, of course, every likelihood that some of this activity will complement the professional development needs of some teaching staff, and where a college is prepared to invest large amounts of money, perhaps to retrain teachers or help them develop their professional competence in order to run courses at higher levels, then 'staff development' becomes indistinguishable from professional development.

Staff development tends to take place within the college's own campus and involve only college staff, though an outside speaker might be called upon. Although there are clearly times when a purely internal arrangement is sufficient, there is a real danger that staff and management become too insular if all their staff development is conducted in this way. Castling (1996: 80) warns:

> There is the risk of staff becoming bogged down in institutional problems which can obstruct progress, and there may be a lack of fresh ideas which would normally come from working with colleagues elsewhere. There might be a reluctance to resource the input by college staff as fully as that by outside experts, and indeed college staff might not command the respect which would have been accorded to visitors purely because they were from outside. The chief danger is probably insularity. The staff developer managing the programme will need to import wider views, either from their own research or by selecting colleague contributions carefully.

Perhaps, then, staff development should come with a health warning or at least those 'being developed' should recognise that the fix they gain from participating in staff development activities may be less than satisfying. Eraut (1994: 10) reminds us that:

> Professionals continually learn on the job, because their work entails engagement in a succession of cases, problems or projects which they have to learn about. This case-specific learning, however, may not contribute a great deal to their general professional knowledge base unless the case is regarded as special rather than routine and time is set aside to deliberate upon its significance. Even then it may remain in memory as a special case without being integrated into any general theory of practice. Thus according to the disposition of individual professionals and the conditions under which they work, their knowledge base may be relatively static or developing quite rapidly. There is little research evidence to indicate the overall level of work-based learning in any profession, but individual examples of both extremes are frequently cited.

As noted in Chapter 1, there is currently a statutory requirement for FE teachers to hold a professional qualification. Many FE teachers will also hold qualifications related to their area of expertise and they may be being 'topped up' by bouts of continuing professional education (CPE) or continuing professional development (CPD). The stage at which these discipline or occupationally based professionals will add a qualification in teaching to their curriculum vitae will depend on the nature of their entry to FE. Norman Lucas has argued that this duality of professional role (that is, of being at one and the same time a teacher and an expert in a professional or craft/trade area) has dogged the development of a statutory qualification structure:

> Management and staff associations have traditionally united against any statutory professional teaching qualification for further education. Historically, lecturers in further education have seen their qualification or expertise in an academic or vocational area as sufficient for teaching. This has placed specialist knowledge of subject or trade above pedagogy. Thus the notion of lecturers being seen as, or seeing themselves as professional teachers with a coherent structure of initial training and professional development has been secondary to a concentration of delivering narrow specialist expertise.
>
> (Lucas, 1996: 69)

In the light of the Lingfield Review, discussed in Chapter 1, Lucas's analysis may have continued relevance (for a critique of the IfL approach to CPD, see also Plowright and Barr, 2012). In their study of the ways in which teachers on in-service ITT programmes were being supported by their colleges, Lucas and Unwin (2009) found that the FE workplace is an actual barrier to professional development. They used Fuller and Unwin's 'Expansive-Restrictive Framework' (see Chapter 4) to analyse the interviews they conducted with teachers across a range of curriculum areas. Teachers told Lucas and Unwin that while, in most cases, their managers were trying to support them, the highly pressurised workplace environment created little space for reflection and even consistent mentoring. Perhaps most importantly, many colleges were failing to afford the trainee teachers the status of having the dual identity of learner (trainee) and worker (teacher), which is one of the key characteristics of an expansive workplace. Lucas and Unwin argue that ITT needs to be integrated within the broader workforce development strategy and practices within colleges so that the workplace context is given sufficient consideration.

Pathways to professional development

Clearly all colleges have their own culture and ethos that may have grown up over a number of years or that may reflect sudden changes introduced by a new senior manager or management team. The level of importance attached to the professional development needs of staff is dependent on that culture so that in some colleges staff may have to fight quite hard to get their real needs met. Throughout a career as a teacher in FE, you will probably want a mix of opportunities to satisfy your professional development needs. As discussed earlier in this chapter, some of your immediate needs might be covered in staff development activities run within the college.

One of the key mechanisms through which you will be asked to try to identify your professional development needs will be through the college's review and appraisal system. If this is not satisfactory in terms of helping you identify and discuss your professional development needs, you will have to find other means for this. Your mentor should play a role here (see Cunningham, 2012; Tedder and Lawy, 2009). This will most likely be an experienced member of staff who provides ongoing support, advice and guidance, and will also be involved in giving feedback from observations of your teaching.

In some colleges, teachers also support each other through peer mentoring. The process of mentoring has to be nurtured, especially in colleges where individuals feel under pressure to compete with each other and feel at the mercy of externally imposed targets and inspections. Cox (1996: 42) advocates peer or collaborative mentoring because:

> In this context, the imbalance of power is less of an issue and the tension generated by the assessment function of the mentor is absent. The discussion of one's own and a collaborative colleague's teaching can be developed in a supportive atmosphere, in a constructive, private dialogue.

As well as helping you to identify and discuss your professional development needs, working with supportive colleagues will also provide tacit doses of professional development, as well as enriching one's day-to-day life in college. Another strategy for considering your professional development needs involves keeping a record of your professional experience in and outside college. This record could take the form of a portfolio, diary or log and could include a combination of examples of your work with students (such as teaching plans, assessments, photographs of students' work, etc.) and more discursive accounts of your development as a teacher (for example, reflections on critical moments, ideas for new ways to teach, etc.). It might also include evidence of your activities related to your area of professional expertise or your links with the local community.

Linked to this notion of recording one's experience is the use of autobiographical writing by teachers throughout all sectors of education. Here, a teacher constructs a narrative of his or her ongoing life as a teacher and uses it to reflect on the extent to which external as well as personal influences determine one's progress and development as a professional. As Bateson argues:

> These resonances between the personal and the professional are the source of both insight and error. You avoid mistakes and distortions not so much

by trying to build a wall between the observer and the observed as by observing the observer – observing yourself – as well, and bringing the personal issues into consciousness.

(Bateson, 1984: 161)

By gaining a better understanding of the personal and the professional, we can then begin to 'map' out our career path and, hopefully, take more control over the nature and scope of the professional development on offer to us. In his highly creative book, *The Man Who Mistook His Wife for a Hat*, the neurologist Oliver Sacks describes a patient of his called Rebecca, a young woman whom he had known for some 12 years and who, after the death of her grandmother, appeared to emerge much more strongly as a person in her own right:

'I want no more classes, no more workshops,' she said. 'They do nothing for me. They do nothing to bring me together . . . I'm a sort of living carpet. I need a pattern, a design like you have on that carpet. I come apart, I unravel, unless there's a design.' I looked down at the carpet, as Rebecca said this, and found myself thinking of Sherrington's famous image, comparing the brain/mind to an 'enchanted loom', weaving patterns ever-dissolving, but always with meaning.

(Sacks, 1986: 175)

Some professional development courses include biographical accounts and portfolios as part of the assessed work submitted by students. There can be problems when personal material of this nature is then used in a public context (for example, in portfolios that will form part of the assessment of teachers). Clearly, if you are preparing an autobiographical account or portfolio for purely personal use, you will not have the problems of ownership. What you might want to do, however, is to use some of that material as the basis for discussions with friends or colleagues about how well you have managed to address your strengths and weaknesses.

Apart from the personal development aspect, there are important pragmatic reasons for building a portfolio or some kind of record of your professional experience. For example, the practice of APL and APEL, discussed in Chapter 6, is used in a number of HEIs and by professional bodies to give exemption from parts of programmes leading to qualifications. Also, you may find that having some physical evidence of your work will come in useful at job interviews or for promotion panels.

Once you have a 'map' or, at least, some idea of your professional development needs, you may wish to pursue a postgraduate course leading to a diploma or master's degree, or you may become a member of a professional body that provides professional development courses. All of these may be available within your own college (if it is linked in some way to an HEI) or you may have to find a course elsewhere. Many HEIs now offer flexible ways to gain a postgraduate qualification (for example, by distance learning or residential weekend study), and, as we noted above, some have introduced APL/APEL procedures to allow experienced people to be exempted from taking the full set of course modules.

Some HEIs have also introduced a structured doctoral programme leading to the Doctorate in Education (or EdD). For this, students take a number of 'taught' modules, some of which will cover research methodology, and then produce a thesis. As noted in Chapter 7, some HEIs are developing research links with FE colleges that go beyond the traditional professional development relationship in which FE staff are merely seen as students working towards an accredited qualification. To this end, master's and EdD programmes often encourage students to conduct action research projects, empirical studies and other forms of analysis based within their professional context.

If you are interested in developing your research potential and feel motivated enough to dedicate some three to five years to one project, you could pursue a research degree (MPhil or PhD). In this case, you would be appointed to a supervisor who has a keen interest in your research ideas and who possibly also carries out research in a similar field. Although all HEIs offer research degrees, it is advisable to gain a good impression of an institution's research rating. In addition, you should also try to find out which academics are in the department in which you would be based, as there may be someone who has published articles and books related to your research interests. Departments differ, too, in their provision for part-time research students in that some bring students together for seminars and social events and may provide access to information technology. A useful way to begin your investigation of an academic department in an HEI is to visit the institution's library, which will house copies of all dissertations and research degree theses. By looking at a sample of this research output for the department you are interested in, you will gain some idea of the nature and scope of projects the department is able to supervise.

If you are a member of a trade union, you should keep in touch with the professional development programmes it offers as well as conferences and discussion group meetings.

In 2007, a number of Centres for Excellence in Teacher Training (CETTs) were established across England with government funding channelled through LSIS as part of a national strategy for improving the quality of teacher training and to support teacher training providers. Although their government funding has now stopped, a number of the CETTs are still operating. They provide a very valuable forum for FE teachers and their websites are full of excellent resources. The following websites were current at the time of writing:

WMCETT: www2.warwick.ac.uk/study/cll/othercourses/wmcett
CETT for Inclusive Living: http://cettil.org.uk

HUDCETT: http://hudcett.hud.ac.uk
SUNCETT: www.sunderland.ac.uk/faculties/es/centres/suncett/
LONCETT: www.loncett.org.uk/
SWITCH: www.switchcett.org.uk/
EMCETT: www.thelearningchain.net/
EECETT: www.acer.ac.uk/EECETT/Success North and
     www.successnorth.org

REFLECTION

The following questions and instructions are designed to help you evaluate and identify your professional development needs. You may find them useful during initial training as well as at different stages during your teaching career:

1   Make a list of the knowledge and skills you would like to gain (or improve) in order to be a more effective teacher. Can you acquire those skills on an in-house staff development programme?
2   Are you comfortable with the curriculum demands imposed on you? Would you feel happier if you could update your skills and knowledge in a particular area of your professional expertise? Have there been recent changes to your professional area (for example, new legislation, new inventions, changes in information technology, etc.)? Can you cope with these changes?
3   Are you aware of the different organisations that could supply you with information and ideas to support and enrich your teaching? Would you gain by joining a professional body? Are there people in neighbouring colleges, schools, HEIs, companies, government agencies and other organisations with whom you should be in contact or with whom you might work in partnership?
4   Will your management support your professional development plans? What will they expect in the form of a proposal (for example, a written proposal with costings) and who is the best person to approach first?
5   Have you considered changing direction? There may be opportunities within the college to try a completely new field (for example, move from teaching into student services) or to set up a new course in a related discipline, or a multi-disciplinary programme.
6   Where do you want to be in five years in terms of your career? Can you identify any professional development issues now so that you can plan your career in advance?

CPD through skills competitions for students

Many FE teachers are involved in preparing their students to take part in skills competitions. In 2011, London hosted WorldSkills (held every two years in different cities round the world) in which young people aged from 16 to 25 from 51 countries took part in 3 days of intensive events competing for Olympic-style medals in the following fields: Transportation and Logistics; Construction and Building Technology; Manufacturing and Engineering Technology; ICLT; Creative Arts and Fashion; and Social and Personal Services. Team UK came fifth, winning 4 golds (in Bricklaying, Plumbing and Heating, Stonemasonry, and Visual Merchandise), 2 silver, 6 bronze, and 12 Medallions of Excellence. The competition was first held in 1950 and has been growing in size ever since. To qualify for the event, young people take part in local, regional and national heats, many of which are hosted in FE colleges.

There are other forms of competitions, often organised by teachers' professional organisations such as the Association of Hairdressers and Therapists (AHT), sometimes in conjunction with product manufacturers. In her research on competitions in hairdressing, Broad (2013 forthcoming) found that participation in skills competitions was regarded as an important form of CPD by hairdressing teachers The events provide opportunities to network with other teachers, sharing expertise not only with students, but with other experts in the field, both within and beyond the teaching environment. The judging is usually done by leading professional hairdressers with national reputations. Broad also reported that teachers valued the competitions because they encourage both student and teacher creativity and enable students to develop expertise beyond the level at which they are studying in college. In addition, students will develop a range of broader skills, including: organisation and planning skills; and the confidence to perform their skills in a public arena.

Life beyond college

FE colleges play a significant role in the life of their local communities and beyond; indeed, some that specialise in certain courses (for example, land-based colleges) attract students on a national and even international basis. The range of people who come through the college doors, as we saw in Chapter 2, represents the diversity of the college's geographical, socio-economic and cultural location. Reaching out from the college, the links into the community will include outreach centres for teaching and access-related services, partnerships with local schools and HEIs, and a range of mechanisms for relating to the world of business and industry. As a college teacher, therefore, you will be constantly aware of the wider world beyond your immediate teaching room.

Part of your duties and responsibilities as a teacher may include liaising with community groups, representing the college on education business and lifelong learning partnership committees and so on. We now discuss the nature of some of the organisations with whom you may be formally required to liaise and work. We also discuss the ways in which these and other organisations can provide you with valuable support in terms of your teaching and professional development.

National and regional bodies

Prior to the 1992 FHE Act, colleges in England were affiliated to their local regional advisory council (RAC), a network of which existed throughout the country. These bodies came within the remit of LEAs but were independent of each other and although they had some activities in common, such as running staff development courses, they were very different in terms of their effectiveness. Where RACs did come together was in their contribution to the work of the FEU, which was set up in 1977, under the auspices of the then Department of Education and Science, to help promote curriculum development initiatives and coordinate and disseminate good practice in teaching and learning. The FEU was particularly active in the late 1970s and early 1980s, when it produced reports such as *A Basis for Choice* (1979) and *Vocational Preparation* (1981), which provided guidance and analysis for colleges in dealing with the sudden dramatic influx of recruits to the newly established government-sponsored youth training schemes. Often working alongside the national Further Education Staff College (FESC), which had been set up in 1963 at Coombe Lodge near Bristol, the FEU produced a wealth of literature, much of it based on action research projects involving colleges.

In April 1995, a new organisation, the Further Education Development Agency (FEDA), replaced both the FEU and FESC. In light of the structural changes to the post-compulsory sector described in Chapter 1, FEDA was renamed the Learning and Skills Development Agency (LSDA) in 2000, signalling that it would now represent a much wider constituency. In April 2006, LSDA was replaced by the Quality Improvement Agency (QIA), which in turn was replaced by the Learning and Skills Improvement Service (LSIS) in 2008. Since the demise of the FEU, the subsequent agencies have been closely tied to supporting the delivery of government policy through staff development programmes and resources. The National Institute for Adult Continuing Education (NIACE) was founded in 1921 and has its headquarters in Leicester and Cardiff. It campaigns for better resources for and access to learning opportunities for adults including in the workplace.

Given the incorporation of colleges in 1993 and the establishment of bodies the role of the RACs became confused and most have either dissolved or transformed into consultancy organisations. In 2009, Scotland's Colleges was formed to play a similar role to LSIS and replaced the Scottish Further Education Unit (SFEU) and a number of other bodies. One organisation that covers the UK and is closely related to the work of colleges is World Skills UK, which, as we saw in Chapter 7, organises annual competitions in a range of vocational areas. The UK CES and the SSCs also have UK-wide remits.

Trade unions, professional organisation and HE

In 2006, the trade union with the largest coverage of FE lecturers in the UK, NATFHE (the National Association of Teachers in Further and Higher Education) merged with the Association of University Teachers (AUT) to form the University and College Union (UCU). The ATL still exists and, in Scotland, lecturers can also join the Educational Institute Scotland (EIS). There is also a trade union in Wales covering both schools and colleges, UCAC (Undeb Cenedlaethol Athrawon Cymru). The Association for College Management (ACM) represents college staff in management positions, though some FE principals also belong to the Secondary Heads Association (SHA). Two membership organisations represent colleges in terms of promoting FE to policymakers and lobbying for change: the AoC in England and Wales; and the Association of Scotland's Colleges. The principals of some of the largest colleges in England belong to the '157 Group'.

As discussed in Chapter 1, many college lecturers have a background in a profession or craft-based occupation and may find it useful to maintain a direct link through an appropriate organisation such as, for example, the Institute of Chartered Accountants or the Association of Construction Heads. Many contemporary occupations can trace their origins back to the medieval craft guilds and the City of London still boasts 107 livery companies, including, for example, the Worshipful Company of Bakers and the Worshipful Company of Tylers [sic] and Bricklayers. The livery companies provide scholarships and bursaries for students and some have close links with colleges.

The Learning and Skills Research Network (LSRN) and the IfL are valuable sources of information for teachers in FE about developments in policy and practice. It is also worth checking if any of the universities in your area host networks to bring together teachers, employers and researchers, and, of course, colleges will have close relationships with universities for the joint delivery of degree and sub-degree programmes. Many universities open their seminars to external visitors and may also have arrangements for FE lecturers to become research associates.

Business- and community-related organisations

There are many different forms of business-related organisation in the UK, stretching from national bodies such as the CBI and the Institute of Directors to local bodies such as Chambers of Commerce and the Round Table. These locally based organisations often have historical roots in their communities, including those which represent the interests of employees rather than those of employers, such as trade councils. The CBI has a regional network of branches that meet regularly for seminars and events at which education and training often feature. There is a wide range of community-based organisations, including, for example, charities, voluntary agencies and single-issue groups.

At a regional level in England, colleges used to have links with one of the nine RDAs established in 1999, but these were abolished in 2010 and replaced by LEPs. It is too early to report on the work of the LEPs, but your college will probably have some involvement. You might also be involved in your local education-business partnership (EBP), which will also include representatives from industry and commerce, the local authority, careers service, local HEIs, private training providers, voluntary organisations, trade unions and schools. EBPs began in 1990 at the same time the TECs were being established. At that time, most EBPs were set up and largely managed by TECs. In the mind of the then Employment Department, EBPs were the means to formalise the largely ad hoc and voluntaristic links between education and business that have been in existence for many years. The very notion of trying to impose a superstructure on relationships that tended to be organic rather than institutionalised has seemed to some on both sides to be too dictatorial and at odds with the concept of partnership. EBPs have, therefore, developed differently throughout the country, ranging from the very successful to those that struggle to get enough people to make meetings quorate. Where an EBP is successful, the local colleges are likely to be heavily involved. An EBP can provide college staff with an excellent forum for liaising with schools over such matters as managing an effective transition for young people transferring to college at 16 or joint initiatives to raise standards in basic skills. Useful relationships with employers can also be established through an EBP.

Because of the need for local organisations to work together to ensure they make the most of limited resources to finance education and training initiatives, EBPs and similar partnerships rely on individuals who are prepared to put their creative energies to work for the collective good.

Gravatt and Silver (2000: 121) argue that partnerships are attractive to government because:

- They bring local organisations together to deliver shared goals.
- They are a way of bridging the public and private sector and of harnessing private sector investment to deliver public goals.
- They can be formed – and dissolved – quickly.
- They make it possible to deliver new programmes without the costs of setting up new organisations or of restructuring existing ones.

Writing from their perspective as registrar and principal, respectively, of Lewisham College in London, Gravatt and Silver (ibid.: 123) highlight the following reasons why community- and business-based partnerships work, or do not work:

Work	Do not work
Shared purpose	Forced geographically
Conscious acceptance	No trust
Voluntary	No guarantees
Respect difference	Own agendas
Shared values	Forced into frameworks
Outward-looking	Resist change
Allowed to evolve	Over-control by external audit

Gravatt and Silver (ibid.: 126) stress that colleges 'need to tread carefully in the matter of partnerships'. They continue, 'Partnerships help organizations achieve objectives and add value to their activities, but they are not a panacea for all public sector problems. Too many partnerships established too hastily with too many overlapping aims just add to the confusion and complexity that gets in the way of education and training' (ibid.).

The term 'partnership' is, of course, a contested one. Partnership suggests an equal relationship, one entered into willingly. Many of the 'partnerships' that exist in the world of education and training are simply gatherings of people who need to ensure their organisations' needs and agendas are represented. As Field (2000: 26–7) argues, 'the discourse of partnership frequently cloaks a profound inequality between the so-called partners'. And the concept of partnership as envisaged by policymakers is a positivist one (that is, the partnerships exist to make the delivery of policy objectives run smoothly). It would be interesting to consider what might happen if, for example, the 'partners' at a meeting of a local Lifelong Learning Partnership decided to use their solidarity to challenge the targets and performance indicators imposed on them from on high. In her study of a partnership between post-16 education and training providers in the English Midlands, Dhillon (2009) found that it was the considerable levels of trust and shared sense of values and norms, built up over a long period, that sustained the collaboration even when funding had been reduced. She argues that this formed the 'social glue' or 'bonding social capital' that kept the partnership alive and also brought benefits to those involved.

Conclusion

As we conclude this book, FE colleges in the UK are fighting for resources in the light of the continuing economic crisis. Many of their students face uncertain futures as unemployment rises and the phenomenon of under-employment (people working part-time and on temporary contracts when they want full-time) grows. We considered writing a completely new chapter on teaching and learning in austerity, but we end where we began with the proposal that the principles of teaching and learning discussed here will and do transcend the turbulent environment in which teachers work.

References

Ainley, P. and Bailey, B. (1997) *The Business of Learning*, London, Cassell.

Ainley, P. and Vickerstaff, S. (1993) Transitions from corporatism: the privatisation of policy failure, *Contemporary Record*, 7(3): 541–56.

Anderson, G., Barton, S. and Wahlberg, M. (2003) Reflection and experiences on further education research in practice, *Journal of Vocational Education and Training*, 55(4): 499–516.

Assessment Reform Group (1999) *Assessment for Learning. Beyond the Black Box*, University of Cambridge, Assessment Reform Group.

Attwood, G., Croll, P. and Hamilton, J. (2004) Challenging students in further education: themes arising from a study of innovative FE provision for excluded and disaffected young people, *Journal of Further and Higher Education*, 28(1): 107–19.

Audit Commission/Ofsted (1993) *Unfinished Business: Full-time Educational Courses for 16–19 Year Olds*, London, HMSO.

Avis, J. (1999) Shifting identity: new conditions and the transformation of practice-teaching within post-compulsory education, *Journal of Vocational Education and Training*, 51(2): 245–64.

Avis, J. and Bathmaker, A.-M. (2006) From trainee to FE lecturer: trials and tribulations, *Journal of Vocational Education and Training*, 58(2): 171–89.

Avis, J., Canning, R., Fisher, R., Morgan-Klein, B. and Simmons, R. (2011) Vocational education teacher training in Scotland and England: policy and practice, *Journal of Vocational Education and Training*, 63(2): 115–27.

Bailey, B. (1983) The technical education movement: a late nineteenth century educational 'lobby', *Journal of Further and Higher Education*, 7(3): 55–68.

Bailey, B. (2002) Further education, in R. Aldrige (ed.) *A Century of Education*, London, RoutledgeFalmer.

Bailey, B. and Unwin, L. (2008) Fostering 'habits of reflection, independent study and free inquiry': an analysis of the short-lived phenomenon of general/liberal studies, *Journal of Vocational Education and Training*, 60(1): 61–74.

Banks, C.N. (2010) *Independent Review of Fees and Co-funding in Further Education in England: Co-investment in the Skills of the Future*, a summary report to Ministers in the DBIS.

Bariso, E.U. (2008) Factors affecting the participation in adult education: a case study of participation in Hackney and Walthan Forest, London, *Studies in the Education of Adults*, 40(1): 110–24.

Bateson, M.C. (1984) *With a Daughter's Eye*, New York, William Morrow.

Bathmaker, A.-M. and Avis, J. (2005) Becoming a lecturer in further education in England: the construction of professional identity and the role of communities of practice, *Journal of Education and Teaching*, 31(1): 47–62.

Bathmaker, A.-M. and Avis, J. (2007) 'How do I cope with that?' The challenge of 'schooling' cultures in further education for trainee FE lecturers, *British Educational Research Journal*, 33(4): 509–32.

Bathmaker, A.-M. and Thomas, W. (2009) Positioning themselves: an exploration of the nature and meaning of transitions in the context of dual sector FE/HE institutions in England, *Journal of Further and Higher Education*, 33(2): 119–30.

Belenky, M.F., Clinchy, M.B., Goldberger, N.R. and Tarule, J.M. (1986) *Women's Ways of Knowing*, New York, Basic Books.

Berne, E. (1970) *Games People Play*, Harmondsworth, Penguin.

Biesta, G. (2008) Pragmatism's contribution to understanding learning-in-context, in R. Edwards, G. Biesta and M. Thorpe (eds) *Rethinking Contexts for Learning and Teaching*, London, Routledge.

Billett, S. and Somerville, M. (2004) Transformations at work: identity and learning, *Studies in Continuing Education*, 26(2): 309–26.

Black, P. and William, D. (1998) *Inside the Black Box*, London, King's College.

Black, P., Harrison, C., Lee, C., Marshall, B. and Wiliam, D. (2003) *Assessment for Learning: Putting it into Practice*, Maidenhead, Open University Press.

Bloom, B.S. (1965) *Taxonomy of Educational Objectives*, London, Longman.

Bloomer, M. (1997) *Curriculum Making in Post-16 Education: The Social Conditions of Studentship*, London, Routledge.

Bloomer, M. and Hodkinson, P. (2000) Learning careers: continuity and change in young people's dispositions to learning, *British Educational Research Journal*, 26(5): 583–97.

Boreham, N. (2002) Work process knowledge, curriculum control and the work-based route to vocational qualifications, *British Journal of Educational Studies*, 50(2): 225–37.

Boud, D. (2010) Relocating reflection in the context of practice, in H. Bradbury, N. Frost, S. Kilminster and M. Zukas (eds) *Beyond Reflective Practice*, London, Routledge.

Boud, D., Keogh, R. and Walker, D. (1985) *Reflection: Turning Experience into Learning*, London, Kogan Page.

Bourdieu, P. and Wacquant, L. (1992) *An Invitation to Reflexive Sociology*, London, Polity Press.

Brandes, D. and Phillips, H. (1985) *Gamesters' Handbook*, London, Hutchinson.

Broad, J. (2013 forthcoming) Unpublished Ed.D Thesis, London, Institute of Education.

Brockmann, M., Clarke, L. and Winch, C. with Hanf, G., Mehaut, P. and Westerhuis, A. (2011) *Knowledge, Skills and Competence in the European Labour Market: What's in a Vocational Qualification?* London, Routledge.

Brookfield, S. (1986) *Understanding and Facilitating Adult Learning*, Milton Keynes, Open University Press.

Brooks, R. (2009) Young people and political participation: an analysis of European Union policies, *Sociological Research Online*, 14(1): 7.

Brooks, V. (2004) Using assessment for formative purposes, in V. Brooks, I. Abbott and L. Bills (eds) *Preparing to Teach in Secondary Schools*, 1st edition, Maidenhead, Open University Press.

Brooks, V. (2007) Using assessment for formative purposes, in V. Brooks, I. Abbott and L. Bills (eds) *Preparing to Teach in Secondary Schools*, 2nd edition, Maidenhead, Open University Press.

Brown, S. (1994) Assessment: a changing practice, in B. Moon and A. Shelton Mayes (eds) *Teaching and Learning in the Secondary School*, London, Open University/ Routledge.

Bryce, T. and Hume, W. (eds) (2009) *Scottish Education*, 2nd edition, Edinburgh: Edinburgh University Press.

Cable, V. (2011) *Letter to the Chief Executive of the Skills Funding Agency*, 3 March, London, DBIS.

Canning, R. (2007) Reconceptualising core skills, *Journal of Education and Work*, 20(1): 17–26.

Canning, R. (2011) Reflecting on the reflective practitioner: vocational initial teacher education in Scotland, *Journal of Vocational Education and Training*, 63(4): 609–17.

Carr, W. (1993) Reconstructing the curriculum debate: an editorial introduction, *Curriculum Studies*, 1(1): 5–9.

Castling, A. (1996) *Competence-based Teaching and Training*, London, City & Guilds Macmillan.

Chowdry, H. and Sibieta, L. (2011) *Trends in Education and Schools Spending*, IFS Briefing Note BN121, London, IFS.

Clarke, J. (2002) Deconstructing domestication: women's experience and the goals of critical pedagogy, in R. Harrison, F. Reeve and J. Clarke (eds) *Supporting Lifelong Learning. Volume 1: Perspectives on Learning*, London, RoutledgeFalmer.

Clough, P. and Barton, L. (1995) Introduction: self and the research act, in P. Clough and L. Barton (eds) *Making Difficulties, Research and the Construction of SEN*, London, Paul Chapman.

Coffield, F., Moseley, D., Hall, E. and Ecclestone, K. (2004) *Should We Be Using Learning Styles? What Research Has to Say to Practice*, London, Learning and Skills Research Centre.

Coffield, F., Edward, S., Finlay, I., Hodgson, A., Spours, K. and Steer, R. (2008) *Improving Learning, Skills and Inclusion*, London, Routledge.

Cole, M. (1985) The zone of proximal development: where culture and cognition create each other, in J. Wertsch (ed.) *Culture, Communication and Cognition: Vygotskian Perspectives*, Cambridge, Cambridge University Press.

Colley, H. (2003) *Mentoring for Social Inclusion: A Critical Approach to Nurturing Mentoring Relationships*, London: RoutledgeFalmer.

Colley, H., James, D., Tedder, M. and Diment, K. (2003) Learning as becoming in vocational education and training: class, gender and the role of vocational habitus, *Journal of Vocational Education and Training*, 55(4): 471–97.

Collinson, D. (ed.) (2009) *Researching Self-regulation in FE Colleges*, Coventry: LSIS.

Corbett, J. (1997) Transitions to what? Young people with special educational needs, in S. Tomlinson (ed.) *Education 14–19 Critical Perspectives*, London, The Athlone Press.

Cort, P. (2009) The EC Discourse on Vocational Training: how a 'common vocational training policy' turned into a lifelong learning strategy, *Vocations and Learning*, 2(2), 87–107.

Cort, P. (2010) Stating the obvious: the European Qualifications Framework is *not* a neutral evidence-based policy tool, *European Educational Research Journal*, 9(3): 304–16.

Cox, A. (1996) Teacher as mentor: opportunities for professional development, in J. Robson (ed.) *The Professional FE Teacher*, Aldershot, Avebury.

Culham, A. (2001) Practitioner-based research in FE: realities and problems, *College Research*, 4(3): 27.

Culham, A. (2003) 'Including' permanently excluded students from pupil referral units in further education, *Journal of Further and Higher Education*, 27(4): 399–409.

Cunningham, B. (2012) *Mentoring Teachers in Post-compulsory Education*, 2nd edition, London, Routledge.

Davies, P. and Owen, J. (2001) *Listening to Staff*, London, LSDA.

DBIS (2010) *Skills for Sustainable Growth: Strategy Document*, London, DBIS.

DBIS (2011a) *White Paper: Students at the Heart of the System*, Cm 8122, London, HMSO.

DBIS (2011b) *New Challenges, New Chances. Further Education and Skills System Reform Plan: Building a World Class System*. London, DBIS.

DCSF/DIUS (2008) *Raising Expectations: Enabling the System to Deliver*, Cm 7348, London, The Stationery Office.

Dearing, R. (1996) *Review of 16–19 Qualifications: Summary Report*, London, School Curriculum and Assessment Authority.

Dee, L. (1999) Inclusive learning: from rhetoric to reality, in A. Green and N. Lucas (eds) *FE and Lifelong Learning: Realigning the Sector for the 21st Century*, London, Institute of Education.

DES/ED/WO (1991) *Education and Training for the 21st Century*, London, HMSO.

DES/WO (1988) *Advancing A Levels (The Higginson Report)*, London, HMSO.

Dewey, J. (1938) *Experience and Education*, New York, Collier.

Dewey, J. (1966) *Democracy and Education*, New York, Free Press.

DfE (2011) *What is Alternative Provision* (available at: www.education.gov.uk/schools/pupilsupport/inclusionandlearnersupport/a0010414/what-is-alternative-provision).

DfEE (1997) *Qualifying for Success: A Consultation Paper on the Future of Post-16 Qualifications*, London, DfEE.

DfEE (1999) *Learning to Succeed*, Cm 4392, London, The Stationery Office.

DfES (2004a) *Every Child Matters: Change for Children in Schools*, London, DfES.

DfES (2004b) *Working Group on 14–19 Reform (2004) 14–19 Curriculum and Qualifications Reform: Final Report of the Working Group*, London, DfES.

DfES (2006a) *Vision Report of the Teaching and Learning in 2020 Review Group*, Nottingham, DfES Publications.

DfES (2006b) *Further Education: Raising Skills, Improving Life Chances*, Cm 6768, London, The Stationery Office.

DfES (2007) *Raising Expectations: Staying in Education and Training Post-16*, Cm 7065, London, HMSO.

Dhillon, J. (2009) The role of social capital in sustaining partnership, *British Educational Research Journal*, 35(5): 687–704.

Dimbleby, R. and Cooke, C. (2000) Curriculum and learning, in A. Smithers and P. Robinson (eds) *Further Education Re-formed*, London, Routledge.

Doughty, H. and Allan, J. (2008) Social capital and the evaluation of inclusiveness in Scottish further education colleges, *Journal of Further and Higher Education*, 32(3): 275–84.

Ecclestone, K. (2000) Assessment and critical autonomy in post-compulsory education in the UK, *Journal of Education and Work*, 13(2): 141–60.

Ecclestone, K. with Davies, J., Derrick, J. and Gawn, J. (2010) *Transforming Formative Assessment in Lifelong Learning*, Maidenhead, Open University Press.

Ecclestone, K. and Hayes, D. (2008) *The Dangerous Rise of Therapeutic Education*, London, Routledge.

Edexcel (2012) *BTEC Qualifications* (available at www.edexcel.com/migration documents/BTEC%20Firsts%20from%202012/BF029945-Specification-BTEC-Level-1-2-First-Award-Business.pdf), accessed 14 May 2012.

Education Scotland (n.d.) *Understanding the Curriculum as a Whole – What is the Curriculum for Excellence?* (available at www.educationscotland.gov.uk/thecurriculum/whatiscurriculumforexcellence/understandingthecurriculumasawhole/index.asp).

Edwards, A. (2001) Researching pedagogy: a sociocultural agenda, *Pedagogy, Culture and Society*, 9(2): 161–86.

Edwards, R. (1993) Multi-skilling the flexible workforce in post-compulsory education, *Journal of Further and Higher Education*, 17(1): 44–51.

Edwards, R. and Miller, K. (2008) Academic drift in vocational qualifications? Explorations through the lens of literacy, *Journal of Vocational Education and Training*, 60(2): 123–31.

Edwards, T., Fitz-Gibbon, C., Hardman, F., Haywood, R. and Meagher, N. (1997) *Separate but Equal? A Levels and GNVQs*, London, Routledge.

Elliott, G. (1996) *Crisis and Change in Vocational Education and Training*, London, Jessica Kingsley.

Elliott, J. (1983) A curriculum for the study of human affairs: the contribution of Lawrence Stenhouse, *Curriculum Studies*, 15(2): 105–23.

Elliott, J.G., Stemler, S.E., Sternberg, R.J., Grigorenko, E.L. and Hoffman, N. (2011) The socially skilled teacher and the development of tacit knowledge, *British Educational Research Journal*, 37(1): 83–103.

Engestrom, Y. (2001) Expansive learning at work: towards an activity – theoretical reconceptualisation, *Journal of Education and Work*, 14(1): 133–56.

Eraut, M. (1994) *Developing Professional Knowledge and Competence*, London, Falmer Press.

Ertl, H. and Stasz, C. (2010) Employing an 'employer-led' design? An evaluation of the development of diplomas, *Journal of Education and Work*, 23(4): 301–17.

ESRC (2007) *Britain Today: The State of the Nation in 2007*, Swindon, Economic and Social Research Council.

Evans, K. (1998) *Shaping Futures*, Ashgate, Aldershot.

Evans, K., Kersh, N. and Sakamoto, A. (2004) Learner biographies: exploring tacit dimensions of knowledge and skills, in H. Rainbird, A. Fuller and A. Munro (eds) *Workplace Learning in Context*, London, Routledge.

Evans, K., Hodkinson, P., Rainbird, H. and Unwin, L. (2006) *Improving Workplace Learning*, London, Routledge.

Evans, K., Guile, D. and Harris, J. (2009) *Putting Knowledge to Work: Integrating Work-based and Subject-based Knowledge in Intermediate Level Qualifications and Workforce Upskilling – the Exemplars*, London, WLE Centre, Institute of Education.

Felstead, A. and Unwin, L. (2001) Funding post compulsory education and training: a retrospective analysis of the TEC and FEFC systems and their impact on skills, *Journal of Education and Work*, 14(1): 91–111.

Felstead, A., Fuller, A., Jewson, N. and Unwin, L. (2009) *Improving Working for Learning*, London, Routledge.

Fettes, T. (2012) Generic skills, in P. Huddleston and J. Stanley (eds) *Work-related Teaching and Learning: A Guide for Teachers and Practitioners*, Abingdon, Routledge.

FEU (1979) *A Basis for Choice*, London, FEU.

Field, J. (2000) *Lifelong Learning and the New Educational Order*, Stoke-on-Trent, Trentham Books.

Field, J. (2004) Articulation and credit transfer in Scotland: taking the highroad or a sideways step in a ghetto? *Journal of Access Policy and Practice*, 1(2): 85–99.

Field, J. (2006) *Lifelong Learning and the New Educational Order*, 2nd edition, Stoke-on-Trent, Trentham Books.

Fieldhouse, R. and Associates (1996) *A History of Modern British Adult Education*, Leicester, NIACE.

Finegold, D., Milliband, D., Raffe, D., Spours, K. and Young, M. (1990) *A British Baccalaureate: Ending the Division between Education and Training*, London, Institute for Public Policy Research.

Finlay, I., Spours, K., Steer, R., Coffield, F., Gregson, M., Hodgson, A. and Edward, S. (2006) 'The heart of what we do': policies on teaching, learning and assessment in the new learning and skills sector, *Research Report 4*, London, Institute of Education, University of London.

Fisher, R. and Webb, K. (2006) Subject specialist pedagogy and initial teacher training for the learning and skills sector in England: the context, a response and some critical issues, *Journal of Further and Higher Education*, 30(4): 337–49.

Fowler, Z. (2008) Negotiating the textuality of further education: issues of agency and participation, *Oxford Review of Education*, 34(4): 425–41.

Freire, P. (1974) *Education: The Practice of Freedom*, London, Writers and Readers Co-operative.

Fuller, A. (2007) Critiquing theories of learning and communities of practice, in J. Hughes, N. Jewson and L. Unwin (eds) *Communities of Practice: Critical Perspectives*, London, Routledge.

Fuller, A. and Unwin, L. (2004) Expansive learning environments: integrating personal and organisational development, in H. Rainbird, A. Fuller and A. Munro (eds) *Workplace Learning in Context*, London, Routledge.

Fuller, A. and Unwin, L. (2010) 'Change and continuity in apprenticeship: the resilience of a model of learning', *Journal of Education and Work*, 25(5): 405–16.

Fuller, A. and Unwin, L. (2011) Vocational education and training in the spotlight: back to the future for the UK's coalition government? *London Review of Education*, 9(2): 191–204.

Fuller, A., Hodkinson, H., Hodkinson, P. and Unwin, L. (2005) Learning as peripheral participation in communities of practice: a reassessment of key concepts in workplace learning, *British Educational Research Journal*, 31(1): 49–68.

Furlong, A. and Cartmel, F. (1997) *Young People and Social Change*, Buckingham, Open University Press.

Gagne, R.M. (1988) *Principles of Instructional Design*, New York, Holt, Rinehart and Winston.

Gale, K., Turner, R. and McKenzie, L.M. (2011) Communities of praxis? Scholarship and practice styles of the HE in FE professional, *Journal of Vocational Education and Training*, 63(2): 159–69.

Gallacher, J. (2006) Blurring the boundaries or creating diversity? The contribution of the further education colleges to higher education in Scotland, *Journal of Further and Higher Education*, 30(1): 43–58.

Giroux, H. (ed.) (1991) *Post-modernism, Feminism and Cultural Politics: Redrawing Educational Boundaries*, Albany, NY, State University of New York Press.

Gleeson, D. (1996) Post-compulsory education in a post-industrial and post-modern age, in J. Avis, M. Bloomer, G. Esland, D. Gleeson and P. Hodkinson (eds) *Knowledge and Nationhood*, London, Cassell Education.

Gleeson, D. (2005) Learning for a change in further education, *Journal of Vocational Education and Training*, 57(2): 239–46.

Gleeson, D. and Shain, F. (1999) By appointment: governance, markets and managerialism in further education, *British Educational Research Journal*, 25(4): 545–61.

Gleeson, D., Abbott, I. and Hill, R. (2011) Governing the governors: a case study of college governance in English further education, *British Educational Research Journal*, 37(5): 781–96.

Gove (2012) Letter from Secretary of State, Rt. Hon. Michael Gove, to Chief Executive of Ofqual, 30 March 2012.

Gravatt, J. and Silver, R. (2000) Partnerships with the community, in A. Smithers and P. Robinson (eds) *Further Education Re-formed*, London, Falmer Press.

Green, A. (1997) Core skills, general education and unification in post-16 education, in A. Hodgson and K. Spours (eds) *Dearing and Beyond*, London, Kogan Page.

Green, A. and Lucas, N. (1999) From obscurity to crisis: the further education sector in context, in A. Green and N. Lucas (eds) *FE and Lifelong Learning: Realigning the Sector for the 21st Century*, London, Bedford Way Papers, Institute of Education.

Griffin, C. (1993) *Representations of Youth*, Cambridge, Polity Press.

Griffiths, C. and Lloyd, M.G. (2009) Degree of success? A review of delivering BSc honours degrees in an FE college, *Journal of Further and Higher Education*, 33(4): 483–92.

Grubb, W.N. and Associates (1999) *Honoured but Invisible: An Inside Look at Teaching in Community Colleges*, London, Routledge.

Guile, D. (2006) What is distinctive about the knowledge economy? Implications for education, in H. Lauder, P. Brown, J.-A. Dillabough and A.H. Halsey (eds) *Education, Globalisation and Social Change*, Oxford, Oxford University Press.

Guile, D. (2010) *The Learning Challenge of the Knowledge Economy*, Rotterdam, Sense Publishers.

Guile, D. (2011) Apprenticeship as a model of vocational 'formation' and 'reformation': the use of foundation degrees in the aircraft engineering industry, *Journal of Vocational Education and Training*, 63(3): 451–64.

Guile, D. and Hayton, A. (1999) Information and learning technology: the implications for teaching and learning in further education, in A. Green and N. Lucas (eds)

FE and Lifelong Learning: Realigning the Sector for the Twenty-first Century, London, Institute of Education.

Guile, D. and Young, M. (1999) Beyond the institution of apprenticeship: towards a social theory of learning as the production of knowledge, in P. Ainley and H. Rainbird (eds) *Apprenticeship: Towards a New Paradigm for Learning*, London, Kogan Page.

Gulikers, J. (2006) *Authenticity is in the Eye of the Beholder: Beliefs and Perceptions of Authentic Assessment and the Influence on Student Learning*, Maastricht, Interuniversity Center for Educational Research, Open-Universiteit-Nederland.

Gulikers, J., Biemans, H. and Mulder, M. (2009) Developer, teacher, student and employer evaluations of competence-based assessment quality, *Studies in Educational Evaluation*, 35(2009): 110–119.

Gunning, D. and Raffe, D. (2011) 14–19 education across Great Britain: convergence or divergence? *London Review of Education*, 9(2): 245–57.

Hager, P. and Hodkinson, P. (2009) Moving beyond the metaphor of transfer of learning, *British Educational Research Journal*, 35(4): 619–38.

Halpin, D. (2008) Pedagogy and the romantic imagination, *British Journal of Educational Studies*, 56(1): 59–75.

Hamilton, M. (2006) Just do it: literacies, everyday learning and the irrelevance of pedagogy, *Studies in the Education of Adults*, 38(2): 125–40.

Hargreaves, D. (2004) *Learning for Life*, Bristol, The Policy Press.

Harkin, J. (2005) Fragments stored against my ruin: the place of educational theory in the professional development of teachers in further education, *Journal of Vocational Education and Training*, 57(2): 165–80.

Harkin, J. (2006) Treated like adults: 14–16-year-olds in further education, *Research in Post-Compulsory Education*, 11(3): 319–39.

Harkin, J., Turner, G. and Dawn, T. (2001) *Teaching Young Adults*, London, RoutledgeFalmer.

Harlen, W. and Deakin Crick, R. (2002) *A Systematic Review of the Impact of Summative Assessment and Tests on Students' Motivation for Learning in Researching Evidence in Education Library*, London, EPPI Centre, Social Science Research Unit, Institute of Education.

Harrow, A.J. (1972) *A Taxonomy of the Psychomotor Domain*, New York, McKay.

Heathcote, G., Kempa, R. and Roberts, I. (1982) *Curriculum Styles and Strategies*, London, FEU.

Hill, R. (2000) A study of the views of full-time FE lecturers regarding their college corporations and agencies of the FE sector, *Journal of Further and Higher Education*, 24(1): 67–76.

Hillage, J., Loukas, G., Newton, B. and Tamkin, P. (2006) *Employer Training Pilots: Final Evaluation Report*, Research Report 774, London, Department for Education and Skills.

Hochschild, A. (1983) *The Managed Heart: The Commercialization of Human Feeling*, Berkeley, CA, University of California Press.

Hodgson, A. and Spours, K. (1997) *Beyond Dearing, 14–19: Qualifications, Frameworks and Systems*, London, Kogan Page.

Hodgson, A. and Spours, K. (1999) *New Labour's Educational Agenda: Issues and Policies for Education and Training from 14+*, London, Kogan Page.

Hodgson, A. and Spours, K. (2001) Part-time work and full-time education in the UK: the emergence of a curriculum and policy issue, *Journal of Education and Work*, 14(3): 373–8.

Hodgson, A. and Spours, K. (2011) Policy for the education and training of 14- to 19-year-olds in the UK – new uncertainties and new divisions? *London Review of Education*, 9(2): 145–51.

Hodkinson, P. (1997) Neo-Fordism and teacher professionalism, *Teacher Development*, 1(1): 69–82.

Hodkinson, P. and Issitt, M. (1995) *The Challenge of Competence*, London, Cassell Education.

Hodkinson, P. and Bloomer, M. (2000) Stokingham Sixth Form College: institutional culture and dispositions to learning, *British Journal of Sociology of Education*, 21(2): 187–200.

Hodkinson, P., Sparkes, A. and Hodkinson, H. (1996) *Triumphs and Tears*, Manchester, David Fulton.

Honey, P. and Mumford, A. (1982) *The Manual of Learning Styles*, Maidenhead, Peter Honey.

Howard, U. (2009) *IFFL Sector Paper 7*, Leicester, NIACE.

Huddleston, P. (2004) *'Learning on the Edge': Second Chance Education for 14–19 Year Olds*, paper presented to the Nuffield Review of 14–19 Education and Training, February 2004.

Huddleston, P. (2011) Vocational pedagogy: bringing it all together? in *National Skills Forum/Associate Parliamentary Skills Group Open to Ideas: Essays on Education and Skills*, London, Policy Connect.

Huddleston, P. (2012) Engaging and linking with employers, in P. Huddleston and J. Stanley (eds) *Work-related Teaching and Learning: A Guide for Teachers and Practitioners*, Abingdon: Routledge.

Huddleston, P., Keep, E. and Unwin, L. (2005) *What Might the Tomlinson and White Paper Proposals Mean for Vocational Education and Work-based Learning?* Discussion Paper 33, Nuffield Review of 14–19 Education and Training.

Hughes, J., Jewson, N. and Unwin, L. (eds) (2007) *Communities of Practice: Critical Perspectives*, London, Routledge.

Hull, G. and Katz, M. (2006) Crafting and agentive self: case studies on digital storytelling, *Research in the Teaching of English*, 41(1): 43–81.

Hull, G., Zacher, J. and Hibbert, L. (2009) Youth, risk and equity in a global world, *Review of Research in Education*, 33: 117–59.

Hyland, T. (1994) *Competence, Education and NVQs: Dissenting Perspectives*, London, Cassell Education.

Hyland, T. (2011) Mindfulness, therapy and vocational values: exploring the moral and aesthetic dimensions of vocational education and training, *Journal of Vocational Education and Training*, 63(2): 129–41.

Ipsos Mori/Social Research Institute (2012) *Fit for Purpose? The View of the Higher Education Sector, Teachers and Employers on the Suitability of A Levels*, Coventry, Ofqual.

Ivanic, R., Edwards, R., Satchwell, C. and Smith, J. (2007) Possibilities for pedagogy in further education: harnessing the abundance of literacy, *British Educational Research Journal*, 33(5): 703–21.

James, D. and Biesta, G. (2007) *Improving Learning Cultures in Further Education*, London, Routledge.

James, D. and Diment, K. (2003) Going underground? Learning and assessment in an ambiguous space, *Journal of Vocational Education and Training*, 55(4): 407–22.

Jaques, D. (1992) *Learning in Groups*, 2nd edition, London, Croom Helm.

Jaquette, O. (2009) Funding for equity and success in English further education colleges, 1998–2003, *Oxford Review of Education*, 35(1): 57–79.

Jarvis, P. (1987) *Adult Learning in the Social Context*, London, Croom Helm.

Jephcote, M. and Abbott, I. (2005) Tinkering and tailoring: the reform of 14–19 education in England, *Journal of Vocational Education and Training*, 57(2): 181–202.

Jephcote, M., Salisbury, J. and Rees, G. (2008) Being a teacher in further education in changing times, *Research in Post-compulsory Education*, 13(2): 163–72.

JISC (2010) *Effective Assessment in a Digital Age: A Guide to Technology-enhanced Assessment and Feedback* (available at: www.jisc.ac.uk/digiassess).

Johnson, M. (2008) Grading in competence-based qualifications – is it desirable and how might it affect validity? *Journal of Further and Higher Education*, 32(2): 175–84.

Johnstone, J.W.C. and Rivera, R.J. (1965) *Volunteers for Learning: A Study of the Educational Pursuits of Adults*, Hawthorne, NY, Aldine.

Keep, E. (2005) Reflections on the curious absence of employers, labour market incentives and labour market regulation in English 14–19 policy – the beginnings of a change? *Journal of Education Policy*, 20(5): 533–53.

Keep, E. (2006) State control of the English education and training system – playing with the biggest train set in the world, *Journal of Vocational Education & Training*, 58(1): 47–64.

Keep, E. (2008) *A Comparison of the Welsh Workforce Development Programme and England's Train to Gain*, ESRC SKOPE Research Paper No. 79.

Kennedy, H. (1997) *Learning Works: Widening Participation in Further Education*, Coventry, FEFC.

Kenway, J. (2001) The information superhighway and postmodernity: the social promise and the social price, in C. Paechter, M. Preedy, D. Scott and J. Soler (eds) *Knowledge, Power and Learning*, London, Paul Chapman.

Kidd, R. (1973) *How Adults Learn*, Chicago, IL, Follett.

Knowles, M.S. (1978) *The Adult Learner: a Neglected Species*, 2nd edition, Houston, Gulf Publishing Company, Book Division.

Kolb, D.A. (1984) *Experiential Learning*, Englewood Cliffs, NJ, Prentice Hall.

Lave, J. (1995) *Teaching as Learning in Practice*, Sylvia Scribner Award Lecture, American Educational Research Association Conference, San Francisco.

Lave, J. and Wenger, E. (1991) *Situated Learning*, Cambridge, Cambridge University Press.

Leitch Review (2006) *Prosperity for All in the Global Economy – World Class Skills*, London, HM Treasury.

Lingfield (2012) *Professionalism in Further Education: Interim Report*, London, Department for Business, Innovation and Skills.

LSIS (2012) *Further Education and Skills Sector: Summary Workforce Diversity Report 2011*, Coventry, LSIS.

Lucas, N. (1996) Teacher training agency: is there anyone there from further education? *Journal of Further and Higher Education*, 20(1): 67–73.

Lucas, N. (1999) Incorporated colleges: beyond the further education funding council's model, in A. Green and N. Lucas (eds) *FE and Lifelong Learning: Realigning the Sector for the 21st Century*, London, Institute of Education.

Lucas, N. (2004) The 'FENTO Fandango': national standards, compulsory teaching qualifications and the growing regulation of FE college teachers, *Journal of Further and Higher Education*, 28(1): 35–51.

Lucas, N. and Nasta, T. (2010) State regulation and the professionalisation of further education teachers: a comparison with schools and HE, *Journal of Vocational Education and Training*, 62(4): 441–54.

Lucas, N. and Unwin, L. (2009) Developing teacher expertise at work: in-service trainee teachers in colleges of further education in England, *Journal of Further and Higher Education*, 33(4): 423–33.

Lucas, N., Nasta, T. and Rogers, L. (2011) From fragmentation to chaos? The regulation of initial teacher training in further education, *British Educational Research Journal*, 38(4): 677–95.

Lumby, J. (2007) 14–16 year olds in further education colleges: lessons for learning and leadership, *Journal of Vocational Education and Training*, 59(1): 1–18.

Lumby, J. (2012) Disengaged and disaffected young people: surviving the system, *British Educational Research Journal*, 38(2): 261–79.

McCrone, T., Wade, P. and Golden, S. (2007) *The Impact of 14-16 Year Olds in Further Education Colleges*, Slough, NFER.

McGiveney, V. (1996) *Staying or Leaving the Course: Non-completion and Retention of Mature Students in Further and Higher Education*, Leicester, NIACE.

McLeod, J., Yates, L. and Halasa, K. (1994) Voice, difference and feminist pedagogy, *Curriculum Studies*, 2(2): 189–202.

McQueen, H. and Webber, J. (2009) What is very important to learning? A student perspective on a model of teaching and learning, *Journal of Further and Higher Education*, 33(3): 241–53.

Maguire, S. and Thompson, J. (2006) *Paying Young People to Stay on at School – Does it Work?* SKOPE Research Paper 69, Oxford, Universities of Oxford and Cardiff.

Marshall, L. and Rowland, F. (1993) *A Guide to Learning Independently*, 2nd edition, Buckingham, Open University Press.

Maslow, A. (1968) *Towards a Psychology of Being*, New York, Van Nostrand.

Mayes, T. (2002) The technology of learning in a social world, in R. Harrison, F. Reeve, A. Hanson and J. Clarke (eds) *Supporting Lifelong Learning. Volume 1: Perspectives on Learning*, London, RoutledgeFalmer.

Minton, D. (1991) *Teaching Skills in Further and Adult Education*, London, City & Guilds.

Mitra, B., Lewin-Jones, J., Barrett, H. and Williamson, S. (2010) The use of video to enable deep learning, *Research in Post-compulsory Education*, 15(4): 405–14.

Murphy, P. (ed.) (1999) *Learners, Learning and Assessment*, London, Paul Chapman/Open University.

NCFE (2010) *Assessing and Assuring the Quality Assessment Guidance for Awarding Organisations*, Newcastle-upon-Tyne.

Neisser, U. (1983) Towards a skilful psychology, in D. Roghers and J.A. Sloboda (eds) *The Acquisition of Symbolic Skills*, New York, Plenum Publishing Corporation.

Nuffield Review of 14–19 Education and Training, England and Wales (2008) *Issues Paper 10 General Education in the 14–19 Phase* (available at www.nuffield14-19 review.org.uk).

OCR (2009) *GCE AS Applied Business Specification*, Coventry, OCR.

Ofqual, WGA, CEA (2009) Functional Skills Criteria for English, Entry 1, Entry 2, Entry 3, Level 1, Level 2. Ofqual/09/4559, Coventry, Ofqual.

Orr, K. (2010) The entry of 14–16-year-old students into colleges: implications for further education initial teacher training in England, *Journal of Further and Higher Education*, 34(1): 47–57.

Osborne, R. (2006) Devolution and divergence in education policy: the Northern Ireland case, in J. Adams and K. Schmuecker (eds) *Devolution in Practice*, Newcastle, IPPR North.

Parry, G. (2005) The Higher Education Role of Further Education Colleges: Think Piece for the Foster Review of FE (available at http://webarchive.nationalarchives.gov.uk/20060214030141/http://dfes.gov.uk/furthereducation/fereview/evidence.shtml).

Parry, G., Callender, C., Scott, P. and Temple, P. (2012) *Understanding Higher Education in Further Education Colleges*, BIS Research Paper Number 69, London, BIS.

Perry, A. (2005) *If I Were You, I Wouldn't Start from Here: Comments on the Structure and Organisation of Further Education for the Foster Review of Further Education* (available at http://webarchive.nationalarchives.gov.uk/20060214030141/http://dfes.gov.uk/furthereducation/fereview/evidence.shtml).

Piaget, J. (1970) *Genetic Epistemology*, New York, Columbia University Press.

Pike, A. and Harrison, J. (2011) Crossing the FE/HE divide: the transition experiences of direct entrants at Level 6, *Journal of Further and Higher Education*, 35(1): 55–67.

Plowright, D. and Barr, G. (2012) An integrated professionalism in further education: a time for phronesis? *Journal of Further and Higher Education*, 36(1): 1–16.

Polanyi, M. (1967) The Tacit Dimension, New York, Anchor Books.

Price, F. and Kaid-Hanifi, K. (2011) E-motivation! The role of popular technology in student motivation and retention, *Research in Post-Compulsory Education*, 16(2): 173–87.

Pring, R. (1997) Aims, values and the curriculum, in S. Tomlinson (ed.) *Education 14–19: Critical Perspectives*, London, The Athlone Press.

Pring, R., Hayward, G., Hodgson, A., Johnson, J., Keep, E., Oancea, A. *et al.* (2009) *Education for All: The Future of Education and Training for 14–19 Year Olds*, London, Routledge.

Quicke, J. (1996) The reflective practitioner and teacher education: an answer to critics, *Teachers and Teaching: Theory and Practice*, 2(1): 11–22.

Raffe, D. (2003) 'Simplicity itself': the creation of the Scottish Credit and Qualifications Framework, *Journal of Education and Work*, 16(3): 239–57.

Raffe, D., Spours, K., Young, M. and Howieson, C. (1998) The unification of post-compulsory education: towards a conceptual framework, *British Journal of Educational Studies*, 4(6): 169–87.

Raggatt, P. and Williams, S. (1999) *Government, Markets and Vocational Qualifications*, London, Falmer Press.

Randle, K. and Brady, N. (1997) Further education and the new managerialism, *Journal of Further and Higher Education*, 21(2): 229–38.

Rees, G., Gorard, S., Fevre, R. and Furlong, J. (2000) Participating in the learning society: history, place and biography, in F. Coffield (ed.) *Differing Visions of a Learning Society, Volume 2*, Bristol, The Policy Press.

Roberts, S. (2012) 'I just got on with it': the educational experiences of ordinary, yet overlooked, boys, *British Journal of Sociology of Education*, 33(2): 203–21.

Robson, J. (ed.) (1996) *The Professional FE Teacher*, Aldershot, Avebury.

Robson, J. (1998) A profession in crisis: status, culture and identity in the further education college, *Journal of Vocational Education and Training*, 50(4): 585–607.

Robson, J. and Bailey, B. (2009) 'Bowing from the heart': an investigation into discourses of professionalism and the work of caring for students in further education, *British Educational Research Journal*, 35(1): 99–117.

Robson, J., Bailey, B. and Larkin, S. (2004) Adding value: investigating the discourse of professionalism adopted by vocational teachers in further education colleges, *Journal of Education and Work*, 17(2): 183–95.

Robson, J., Bailey, B. and Mendick, H. (2006) *An Investigation into the Roles of Learning Support Workers in the Learning and Skills Sector*, London, Learning and Skills Network.

Robson, J., Bailey, B. and Mendick, H. (2008) Learners' emotional and psychic responses to encounters with learning support in further education and training, *British Journal of Educational Studies*, 56(3): 304–22.

Roe, W. (2011) *Review of Post-16 Education and Vocational Training in Scotland* (available at www.scotland.gov.uk/Resource/Doc/355876/0120235.pdf).

Rogers, A. (1986) *Teaching Adults*, Milton Keynes, Open University Press.

Rogers, A. (2002) *Teaching Adults*, 3rd edition, Buckingham, Open University Press.

Rogers, J. (1992) *Adults Learning*, 3rd edition, Buckingham, Open University Press.

Rommes, E., Faulkner, W. and Van Slooten, I. (2005) Changing lives: the case for women-only technology training revisited, *Journal of Vocational Education and Training*, 57(3): 293–317.

Rowland, S. (1993) *The Enquiring Tutor*, London, Falmer Press.

Russell, L., Simmons, R. and Thompson, R. (2011) Ordinary lives: an ethnographic study of young people attending entry to employment programmes, *Journal of Education and Work*, 24(5): 477–99.

Russell, M. (2010) The formation of effective work groups within an FE classroom, *Research in Post-compulsory Education*, 15(2): 205–21.

Sacks, O. (1986) *The Man Who Mistook His Wife For a Hat*, London, Pan Books.

Sanderson, B. (2001) Branding education, *RSA Journal*, 3(4): 22–5.

Schofield Review (2009) *A Review of Governance and Strategic Leadership in English Further Education*, London, AoC/LSIS.

Schön, D. (1983) *The Reflective Practitioner: How Professionals Think in Action*, New York, Basic Books.

Schön, D. (1987) *Educating the Reflective Practitioner*, San Francisco, CA, Jossey-Bass.

Schuller, T. and Watson, D. (2009) *Inquiry into the Future for Lifelong Learning*, Leicester, NIACE.

Scott, I. (2010) But I know that already: rhetoric or reality? The accreditation of prior experiential learning in the context of work-based learning, *Research in Post-Compulsory Education*, 15(1): 19–31.

Scottish Government (2011) *Putting Learners at the Centre: Delivering our Ambitions for Post-16 ESEU (1999) Bridging the Gap: New Opportunities for 16–18 year olds Not in Education, Employment or Training*, London/Edinburgh, The Stationery Office/Scottish Government.

Sennett, R. (2008) *The Craftsman*, London, Allen Lane.

SEU (1999) *Bridging the Gap: New Opportunities for 16–18 Year Olds Not in Education, Employment or Training*, London, The Stationery Office.

Sharp Commission (2011) *A Dynamic Nucleus: Colleges at the Heart of Local Communities*, Leicester, NIACE.

Shattock, M. (2000) Governance and management, in A. Smithers and P. Robinson (eds) *Further Education Re-formed*, London, Falmer Press.

Silver, R. and Forrest, W. (2007) Learning to become, in D. Kehoe (ed.) *Practice Makes Perfect: The Importance of Practical Learning*, London, The Social Market Foundation.

Simmons, R. (2008) Golden years? Further education colleges under local authority control, *Journal of Further and Higher Education*, 32(4): 359–71.

Simmons, R. (2009) Further education and the lost opportunity of the Macfarlane Report, *Journal of Further and Higher Education*, 33(2): 159–69.

Simon, B. (1999) Why no pedagogy in England? in J. Leach and B. Moon (eds) *Learners and Pedagogy*, London, Paul Chapman Publishing.

Simpson, L. (2009) *The Private Training Market in the UK, Inquiry into the Future of Lifelong Learning Sector Paper 2*, Leicester, NIACE.

Skinner, B.F. (1968) *The Technology of Teaching*, New York, Appleton-Century-Crofts.

Smith, J.J. (1989) Judgements in educational assessment, *Journal of Further and Higher Education*, 13(3): 115–19.

Squires, G. (1987) *The Curriculum Beyond School*, London, Hodder and Stoughton.

Stasz, C. (2011) *The Purposes and Validity of Vocational Qualifications*, ESRC SKOPE Research Paper No.105, Universities of Oxford and Cardiff.

Stenhouse, L. (1975) *An Introduction to Curriculum Research and Development*, London, Heinemann.

Stoten, D.W. (2011) Education, leadership and the age of austerity: an investigation into the experiences at college level, *Research in Post-Compulsory Education*, 16(3): 289–301.

Stronach, I., Corbin, B., McNamara, O., Stark, S. and Warne, T. (2002) Towards an uncertain politics of professionalism: teacher and nurse identities in flux, *Journal of Education Policy*, 17(1): 109–38.

Swan, M. and Swain, J. (2010) The impact of a professional development programme on the practices and beliefs of numeracy teachers, *Journal of Further and Higher Education*, 34(2): 165–77.

Taubman, D. (2000) Staff relations, in A. Smithers and P. Robinson (eds) *Further Education Re-formed*, London, Falmer Press.

Tedder, M. (1994) Appraisal and professionalism in colleges, *Journal of Further and Higher Education*, 18(3): 74–82.

Tedder, M. and Lawy, R. (2009) The pursuit of 'excellence': mentoring in further education initial teacher training in England, *Journal of Vocational Education and Training*, 61(4): 413–29.

THES (1998) Doubts over who foots the bill for the University of Industry, Editorial, *Times Higher Education Supplement*, 20 November.

Thompson, R. (2011) Individualisation and social exclusion: the case of young people not in education, employment or training, *Oxford Review of Education*, 37(6): 785–802.

Tomlinson, J. (1996) *Inclusive Learning: Report of the Learning Difficulties and/or Disabilities Committee*, London, The Stationery Office.

Tough, A. (1971) *The Adult's Learning Projects*, Toronto, Ontario Institute for Studies in Education.

Towler, C., Woolner, P. and Wall, K. (2011) Exploring teachers' and students' conceptions of learning in two further education colleges, *Journal of Further and Higher Education*, 35(4): 501–20.

UKCES (2009) *The Employability Challenge Full Report*, Wath-upon-Dearne, UKCES.

UKCES (2010) *Ambition 2020: World Class Skills and Jobs for the UK: 2010 Report*, Wath-upon-Dearne, UKCES.

Unwin, L. (1997) Reforming the work-based route: problems and potential for change, in A. Hodgson and K. Spours (eds) *Dearing and Beyond*, London, Kogan Page.

Unwin, L. (1999) 'Flower arranging's off but floristry is on': lifelong learning and adult education further education colleges, in A. Green and N. Lucas (eds) *FE and Lifelong Learning: Realigning the Sector for the 21st Century*, London, Bedford Way Papers.

Unwin, L. (2004) Growing beans with Thoreau: rescuing skills and vocational education from the UK's deficit approach, *Oxford Review of Education*, 30(1): 147–60.

Unwin, L. (2009) *Sensuality, Sustainability and Social Justice: Vocational Education in Changing Times*, London, Institute of Education.

Unwin, L. (2010) Learning and Working from the MSC to New Labour: Young People, Skills and Employment, *National Institute Economic Review*, No. 212, April 2010.

Unwin, L. and Edwards, R. (1990) The tutor–learner relationship: making sense of changing contexts, *Adults Learning*, March: 197–9.

Unwin, L. and Wellington, J. (2001) *Young People's Perspectives on Education, Employment and Training*, London, Kogan Page.

Unwin, L., Fuller, A., Turbin, J. and Young, M. (2004) *The Impact of Vocational Qualifications*, DfES Research Report 522, Nottingham, DfES.

Usher, R., Bryant, I. and Johnston, R. (2002) Self and experience in adult learning, in R. Harrison, F. Reeve, A. Hanson and J. Clarke (eds) *Supporting Lifelong Learning, Volume 1*, London, RoutledgeFalmer.

Vygotsky, L.S. (1978) *Mind in Society*, edited by M. Cole, V. John-Steiner, S. Scribner and E. Souberman, Cambridge, Harvard University Press.

Wahlberg, M. (2007) *What Works, What Matters? Evaluations of Centres of Vocational Excellence in FE: Full Research Report*, ESRC End of Award Report, RES-000–22–1728, Swindon, ESRC.

Watson, C. (2006) Narratives of practice and the construction of identity in teaching, *Teachers and Teaching: Theory and Practice*, 12(5): 509–26.

Whitty, G. (2012) A life with the sociology of education, *British Journal of Education Studies*, 60(1): 65–75.

Wildemeersch, D. (1989) The principal meaning of dialogue for the construction and transformation of reality, in S.W. Weil and I. McGill (eds) *Making Sense of Experiential Learning*, Milton Keynes, SRHE/Open University Press.

Wilkins, S. and Walker, I. (2011) Applied and academic A levels: is there really a need for the applied track in UK further education? *Journal of Further and Higher Education*. doi: 10.1080/0309877X.2011.584967.

Williams, J. (2008). Constructing social inclusion through further education – the dangers of instrumentalism, *Journal of Further and Higher Education*, 32(2): 151–60.

Wilson, A. and Wilson, B. (2011) Pedagogy of the repressed: research and professionality within HE in FE, *Research in Post-compulsory Education*, 16(4): 465–78.

Wolf, A. (1995) *Competence-based Assessment*, Buckingham, Open University Press.

Wolf, A. (2002) *Does Education Matter? Myths About Education and Economic Growth*, London, Penguin.

Wolf, A. (2009) *An Adult Approach to FE*, London, Institute for Economic Affairs.

Wolf, A. (2011) *Review of 14–19 Vocational Education (The Wolf Review)*, London, Department for Education.

Wolf, A., Jenkins, A. and Vignoles, A. (2006) Certifying the workforce: economic imperative or failed social policy? *Journal of Education Policy*, 21(5): 535–65.

Young, M. (1993) A curriculum for the 21st century? Towards a new basis for overcoming academic/vocational divisions, *British Journal of Educational Studies*, 40(3): 203–22.

Young, M. (1998) *The Curriculum of the Future*, London, Falmer Press.

Young, M. (2003) National qualifications frameworks as a global phenomenon, *Journal of Education and Work*, 16(3): 223–37.

Young, M. (2008) *Bringing Knowledge Back In: From Social Constructivism to Social Realism in the Sociology of Education*, Abingdon, Routledge.

Young, M. and Leney, T. (1997) From A-levels to an Advanced Level curriculum of the future, in A. Hodgson and K. Spours (eds) *Dearing and Beyond*, London, Kogan Page.

Young, M., Lucas, N., Sharp, G. and Cunningham, B. (1995) *Teacher Education for the Further Education Sector: Training the Lecturer of the Future*, London, Institute of Education, University of London.

Zukas, M. (2006) Pedagogic learning in the pedagogic workplace: educators' lifelong learning and learning futures, *International Journal of Pedagogies and Learning*, 2(3): 71–80.

Zukas, M. and Malcolm, J. (2002) Pedagogies for lifelong learning: building bridges or building walls? in R. Harrison, F. Reeve and J. Clarke (eds) *Supporting Lifelong Learning. Volume 1: Perspectives on Learning*, London, RoutledgeFalmer.

Zukas, M., Bradbury, H., Frost, N. and Kilminster, S. (2010) Conclusions, in H. Bradbury, N. Frost, S. Kilminster and M. Zukas (eds) *Beyond Reflective Practice*, London, Routledge.

Further reading

Here we recommend a number of books that are relevant to FE teachers, but that are not cited in the text. There are also several academic and professional journals where you will find reports on the latest research and developments in theories of teaching, learning and assessment, as well as practical resources.

I Where will I teach?

Ball, S.J. (2008) *The Education Debate*, Bristol, Policy Press.

Coffield, F. and Williamson, B. (2012) *From Exam Factories to Communities of Discovery: The Democratic Route*, London, Institute of Education.

Dorling, D. (2011) *So You Think You Know About Britain?* London, Constable.

Pilz, M. (ed.) (2012) *The Future of Vocational Education and Training in a Changing World*, Dordecht, Netherlands, Springer.

2 Who will I teach?

Ecclestone, K., Biesta, G. and Hughes, M. (eds) (2009) *Transitions and Learning Through the Lifecourse*, London, Routledge.

Furlong, A. (ed.) (2009) *Handbook of Youth and Young Adulthood*, London, Routledge.

Hagell, A. (ed.) (2012) *Changing Adolescence*, Bristol, Policy Press.

Schuller, T. and Watson, D. (2009) *Learning Through Life. Inquiry into the Future of Lifelong Learning*, Leicester, NIACE.

3 What will I teach?

Huddleston, P. and Stanley, J. (eds) (2012) *Work-related Teaching and Learning: A Guide for Teachers and Practitioners*, London, Routledge.

Nuffield Review (2009) *Education for All: The Future of Education and Training for 14–19 Year Olds – Summary, Implications and Recommendations*, Oxford, Department of Education.

Stanton, G. (2008) *Learning Matters: Making the 14–19 Reforms Work for Learners. Summary Report*, CfBT Education Trust (available at: www.cfbt.com/evidence foreducation/pdf/LearnMatSum_WEBv4%20FINAL.pdf).

Taylor, C. (ed.) (2012) *Teaching and Learning on Foundation Degrees*, London, Continuum.

4 Approaches to learning

Aspin, D.N., Chaman, J., Evans, K. and O'Connor, B. (2012) *Second International Handbook on Lifelong Learning*, Dordecht, Netherlands, Springer.

Dolphin, T. and Lanning, T. (2011) *Rethinking Apprenticeships*, London, IPPR.

Hillier, V. (2011) *Reflective Teaching in Further and Adult Education*, 3rd edition, London, Continuum.

Malloch, M., Cairns, L., Evans, K. and O'Connor, B.N. (2012) *The SAGE Handbook of Workplace Learning*, London, SAGE.

Sennett, R. (2008) *The Craftsman*, London, Penguin.

Winch, C. (2012) *Dimensions of Expertise: A Conceptual Exploration of Vocational Knowledge*, London: Continuum.

5 Teaching strategies

Bostock, J. and Wood, J. (2012) *Teaching 14–19: A Handbook*, London, Open University Press.

Coffield, F. (2008) *Just Suppose Teaching and Learning Became the First Priority*, London, LSN.

QCA (2008) *The Diploma and its Pedagogy*, London, QCA (available at: http://web archive.nationalarchives.gov.uk/20081112162229 and http://qca.org.uk/qca_19933. aspx).

Starkey, L. (2012) *Teaching and Learning in the Digital Age*, London, Routledge.

6 Assessment and recording achievement

Gipps, C. (2011) *Beyond Testing*, London, Routledge.

Stobart, G. (2008) *Testing Times: The Uses and Abuses of Assessment*, London, Routledge.

7 Evaluation, reflection and research

Bolton, G. (2010) *Reflective Practice: Writing and Professional Development*, London, SAGE.

Livingstone, D. and Guile, D. (eds) (2012) *The Knowledge Economy and Lifelong Learning: A Critical Reader*, Rotterdam, Netherlands, Sense.

Skills Commission (2009) *Teacher Training in Vocational Education*, London, Policy Connect.

8 Professional development

Cunningham, B. (ed.) (2008) *Exploring Professionalism*, London, Institute of Education.

Edwards, A. (2010) *Being an Expert Professional Practitioner: The Relational Turn in Expertise*, Dordrecht, Netherlands, Springer.

Index

Page numbers in *italics* refer to figures.